THE NEW AMERICANS

THE NEW AMERICANS

How the Melting Pot Can Work Again

Michael Barone

Since 1947
REGNERY
PUBLISHING, INC.
An Eagle Publishing Company • Washington, DC

OCM 46385961

Copyright © 2001 by Michael Barone

Cataloging-in-Publication Data on file with the Library of Congress

Published in the United States by
Regnery Publishing, Inc.
An Eagle Publishing Company
One Massachusetts Avenue, NW
Washington, DC 20001

Visit us at www.regnery.com

Distributed to the trade by
National Book Network
4720-A Boston Way
Lanham, MD 20706

Printed on acid-free paper
Manufactured in the United States of America

10 9 8 7 6 5 4 3 2 1

BOOK DESIGN BY JULIE LAPPEN

SET IN JANSON

Books are available in quantity for promotional or premium use. Write to Director of Special Sales, Regnery Publishing, Inc., One Massachusetts Avenue, NW, Washington, DC 20001, for information on discounts and terms or call (202) 216-0600.

CONTENTS

☆　☆　☆　☆　☆　☆　☆　☆　☆

INTRODUCTION

THE NEW AMERICANS

In January 1994, speaking in Milwaukee, Vice President Al Gore gave a speech in which he translated the national motto *E pluribus unum* as "out of one, many."[1] One might guess that this was an inadvertent error, or evidence that Gore did not take Latin at St. Albans or Harvard. Except that in the words that followed he made it clear that the words had come out as intended. "You all share the American belief that there is strength in all our differences," he said, "that we can build a collective civic space large enough for all our separate identities." *Separate identities*: Here Gore aligned himself with a view widely prevalent, and not just among his fellow partisans, of the course of American history. America in this view was for a very long time monocultural, a white-bread nation in which just about everyone was like everybody else (with the one important exception, as

Gore would surely agree, of blacks). Immigrants, in this view, were white Europeans—pretty much like everybody else. But now, with the influx of immigrants from Latin America and Asia, and with our laws classifying people by race, we have suddenly become a multicultural society. White-bread America has become multigrain.

For someone Gore's age and with no knowledge of the longer run of American history, this view superficially makes sense. America in the 1950s was famously called a conformist society, a nation of organization men. Immigration from Europe had been cut close to zero by the Immigration Act of 1924; old ethnic neighborhoods seemed to be dying out. The percentage of foreign-born residents, which was 15 percent in 1910, dropped steadily to 4.7 percent in 1970.[2] Most Americans, until the civil rights movement of the late 1950s and early 1960s, paid little attention to the legally enforced racial segregation of the South or the racial discrimination prevalent in the North. It was possible, though not entirely accurate, to think of America as "one."

But these years were the exception, not the rule, in American history. The United States has never been a monoethnic nation. The American colonies, as historian David Hackett Fischer teaches in *Albion's Seed*, were settled by distinctive groups from different parts of the British Isles, with distinctive folkways, distinctive behaviors in everything from politics to sexual behavior. And this is not to mention the German immigrants who formed 40 percent of Pennsylvania's population in the Revolutionary years and who, Benjamin Franklin feared,[3] would never be assimilated. Many different religious groups—Catholics and Mennonites, Shakers and Jews—established communities and congregations, making the thirteen colonies and the new nation more religiously diverse than any place in Europe. We were already, in John F. Kennedy's phrase, a nation of immigrants.

One who understood this was George Washington. In August 1790, the first president wrote a letter to the Touro Synagogue in

Newport, Rhode Island. Always aware that he was setting precedent for a republic that he believed would someday encompass
more than 100 million people, Washington used this occasion to
set forth his vision of civic equality and of how people with
diverse backgrounds should live together as Americans. Jews
everywhere in Europe had lived for centuries under civil disabilities, unable to participate in politics and government, limited in
their right to own land and to travel outside their ghettoes.
Washington opposed such barriers to citizenship, and went further. Responding to the congregation's letter congratulating him
on his election to the presidency, he wrote, "It is now that tolerance is no more spoken of, as if it was by the indulgence of one
class of people, that another enjoyed the exercise of their inherent natural rights. For happily the government of the United
States, which gives to bigotry no sanction, to persecution no
assistance, requires only that they who live under its protection
should demean themselves as good citizens, in giving it on all
occasions their effectual support."4 Here, in Washington's ornate
eighteenth-century prose, was the idea of the Melting Pot, long
before it received its name. Anyone could become an American.
The nation would welcome newcomers of all backgrounds—
there were no restrictions on immigration then—and treat them
as equals, not out of generosity but on principle. A diverse people would share a common citizenship. America would be a
proudly multiethnic nation. But it would also be a nation with a
common civic culture.5

Washington provided Americans with a good working formula
for assimilating the tens of millions of immigrants who would
come here over the next two centuries. They would be eligible
for citizenship, entitled to be treated as the equal of every
other American, provided that they accepted civic obligations and
the civic culture. During most of the succeeding two centuries,
mass immigration has been the rule, not the exception, in
American life. The reason for much of this immigration was

simple economics, for even in the 1790s the United States was, for ordinary people, the most economically bountiful nation in the world. But economics cannot explain everything. There was never mass immigration to the United States from some countries that had lower incomes—France, for example, or Spain, or northern Italy. Mass immigration has come from only a few places—Britain and Ireland, southern Italy and parts of Germany and Scandinavia, the Russian Pale of Settlement within which Jews were confined a century ago, Poland and other countries in eastern Europe. Immigration has been prompted sometimes by terrible events—the Irish potato famine, the Russian pogroms— and sometimes by the pressure that population growth unaccompanied by economic growth puts on a peasantry.

But it is usually sustained—it only becomes chain migration, with one relative and family and neighbor following another— when there is a sense that the way of life in the old country is in some fundamental way unfair or dysfunctional, a sense strong enough to overcome the usual human desire to live where one grew up. And it sometimes happens that different countries are dysfunctional in similar ways—southern Italy and Mexico, for example. Coming to America gives immigrants a chance to get away from a dysfunctional society, but they also bring with them habits of mind they developed to adapt to that society, habits of mind that turn out to be dysfunctional in the United States—the deep distrust of institutions among southern Italians and Latinos,* for instance. These habits of mind are not easily discarded; they are handed down from parents to children, generation to generation.

---

* I use the term "Latino" to describe Latin American immigrants for several reasons. The term "Hispanic," invented by the Census Bureau, is seldom used in everyday conversation. In California, the state with the largest number of Latinos, "Hispanic" is almost never used, and in Texas, the state with the second largest number of Latinos, "Latino" is used far more often than "Hispanic." Also, "Hispanic" is imprecise: does it include the Portuguese-speaking Brazilians? Does it include Spaniards? "Latino," in contrast, refers to all of Latin America and the Spanish-speaking Caribbean as well—the old countries of the immigrants we are talking about.

But in time the environment of the United States fosters different, more functional habits of mind—a process that can be called assimilation.

Many savants predicted a hundred years ago that the immigrants of their day could never be assimilated, that they would never undertake the civic obligations and adapt to the civic culture of the United States.[6] History has proven them wrong. American democracy emerged strengthened from the tests of depression and war, the American economy has proved to be the strongest and most supple in the world, and if the American common culture is not in as good a condition as many would like, no one can seriously argue that it is because of the ethnic separatism of Irish, Italians, or Jews. Today we hear similar predictions about contemporary immigrants and minority groups. Those predictions, too, will in time be proven wrong.

The spirit of welcoming immigrants, enabling and expecting them to become Americans, was set early on, as witness George Washington's words to the congregation of the Touro Synagogue. Over the past two centuries the United States has attracted immigrants more than any other nation. It has also generated a vast internal migration—the movement of blacks from the rigidly segregated, rural South to the great cities of the North from 1940 to 1965—that in many ways resembles the mass migrations from Europe, Latin America, and Asia to large American cities. Overall, 35 million immigrants arrived from 1840 to 1924, in the first wave of mass immigration, and the percentage of foreign-born residents ranged between 13 and 15 percent from 1850 to 1920. Then the 1924 immigration act virtually shut down immigration, and as a result the percentage of foreign-born residents dropped to the 1970 low of 4.7 percent. The Immigration Act of 1965 and successive immigration laws have opened up the door again, and the percentage of foreign-born residents rose to 10 percent in 2000. Ethnic diversity is as American as apple pie—or pizza or bagels, or soul food or tacos or dim sung.

The thesis of this book is that minority groups of 2000 resemble in important ways immigrant groups of 1900. In many ways blacks resemble Irish, Latinos resemble Italians, Asians resemble Jews. Thus, in seeking to assimilate the peoples of the great migrations of our times, we need to learn from America's success in assimilating these earlier immigrants, as well as from the mistakes that were made along the way. This does not mean obliterating their original identities or cutting off people entirely from their heritage; it does mean helping them to transform dysfunctional habits of mind into those that are functional in this new country. Immigrants and minorities need to be interwoven into the fabric of American life, but the process of interweaving means that the fabric itself will change in subtle ways over time. One cannot understand the character of American life today without understanding the contributions of the Irish, Italian, Jewish, and other immigrant groups of a hundred years ago. One will not be able to understand the character of American life in 2100 without understanding the contributions of the blacks, Latinos, and Asians of today. America in the future will be multiracial and multiethnic, but it will not—or should not—be multicultural in the sense of containing ethnic communities marked off from and adversarial to the larger society, any more than today's America consists of unassimilated and adversarial communities of Irish, Italians, or Jews. Some claim that today's minorities are different because they are different races, but a hundred years ago the Irish, Italians, and Jews were considered to be other races. Contrary to what Vice President Gore implied in 1994, we are not in a wholly new place in American history. We've been here before.

We should not make the mistake of assuming that assimilation was painless or that the way Americans dealt with the immigrant groups of a hundred years ago was flawless. The pointed and often hurtful ethnic stereotyping that was so prominent in American popular culture a century ago has little equivalent today. There were plenty of examples of bigotry and discrimination that any decent-minded person today must abhor. On the whole, however, assimilation was successful. It has made us a strong, creative, tolerant nation. We should not forget the lessons our history teaches.

I came to write this book partly out of my personal background and experience. My own life is linked to each of the three immigrant groups of 1900 mentioned here. I am of Italian and Irish ancestry; my former wife is Jewish. My paternal grandfather was the son of Italian immigrants, born the year after his parents left Sicily for Buffalo, New York. (What did they think of the climate?) He married my grandmother, born in West Virginia, the descendant of Scots and Germans who had come to America in colonial days. My maternal grandfather was born in Canada, in a farming town full of Irish whose forebears had moved there shortly after the Irish potato famine of the 1840s; he immigrated to Michigan in the 1890s. He married my grandmother, born in Detroit, the descendant of Irish Catholics who had come to Boston in the famine years. As it happened, the public school I attended in Detroit in the early 1950s had a student body about one-third Catholic, one-third Protestant, and one-third Jewish: the Melting Pot. The private schools I later attended— Cranbrook School in the Detroit suburbs, Harvard College, and Yale Law School—had student bodies about one-third Jewish, much more than one-third Protestant, and much less than one-third Catholic, plus small numbers of blacks. My school years spanned the 1950s and the first half of the 1960s, in many ways America's most culturally homogenous, white-bread years. Yet I was conscious from my very early years of America's ethnic and religious diversity, aware that we were part of one country yet of many different backgrounds.

One could not grow up in Detroit in those years unaware of the vast migration of southern blacks into northern cities. Large parts of Detroit were undergoing racial change as many blacks moved into formerly white neighborhoods. The Detroit newspaper classified ads had separate sections for apartments—"white" and "colored"—and whole square miles would change from all-white to mostly black within a year or two. When I became active in politics in the mid-1960s, I learned how different ethnic and racial groups had very different party preferences. Hopeful that blacks and whites could work together despite racial animosities, I canvassed white neighborhoods for black candidates and black neighborhoods for white candidates. In the summer of 1967, I worked as an intern in the office of Detroit mayor Jerome Cavanagh, and in the riot that year I was a witness to the destruction of the city, large parts of which I knew block by block. Since 1969 I have lived in two cities, Detroit and Washington, with black majorities.

More recently, in the 1990s, I have worked to learn more about the new immigrant communities of America. In 1998 *Reader's Digest* assigned me to write a story on America's Latinos, with the *Digest* characteristically encouraging me to travel to Los Angeles, Houston, El Paso, New York, Chicago, and Miami to see how Latinos are living, how they are coping and moving upward. I have continued to cover Latino immigrants and Asian immigrants as well. In addition, I have been coauthor since 1971 of *The Almanac of American Politics* with Grant Ujifusa, the grandson of Japanese immigrants, who grew up in Wyoming near one of the camps where Japanese-Americans were interned during World War II.

So I have had a close acquaintance with all six of the ethnic groups that are the subject of this book. I began to notice the resemblances between each of the three pairs in the 1990s. It started with the Italians, when friends at the National Italian American Foundation and other organizations asked me to comment on the political experiences of Italian-Americans. What became immediately obvious was the difference between the mostly apolitical Italians, who never wholeheartedly embraced either major American political party, and the highly political and, for most of a century, almost entirely Democratic Irish. That led me to look into the background of Italians in politically dysfunctional southern Italy. Then, as I began researching the *Reader's Digest* piece, it struck me that today's Latinos were very much like the Italians of a hundred years before. They both came from politically dysfunctional countries whose major institutions had their roots in the sixteenth-century governance of Emperor Charles V; they had low levels of trust in large institutions; they came to America with little in the way of a political agenda and often with an intention to return to the old country; they worked hard, stayed close to their families, and had little involvement in politics. Indeed, the resemblance between the Latinos and the Italians is the closest of any of the three in this book.

The resemblance between blacks and the Irish is obvious to anyone with a knowledge of, and affection for, the works of Daniel Patrick Moynihan. In his controversial report on the black family, issued in 1965, Moynihan wrote of "important differences in family patterns surviving from the age of the great European migrations to the United States, and these variations account for notable differences in the progress and assimilation of various ethnic and religious groups."[7] There is no doubt which ethnic group Moynihan had in mind: his own, the Irish. Moynihan's father, a talented man given to drink, abandoned his family. This was not at all uncommon for the Irish; it is the theme of a popular book of the 1940s, *A Tree Grows in Brooklyn*, and a popular book of the 1990s, *Angela's Ashes*. In his brilliant and heartbreaking chapter on the Irish in *Beyond the Melting Pot*, published in 1963, Moynihan wrote, "There was a touch of Sambo in the professional Irishman: he was willing to be welcomed on terms that he not forget his place."[8] The Irish in British-ruled Ireland and the blacks in the rural, segregated South lived in societies whose fundamental unfairness they could never ignore: they were barred entirely from politics and kept almost entirely from the market economy; their men, barred from discharging their responsibilities, were left to behave irresponsibly in ways that hurt those around them. Today, of course, it is natural to say that their experiences could not have been similar (and in fact they were far from identical) because blacks are members of a different race. But we must recall that the Irish immigrants of the nineteenth century were widely considered to be of another race, a fact reflected in the wry title of a recent book, *How the Irish Became White*.[9] While the resemblance between Irish and blacks is not as close as that between Italians and Latinos, their experiences are still in many ways eerily similar.

Anyone familiar with elite American universities, where Jews and Asians are found in proportions enormously higher than their share of the population, will recognize the resemblance between those two groups. Indeed, both Jews and Asians have been victims of university-imposed quotas: Jews were often kept out of prestigious universities from the 1920s to the 1960s, and Asians have been denied places at elite universities by means of racial quotas and preferences since the 1970s. Even so, they excel: it is said, perhaps apocryphally, that two decades ago the most common last name in the Harvard faculty directory was Cohen, and now it is Chen. The resemblance between Jews and Asians is the least close of the three examined here, however. The Jews who immigrated in vast numbers from 1890 to 1924 were almost all Yiddish-speaking Ashkenazim from the Russian and Austro-Hungarian empires, with a similar cultural background; they quickly outnumbered the German Jews who had come over in much smaller numbers earlier. In contrast, Asians come from many different countries and cultures. The concentration here will be on the Chinese and other East Asian groups that have been subject, in different ways, to persecution and the vicissitudes of war, as were the Jewish immigrants of a century ago.

It should be added that some groups of immigrants have been left out, not because they were or are unimportant, but because I do not see resemblances between those of earlier times and those of today. For instance, there seem to be today no equivalents to the German, Scandinavian, Polish, and other non-Jewish eastern European immigrants of a hundred years ago, and the South Asian or Middle Eastern immigrants of today seem to have no parallels from a century ago.

If there are great resemblances between the immigrants of 1900 and 2000, there is a great difference in the responses of the American elite then and now. In the early twentieth century, elite Americans were preoccupied with immigration. This was perhaps because immigrants were so numerous and visible in the center of the great cities where the elite was concentrated—New York, Boston, Philadelphia, Chicago. These elites responded with a call for "Americanization." Foremost among the advocates of Americanization was Theodore Roosevelt, who said in 1915, "We cannot afford to use hundreds of thousands of immigrants merely as industrial assets while they remain social outcasts and menaces any more than 50 years ago we could afford to keep the black man merely as an industrial asset and not as a human being."[10] The answer was not to end immigration: Presidents William Howard Taft and Woodrow Wilson, an elite Republican and an elite Democrat, both vetoed bills that would have restricted the numbers allowed in. Americanization, they felt, was the appropriate solution, and they saw the process as a mutually beneficial bargain. John Miller describes its terms: "Immigrants needed to become a part of American society, not mere sojourners in it. They had responsibilities to their new home. In a rough order of priority, these included living by its laws, working at jobs, learning English, and earning citizenship. The native-born population would reap some reward when immigrants performed any of these duties, ranging from simple matters like the preservation of the peace to more complex benefits like economic gain, national cohesion, and domestic tranquility. The immigrant would profit as well, went the thinking, since assimilation underwrote success in the United States."[11] Elite organizations and government agencies fostered the teaching of English and appreciation of American civic ideals.[12] Of course, the elites did not entirely welcome immigrants into their midst; Jews especially were excluded from elite corporations, law firms, universities, and clubs. Even so, by any measure Americanization was an overwhelming success.

In the last third of the twentieth century, however, elite Americans have not been preoccupied with immigration and have tended to regard "Americanization" as an uncouth expression of nationalistic pride or a form of bigotry. Although immigrants have again moved in large numbers to our great cities, they tend to live in outlying neighborhoods that members of the elite, speeding by on freeways or in train tunnels, seldom see—South Central and East Los Angeles, the outer boroughs of New York City, and so forth. The vast immigration of the late twentieth century, which elite opinion did not anticipate, has been seen through the prism of the civil rights experience; indeed, President Lyndon Johnson made immigration reform a priority in 1965 because he saw the old system of national origin quotas as a form of unfair discrimination. Based on the assumption that Latino and Asian immigrants would face the same problems as blacks—that they would be met with racial or ethnic discrimination in employment, housing, public accommodations, and admission to elite institutions; that they would be plagued by poverty—the solutions became to give immigrants the protections of civil rights legislation. This quickly came to mean granting them the benefits of racial quotas and of massive government spending programs. At the same time, the civil rights movement and the turmoil of the late 1960s filled the elite with doubt about basic American values, even as that movement prompted the country to live up to those values as it never had before. Elites came to see Americanization as the unfair subjection of members of other races and cultures.[13] They came to celebrate, as Al Gore did in 1994, an America that would be made up of separate and disparate "multicultural" groups, fenced off in their own communities, entitled to make demands on the larger society but without any responsibility to assimilate to American mores.[14] This outlook, along with the governmental policies and administrative practices it fosters, has in many cases retarded assimilation.

We risk forgetting the lessons our history teaches when we say that America suddenly and for the first time has become a multicultural nation. Though it may have seemed natural in the wake of the civil rights experience to view Latino and Asian immigrants as new races whose experience and whose problems would be similar to those of blacks, the needs and experiences of blacks are very different from those of Latinos and Asians. Ethnic or racial discrimination has been only a small obstacle to the success of these immigrant groups. It is far more instructive to observe that the experiences and problems of Latinos and Asians more closely resemble those of Italians and Jews a century before, just as the experiences and the problems of the blacks who moved out of the rural, segregated South to the urban centers of the North more closely resemble those of the Irish Catholics who left British-ruled Ireland.

By stepping back from the prevalent view of the immigrant and minority groups, we see how misguided some of our policies and programs are. It is absurd, for instance, to grant immigrants quotas and preferences that are based on past discrimination because, as John Miller points out, "foreign-born newcomers almost by definition cannot have experienced a past history of discrimination in the United States."[15] Even more absurd and counterproductive have been the so-called bilingual education programs, which have kept Latino immigrants' children in Spanish-language instruction and denied them the knowledge of English that they need to advance in American society. What these immigrants need is what Americanization supplied the immigrants of a hundred years ago—a knowledge of English and basic reading and mathematics skills, an appreciation of the American civic culture, a fair chance at moving ahead as far as their abilities will take them. We need to learn the good lessons our forebears taught, even as we strive to avoid their mistakes.

A word about the title. Many may object that blacks are not new Americans. They are of course right. Americans of African descent tend to have ancestors who arrived earlier in this country than most Americans. But it is also true—indeed it is the central tragedy of American history—that blacks did not enjoy the full rights of American citizenship until the 1960s. In that sense, and that sense only, they qualify as new Americans for the purpose of this book.

PART 1

IRISH AND BLACKS

"We are a primitive people, wandering wildly
in a strange land, the nineteenth century."
—**ANONYMOUS IRISH IMMIGRANT**

"Perhaps never in history has a more utterly
unprepared folk wanted to go to the city;
we [southern blacks] were barely born as a folk
when we headed for the tall and sprawling centers
of steel and stone."
—**RICHARD WRIGHT**

To most Americans today, it is not immediately obvious that the black migrants who left the rural South for the industrial cities of the North starting in the 1940s resemble the Irish immigrants who left rural Ireland and crossed the ocean to the great cities of the Atlantic seaboard starting in the 1840s. Yet the resemblances are many.

Both the Irish and the blacks came from an old country where they were second-caste citizens—the Irish from "Britain's other island," the blacks from the segregated American South. Both were barred, because of their religion or their race, from government and politics. As tenant farmers many Irish and as sharecroppers many blacks were effectively excluded from the market economy. Both were ordinarily denied all but a rudimentary education. "The movement of the progressive societies," wrote the English legal historian Sir Henry Maine a century ago, "has hitherto been a movement from Status to Contract."[1] That is to say, it was a movement from a society in which how you were treated depended on who you were—free or unfree, Protestant or Catholic, white or black—to a society in which how you were treated depended on voluntary agreements between you and others. But British-ruled Ireland and the segregated South were not progressive societies in Maine's sense. Irish Catholics in the 1840s and southern blacks in the 1940s lived in societies where on important matters they were defined by status, not contract. They could never escape the adverse consequences of being Catholic or being black. They might be guaranteed subsistence by the owners of the land they worked, but they could expect to reap no other benefits: there was no reliable connection between effort and reward. Their subordinate status inevitably had an impact on their personal lives. Their males were demeaned and denied respect because of their subservient economic status, and fathers often deserted their families.

These were peoples whose experiences infected them with fatalism: they did not do things, things happened to them. But one aspect of their lives they controlled: their religion. The Irish had the Catholic Church, which was not controlled by the ruling Protestants; southern blacks had their own Protestant sects, with ministers who were not controlled by the ruling whites. For all their religious faith, violence and crime were common in their communities, with the ruling class indifferent to Irish-on-Irish or black-on-black crime. Yet in these difficult circumstances the Irish and blacks nevertheless managed to develop a protest politics of great strength and moral force, a movement in which their churches played leading roles, before their respective great migrations began.

Both began leaving the old country in large numbers in a moment of crisis, when their old way of life suddenly became unfeasible—with the outbreak of the potato famine in the 1840s and the introduction of the mechanical cotton picker and the onset of World War II in the 1940s. In the new country of the American North, both the Irish and blacks were unsophisticated rural people suddenly thrust in very large numbers into the nation's most sophisticated great cities. Both were noticeably different from others in these cities—different in appearance, different in accent and their use of language, different in behavior. Both met with discrimination. The Irish and blacks worked mostly at unskilled jobs and earned low incomes compared to others, though economically they were significantly better off than in the old country. Neither showed much entrepreneurial impulse; with no experience in economic activity, few started their own businesses.

Both groups were also in many ways fenced off from the larger society. For several generations, the Irish and blacks had continuing contact with the places from which they came, and few intermarried with other groups. To be sure, however, the consequences of intermarriage in America were very different: the children of Irish/non-Irish marriages often found their Irish identification obscured, while the children of black/white marriages to this day are almost invariably classified as black.

The Irish and blacks each created and dominated their own churches, the Irish within the hierarchical structure of the Catholic Church, where in America they usually encountered non-Irish Catholics, blacks in the more entrepreneurial setting of churches that have had few if any non-black members.

Even in the new country, family ties among both groups proved to be weak; fatherlessness was common, as many men abandoned their wives and children or were victims of work accidents and crime. Crime rates among both groups were high, significantly higher than among other groups in the city, with crime becoming markedly more visible about a decade after the great migrations began. And about twenty years after the migrations started, large numbers of both groups took part in bloody urban riots—the draft riots of the 1860s and the urban riots of the 1960s. (More people died in the New York draft riot of 1863 than in the Watts riot of 1965 and the Detroit riot of 1967 combined.) Both groups had high rates of substance abuse—alcohol with the Irish, alcohol plus marijuana and crack cocaine with blacks.

Despite all these disadvantages, both groups produced many examples of excellence. The Irish and black communities produced many notable sports heroes and entertainment figures. Both, that is, put an indelible imprint on American popular culture long before they became fully interwoven into the fabric of American life.

With their traditions of peaceful protest and their sense of grievance against an unfair larger society, both groups looked to control of government as a means of advancement, and both excelled at politics. They built their own political organizations, modeled on their churches: the Irish, hierarchical political machines; blacks, ad hoc organizations assembled by charismatic local leaders. They were initially the object of competition between Democrats and Whigs or Republicans, but within about twenty years both became heavily, almost unanimously, Democratic. Both used politics to create large numbers of public sector jobs for their own people. In some cities where they were majorities—Boston and Jersey City for the Irish, Detroit and Washington for blacks—they created a predatory politics, which overloaded the public payroll and neglected to enforce the law, ultimately damaging the cities' private economies. But in other cities and in state and national politics, members of these groups also provided competent and constructive political leadership.

Convergence to the American mean—rising to levels of average income and education—was for both groups very slow. They were handicapped by the habit of mind that cherished grievances against a fundamentally unfair society whose rules they saw no reason to obey. This habit of mind, functional in the genuinely unfair status societies of Ireland and the American South, proved dysfunctional in the more ambiguous—partly fair, partly unfair—contract society of the northern American city. A continuing preoccupation with religious, ethnic, or racial grievance persisted for many years, understandably so given the viciously discriminatory character of the old country and the continuing discrimination in the new. The Irish bemoaned "No Irish need apply" signs long after most had disappeared and insisted that Al Smith had been defeated in 1928 only because he was an Irish Catholic, though there is no reason to believe any Democrat could have won the White House that year. Blacks remained alert for signs of racism and discrimination even as these became less common, and many were fixated on charges of white mass killings of black children in Atlanta or the burning of black churches in the rural South, though the Atlanta killer turned out to be black and most of the churches were burned in accidents or by blacks.

But both groups, like almost all migrants and immigrants, had headed to areas of rapid economic growth and partook of at least some of the benefits. Within fifty years of the initial migrations, there were many lace-curtain Irish and middle-class blacks. Discrimination held back many members of both groups, but so did the widespread fatherlessness, which tended to produce economic dependency and crime—the characteristics of a stubbornly persistent underclass. Still, dysfunctional habits of mind tend to grow weaker over the generations. America's elites, never much bothered by discrimination against the Irish, caustically scorned Irish cultural behavior and Irish patronage politics, to the point that Irish leaders felt obliged to pretend at least to adhere to the standards of the larger society. Over time, this presumably weakened the sense of grievance and the dysfunctional habits of mind brought over from the old country. Society addressed the ills of the Irish through private charities, the settlement house movement, temperance societies, and police forces, all of which tried to improve individuals' conduct and to help people conform to the standards of the larger society. The Irish rose to average levels of income and education by the 1950s, and in 1960 an Irish Catholic was elected president of the United States. The Irish had finally become interwoven into the fabric of American life.

In contrast, America's elites, who from the 1870s to the 1960s had generally ignored racism and segregation, in the early 1960s took a strong stand against discriminating against blacks—a great improvement over their predecessors' treatment of the Irish. Starting in the late 1960s and early 1970s, these elites championed programs of vast public spending and lenient law enforcement. These programs purposefully avoided trying to improve individuals' conduct and to help them conform to the standards of the larger society—that was called "blaming the victim"—and gave sanction to behaviors that resulted in the tripling of crime and welfare in the decade after 1965—trends that gravely harmed many black Americans. In the 1970s, 1980s, and 1990s, America's corporate, university, and media elites gave their imprimatur to the system of racial quotas, preferences, and set-asides that has strengthened the sense of grievance, racial consciousness, and, on elite campuses and in workplaces, the dysfunctional habit of mind which holds that the larger society is fundamentally unfair and that one has no obligation to obey it. These policies resulted from the same good motives that prompted civil rights laws and an end to legal segregation in the South. Unlike those measures, however, the new system had bad as well as good effects on black Americans and has probably retarded their movement toward becoming interwoven into the fabric of American life.

Nevertheless, there is much reason for optimism. In the 1990s the black middle class continued to expand, while crime and welfare dependency trended sharply downward. Moreover, as the experience of the Irish shows, this country is by its nature far readier than any other to interweave peoples of different background and sometimes dysfunctional behavior into the national fabric. It took 120 years for the Irish; it may not take as long for blacks.

CHAPTER 1

IRISH

THE OLD COUNTRY

A traveler in western Ireland today sees hundreds of stone walls dividing the green land into thousands of tiny plots. In some plots are the ruins of stone houses, long ago abandoned; in others, a few animals graze; most are simply vacant. But once they were separate farms—mute evidence that at one time this was a much more thickly populated land, with thousands of tenant farmers raising potatoes until the crop failed in the potato famine of 1846. There were 8.2 million people counted in Ireland in the 1841 census, many more than the 5.2 million on the island today. These numbers tell a story of demographic disaster and mass emigration. More than 1 million people in Ireland died in the years of the famine; some 4 million emigrated over the next fifty years, the very large majority of them going to the United

States. Ireland was the source of the first mass migration of seemingly alien immigrants to the young republic.

This did not seem foreordained to the Americans or the Irish in the years before the famine. Fifty years earlier, Ireland had not been so very different from England in population or industrial development. Travelers today can see the eighteenth-century row houses that made Dublin the second largest Georgian city in the British Empire, and in the countryside beyond, the canals built then are still operating. In 1800 Ireland had 5 million people, not that much less than England's 10 million. But England had an industrial revolution and Ireland a famine; by 1900 the figures were 4 million for Ireland and 32 million for England.[1] The textile loom succeeded and the potato failed.

But there was another important difference between England and Ireland. Ireland was a possession of the king of England, and after the Protestant William III defeated the Catholic James II at the Battle of the Boyne in 1690, severe laws were passed against the large majority of Irish who were Catholic. Catholics were forbidden from voting for or serving in Parliament; they could not be lawyers or serve in local government (Edmund Burke's father converted to Protestantism and became a lawyer).[2] Many restrictions on Catholics' freedom of worship, education, entering the professions, and owning land were removed between 1778 and 1792, and in 1793 Catholic forty-shilling freeholders were given the right to vote.[3] But full Catholic emancipation did not follow; in 1801 Prime Minister William Pitt of Britain promised to enact it, but King George III insisted on his veto, and Pitt resigned in protest. The remaining restrictions made it clear that Catholics were second-class citizens. The courts were famously unfair, and in response the Irish developed, in the words of author William V. Shannon, "the art of soft deception ('blarney') and the disingenuous oath which is not really an oath at all. These were acts of the imagination designed to oblige the hearer with the fiction of compliance while preserving fidelity to one's own conception of justice."[4]

So in the early nineteenth century, Catholic landholding was still sharply limited; on death, a Catholic's land was divided among his sons, unless the oldest son converted to Protestantism, in which case he inherited it all. Most Irish peasants rented their land from large Protestant landholders, at terms the landowners set. Typically they lived in a traditional village or *clachan*, which Peter Quinn calls "a clump of cabins that leaned on one another," where there was an "incessant emphasis on singing, dancing, and story-telling."[5] Catholic schools and education abroad were prohibited, the public display of crosses was banned, and Catholic priests were barred from stepping outside their parishes.[6] Despite British restrictions, Catholic priests were typically trained at the seminary in Douai in northern France. After the French Revolution, the British allowed the establishment of seminaries in Maynooth and Carlow, not far from Dublin—and, presumably to gain leverage, granted them a government subsidy. The Catholic priest was the one figure who could provide rapid communication between Irish Catholics and articulate Catholic complaints against British rule. Indeed, the Church was the one institution Irish Catholics effectively controlled. Hence the British attempts to restrict the Church. Over time, however, these efforts became less effective, and the Church became more influential during the political agitation in the 1820s and in the famine years of the 1840s.[7]

Irish Catholics were considered a lower caste, excluded from government and forced to live mostly as tenant farmers, with little access to the economic marketplace. This was "a classic case of racial oppression," writes one historian. "Native Irish, Celts, or Gaels (as well as 'Papists' and other equally derogatory names) ... were regarded, and frequently spoke of themselves, as a 'race,' rather than a nation."[8] For the large majority of the Irish there was, to use Sir Henry Maine's terms, little progress from status to contract. Irish Catholics were stuck in a condition where their status determined everything and afforded them little opportunity to make their way ahead.

This had its effect on family life, summed up in a pithy phrase in the *Harvard Encyclopedia of American Ethnic Groups*: "permanent celibacy and delayed marriage."[9] Men, unable to own property and severely restricted in their ability to make a living, often married late or not at all.[10] The system encouraged irresponsible behavior and a servility that must have deprived men of moral authority inside the home as well as outside. In the early 1800s, historian Charles Morris writes, "Ireland was still mostly a primitive, preliterate society, notable for its charm, its music, and its tall tales, and the utter shiftlessness of its rural masses. The Irish peasant character that emerges from these accounts is much like that of the Sambo archetype in the American South—oppressively servile ... but watchful and crafty, master of the indirect statement and the half-truth, comically lazy, and occasionally dangerous."[11] Even men who did marry or father children did not take a lead role in their families and often were absent.

Over the course of the eighteenth century, the religious and land restrictions imposed on Irish Catholics met with "sporadic terror" from rural vigilante groups,[12] but with no political revolt. (The unsuccessful 1798 revolt against the British government was led mostly by Irish Protestants, who tended to oppose votes for Catholics.)[13] But there was still memory of a time when a different order had seemed possible. Even today, Catholics in Northern Ireland consider it a grievous provocation when Protestants march through Catholic neighborhoods celebrating William III's victory—and the Catholic James II's defeat—at the Battle of the Boyne more than three hundred years ago. They remain aware that, had the battle gone the other way, they might not have had to live under Protestant rule. The failure of the 1798 uprising, the passage in 1801 of the Act of Union, which abolished the separate Irish Parliament, the British victory over Napoleon's France—all made it seem extremely unlikely that British rule could be ended. But the terms of British rule might change: many British leaders from Pitt on favored Catholic emancipation, and the enfranchisement of forty-shilling life tenants gave at least some Catholics the vote. As a result, by the nineteenth century Irish Catholics were aware that government action could change the system they hated, which focused their attention on the political realm.

"There is a moral electricity in the continuous expression of public opinion concentrated on a single point," said Daniel O'Connell, the organizer of Irish mass politics in the 1820s. O'Connell was a west Ireland landowner, a Catholic who spoke Irish (Americans commonly refer to this language as Gaelic) and was educated in France, a lawyer elected to Parliament in 1828 who became one of the great orators of the House of Commons. In 1823 he formed the Catholic Association, which, with strong support from the Catholic Church, quickly became a mass orgaization capable of raising 20,000 pounds a year. This was arguably the first European mass political party, developed around the same time Martin Van Buren was organizing the supporters of Andrew Jackson into the Democratic Party in the United States. O'Connell, writes historian William O'Connor Morris, "formed the bold design of combining the Irish millions, under the superintendence of the native priesthood, into a vast league against the existing order of things, and of wresting the concession of the Catholic claims from every opposing party in the state by an agitation, continually kept up, and embracing almost the whole of the people, but maintained within constitutional limits, though menacing and shaking the frame of society."[14] He led monster rallies, "backed up," as historian R. F. Foster writes, "by the implicit threat of mass disobedience, of unilateral withdrawal of allegiance, even of a refusal to recognize the legitimacy of the state."[15] A Catholic Association candidate was elected to Parliament in 1826; the Catholic Association had deployed priests, hired salaried agents, established travel facilities for outlying voters, and provided alternative jobs or housing to tenant voters harassed by their landlords.[16] O'Connell, elected two years later, led a bloc of thirty-six Irish members to force passage of the Catholic Emancipation Act of 1829, which removed restrictions against Catholics in politics and landholding, but at the price of the dissolution of the Catholic Association and raising the requirement for life tenants' voting from 40 shillings to 10 pounds.[17] Maintaining his Irish MPs as a key balancing force in the 1830s, O'Connell began to demand repeal of the 1801 Act of Union, though he was careful to remain ambiguous about an alternative. In 1843 he planned a massive rally for repeal in Clontarf, near Dublin, then cancelled it under pressure from Prime Minister Robert Peel. He was prosecuted anyway and sentenced to a year in jail, but the House of Lords quashed his conviction. O'Connell took no part in politics after the famine of 1846—he died on a pilgrimage to Rome in 1847—but he had developed a sectarian Catholic mass political party as well as what Foster calls a "lively culture of political engagement."[18] By the famine year of 1846, Catholic Ireland was economically stagnant but politically vibrant.

THE CRISIS: THE 1840s

In July 1845 disaster struck Ireland. Just before harvest time, the green leaves on the potato plants in field after field suddenly turned black. Farmers frantically tried to pare off the black leaves, but even when they could they found the potatoes underground already putrid. Fortunately the famine struck only 30 percent to 40 percent of the potatoes, and relief efforts—government workhouses fed American corn to nearly 10 percent of the population—were able to feed most of the peasants threatened with starvation. But in the summer of 1846 the potato blight returned—and this time it destroyed almost all the potato crop. This meant disaster for Ireland: except in eastern Ulster, where the poor subsisted on oatmeal, Ireland's rapidly growing peasantry lived almost entirely on potatoes. The new English ministry of Lord John Russell distributed food on more stringent terms than the old ministry of Sir Robert Peel, and so, despite the efforts of some landlords, Catholic and Protestant clergymen, Irish and British Quakers, and Irish-Americans, between 1.1 and 1.5 million Irish people died from starvation and famine-related disease. Ireland lacked the infrastructure to transport and distribute food in amounts needed to relieve everyone, and, in the huts between the tiny fields bounded by stone walls, many peasants simply huddled and died. In 1847 the potato blight abated, but it returned in full force in 1848 and continued to afflict the potatoes for six more years. Not until 1855 did the potato harvest return to the levels of the early 1840s—far too late for hundreds of thousands of Irish peasants.[19]

Even before the famine, many peasants were leaving overcrowded Ireland, with most going to the United States. Between 1834, when emigration suddenly stepped up, and 1845, 367,000 Irish immigrants came to America. That flow of immigration would surely have continued even if the potato blight had not appeared,[20] but the famine increased it by astonishing proportions. More than 2 million Irish—a quarter of the pre-famine population—left for the United States, Britain, Canada, and, in a few cases, Australia;[21] 1,238,000 million Irish arrived in the United States in the nine years from 1846 to 1854. Many risked the perils of a winter crossing. Weakened by hunger and disease, some 30 percent of those headed to British North America and 9 percent headed to the United States died on "coffin ships" during the voyage[22]—levels of mortality reminiscent of the slave ships of the late eighteenth and early nineteenth centuries. Another 269,000 Irish came to America from 1855 to 1860, before the Civil War cut down (but by no means ended) the migration. In only fifteen years, 1.5 million Irish moved to a country that, at the beginning of the period, had only 20.8 million people.[23]

The numbers abated, but the pattern had been set. Chain migration naturally followed: Irish emigrants crossed the ocean and headed to the neighborhoods where relatives, friends, and neighbors had already established a beachhead. Between 1861 and 1899 another 2,164,000 Irish immigrated to the United States; between 1900 and 1914, when World War I virtually shut down transatlantic migration, 482,000 more arrived. The total Irish immigration from 1846 to 1914 was 4,153,000.

THE NEW COUNTRY

"The Irish were a rural people in Ireland and became a city people in the United States," writes author William V. Shannon.[24] From the very start of mass migration, very few Irish immigrants moved to the interior of the country and became farmers, as many Germans did. They headed to Boston and Philadelphia and, especially, New York. This sudden mass immigration had a massive effect on the big cities. By 1850, 26 percent of New York City's residents were born in Ireland; by 1855, 28 percent of the residents of New York State were Irish-born—and this did not include the immigrants' young children born in the United States.[25] Although some Irish immigrants did head west, almost all settled in cities; 90 percent of Irish-Americans lived in urban areas in 1920.[26]

Why did the Irish stay in the cities, when nearly all had worked as farmers? For one thing, it was lonely on the prairie, the new frontier lands, Shannon points out.[27] But it wasn't too lonely for other immigrants of the day. Also, it required capital to move west in those days before the Homestead Act, and many Irish immigrants had barely scraped together enough cash to get across the ocean. Of course, few immigrants arrived laden down with cash. Probably the strongest explanation is that the Irish simply didn't want to farm. In Ireland they had been tenants, with few rights and few opportunities to learn how to manage a farm. The one crop they knew well, potatoes, had failed them dismally. As Pulitzer Prize–winning author Frank McCourt puts it, "Our forebears, landing on the eastern seaboard of the United States, hesitated to move inland, where they could have farmed to their hearts' content. Oh, no, they weren't going to be caught again. Look at what the land had done to them in Ireland. They'd stay in the big cities, never again be victims of the treacherous spud."[28] And when given a chance, they were not very good farmers. In 1880, long after the famine, Bishop John Ireland of St. Paul imported two dozen families from Connemara in the far west of Ireland and settled them on Minnesota farms; they planted no crops, built no buildings, ate their seed, and slaughtered many animals. To save them from starving in the northern winter, Bishop Ireland brought them back to St. Paul and put them on diocesan welfare.[29] The Irish naturally associated farming with a tenant system they hated and with a crop that produced disaster. They wanted no part of it. So in a nation where the large majority lived on farms, they stayed in the big cities.

Certainly they did not settle in cities because they had any experience with city life or because they fit easily into urban America. To the contrary: there was an enormous cultural gap between urban American and traditional Irish societies.[30] As historian Kerby Miller writes, "In 1845–55, an unprecedented proportion of the Irish immigrants were traditionalist peasants, often Irish-speakers, who might never have emigrated under normal circumstances and who carried to the New World premodern attitudes and behavior patterns diametrically opposed to those ... characterized as typically American."[31] Perhaps one-third of the first huge wave of immigrants spoke Irish and had little or no English.[32] That changed within a few decades, as the people of Ireland abandoned the Irish language; by 1900 Ireland was almost entirely English-speaking. But the cultural gap remained for many years. "All things nearly are done in this

country in a different way," Miller quotes one immigrant as saying. "Had I fallen from the clouds amongst this people, I could
not feel more isolated, more bewildered," said another. "We are
a primitive people," said a third, "wandering wildly in a strange
land, the nineteenth century."[33]

That primitiveness was apparent in the most concrete ways.
American cities in this period were developing municipal water
systems, building sewers, paving streets, and working to keep pigs
and other animals from roaming the streets freely. Civic elites
realized that for a city like New York, with more than 400,000
people crowded onto Manhattan Island below 14th Street, such
measures were necessary to maintain public health. The Irish,
fresh from their well-watered green fields, accustomed to living in
the tight quarters of the *clachan*, had no such understanding. As
Thomas Sowell writes, "The importance of proper garbage dis-
posal, to keep the neighborhood from being overrun with rats,
was one of the many similar facts of urban life that every rural
group new to the city would have to learn over the years, beginning with the Irish and continuing with many others to the present day. None paid a higher price than the Irish in their years of
adjustment. Cholera, which had been unknown before, swept
through Boston in 1849, concentrated almost exclusively in Irish
neighborhoods. In New York, cholera was also disproportionately
observed in Irish wards."[34] Irish immigrants also had New York's
highest rates of typhus and typhoid fever.[35] Infant mortality was
appalling, even by the standards of the time, and the conditions of
life degrading.[36] As Charles Morris notes, "Even Irish apologists
like Thomas D'Arcy McGee admitted that the Irish needed time
and understanding to learn the habits and discipline required in
their new country."[37]

This fast-arriving flood of hundreds of thousands of immigrants, with their strange speech and strange habits, aroused
revulsion among native-born Americans. These new arrivals far
outnumbered pre-famine Irish immigrants, who had come better

prepared to accommodate themselves to American ways. Sowell writes, "They crowded into the poorest quality housing—far worse than slum housing today—and lived under conditions that readily communicated disease, fire, and such social problems as violence, alcoholism, and crime. The native public's reaction to the Irish included moving out of neighborhoods en masse as the immigrants moved in; stereotyping them all as drunkards, brawlers, and incompetents; and raising employment barriers exemplified in the stock phrase, 'No Irish need apply.' The jobs the Irish did find were those considered too hard, too menial, too dirty, or too dangerous for others. The hardships of their lives may be summed up in the nineteenth-century observation, 'You seldom see a gray-haired Irishman.'"[38] Traveling through upstate New York on his tour of America in the 1840s, Charles Dickens recorded his impression of Irish canal laborers: "clumsy, rough, and wretched hovels ... all were very ... filthy. Hideously ugly old women and very buxom young ones, pigs, dogs, men, children, babies ... all wallowing together in an inseparable heap."[39] "Irish pigs running loose were the despair of New York health authorities," reports Charles Morris.[40] Even Bishop John Hughes, the most effective Irish leader in the 1840s, described the New York Irish as "the poorest and most wretched population that can be found in the world—the scattered debris of the Irish nation."[41]

The Irish tended to live in neighborhoods that were heavily, though seldom totally, Irish. Just as many native-born Americans shunned them, so did other distinctive ethnic groups have poor relations with the Irish. Competition for jobs led to deep hostility between blacks and Irish, and relations between Germans and Irish, and later between Italians and Irish, were not good.[42] Their Catholicism became an issue, and not solely for native-born Americans. Protestant Irish, much more well established in the United States, took to calling themselves Scots-Irish to distinguish themselves from the widely disliked Irish Catholics.[43]

WORK

Irish immigrants made their livings mostly through hard labor. From Ireland they brought no experience of entrepreneurship and often no acquaintance with the cash economy. Unwilling to go back to farming, uninterested in taking a chance on the frontiers of the Middle West, they lodged in the cities that had the fastest-growing economies in the nation and supplied the workforce that was, unbeknownst to them, an essential ingredient in that growth. "For the most part, the Irish did the heavy, hard, dirty work of the city," writes historian Carl Wittke. "Although among the first generation there were masons, bricklayers, plasterers, carpenters, and tailors who worked in sweatshops, there were more helpers and hodmen, porters, street cleaners, waiters, hostlers, bartenders, boatmen, stevedores, and longshoremen, and unskilled, brawny laborers who did the digging, blasting, and laying of pipes for the city. Others worked in warehouses, quarries, and shipyards.... Many Irishmen, with their innate love for animals, went to work in livery stables. It was not an uncommon experience for the immigrant to begin by cleaning horses and washing carriages in livery stables, then become a driver, fitting up 'shanty stables' on vacant lots, and finally managing his own cabs and wagons. They hauled freight from the wharves and depots or drove patrons to the theater in Dublin 'covered cars.'"[44] Irish-Americans, reports the *Harvard Encyclopedia of American Ethnic Groups*, were the only immigrant group whose upward mobility during most of the nineteenth century was as limited as that of blacks.[45]

In contrast to other groups, before or after, a majority of early Irish immigrants were women,[46] and many of them worked—as domestic servants, sewing, taking in boarders, selling fruit and vegetables, and so forth.[47] By 1855, 74 percent of domestics in New York were Irish, and in 1880, 44 percent of Manhattan's and Brooklyn's servants were still Irish.[48] This pattern persisted well into the twentieth century.[49]

Despite all this hard work, and even though the immigrants' condition was better than in Ireland, where many faced starvation, many Irish-Americans found themselves destitute. From 1849 to 1891, about 60 percent of those in the New York City Alms House were Irish immigrants.[50] There were more Irish immigrants in lunatic asylums, charity hospitals, prisons, and almshouses than any other group.[51] Poor-relief expenditures in Boston quadrupled between 1840 and 1860; the Irish accounted for three-quarters of Boston's arrestees and police detainees, and 55 percent of New York's, by 1860.[52] As Thomas Sowell summarizes, "No other immigrant group was so concentrated at the bottom of the economic ladder."[53]

The situation did improve for some Irish in the post–Civil War era. As Daniel Patrick Moynihan writes, "With the coming of the Gilded Age, middle-class and even upper-class Irish appeared. For a period they ranged across the social spectrum, and in this way seemed to dominate much of the city's life."[54] Still, most of the Irish continued to lag far behind economically. In 1880, 59 percent of the Irish in Detroit held unskilled jobs; only the then few Polish and blacks and Canadians (many of them of Irish descent) had a similarly low job profile.[55] In Boston in 1890, 65 percent of Irish held low manual jobs; the percentage was no higher than 36 percent for other groups. "The Irish," notes Donald L. Miller, "came to Chicago in the 1830s to dig the Illinois and Michigan Canal and settled in a waste-board shantytown, Chicago's first slum, on the mudflats where the canal met the South Branch of the Chicago River, a place called Bridgeport, to this day the emotional center of Chicago's Irish community." While Bridgeport produced the mayors of Chicago from 1933 to 1979, for a century its residents were much more likely to work on railroad construction jobs and in the brickyards, slaughtering mills, and glue factories.[56] The Irish also lagged behind in entrepreneurship: in 1909 Boston Irish had higher incomes than Jews, but Jews produced nine times as many business owners (though of course many of the businesses were nothing more than peddling from pushcarts).[57] As late as 1910, nearly half of first-generation Irish immigrants worked as laborers and operatives, and only 6 percent as managers or professionals, 11 percent in sales or technical jobs, and 22 percent as craftsmen.[58]

It is tempting to ascribe these patterns to religious and ethnic discrimination, and, as we will see, discrimination indeed existed. But the habits of mind the Irish brought with them from the old country were a powerful impediment to economic success and a heavy bar to entrepreneurship. One reason such habits of mind persisted was that, despite the length and difficulties of ocean voyages, contact with Ireland was not completely cut off. As author Patrick Blessing writes, "The steady arrival of newcomers, contact with the homeland through the immigrant press, the regular exchange of letters, and frequent lecture tours by nationalists from Ireland perpetuated the inherited culture. Textbooks in Catholic schools provided children with stories about the history and culture of Ireland. When ocean travel became relatively easy around the turn of the century, more and more Irish visited home: between 1899 and 1910 over 18 percent of those arriving had previously resided in the United States."[59] Starting in the middle of the nineteenth century and continuing until the Irish Free State was created in 1921, many Irish in America supported the Fenian movement against British rule in Ireland. Afterwards, Irish-Americans provided much of the funding of the Irish Republican Army. Irish consciousness persisted long after the percentage of Irish-born immigrants declined.[60]

It is perhaps unsurprising that, coming from a society where everything was determined by status, not contract, the Irish with very few exceptions did not move up through entrepreneurship.[61] Kerby Miller quotes one Irish immigrant as saying that American businessmen "were full of business enterprise, while unenterprise was much more our specialty."[62] Miller also cites a turn-of-the-century observer who said that the Irish of Boston's

South End seemed "severely out of touch with the American cultural environment to which they were at the same time so vulnerable." The "ordinary Irishman," the observer said, "lives in the present and worries comparatively little about the future. He is not extravagant in any particular way, but he is wasteful in every way; it is his nature to drift when he ought to plan and economize. This disposition, combined with an ever-present tendency to drink too much, is liable to result in insecure employment and a small income."[63] In New York, the Irish moved up economically much more slowly than the Germans, and most were still working class in 1914, living in rough neighborhoods like Hell's Kitchen on Manhattan's West Side.[64]

With their working-class jobs and their gifts of political organization, Irish-Americans from early on became leaders of labor unions. The first Labor Day, in 1882, was organized by one P. J. McGuire. Though there were some Irish radicals and socialists, notably the orator Mother Jones and the Communist Elizabeth Gurley Flynn, most Irish labor leaders were meat-and-potatoes unionists, interested in raising wages and improving living conditions, and aware that the Catholic Church was in many ways sympathetic to the labor movement. Their greatest leader was George Meany, a onetime Bronx plumber who headed the AFL-CIO from 1955 until 1979.[65]

Some Irish, of course, did break out of the working class. As Thomas Sowell writes, "There have been some highly successful businesses founded by Irish-Americans, such as the Grace Steamship Lines, and Irish-Americans invented the Sullivan rubber heel and the 'hurricane lamp' for use on railroads." But, quoting Daniel Patrick Moynihan from the early 1960s, Sowell notes that "the types of businesses in which the Irish have done well have typically been 'businesses such as banking, where there is stress on personal qualities and the accommodation of conflicting interests, and not a little involvement in politics.' Bars and saloons are also businesses requiring a human touch, and the Irish have thrived in such businesses."[66] One dazzling example is Joseph P. Kennedy, the son of a saloonkeeper and ward heeler in East Boston who married the daughter of the mayor of Boston and embarked on a spectacular financial career in the 1910s to become probably the richest Irish Catholic in America. Kennedy himself had "not a little involvement in politics" and used his money to win high office from Franklin D. Roosevelt and to secure the election of his son to the House of Representatives, the Senate, and the presidency of the United States.

But Kennedy and the others were the exceptions that proved the rule. Moynihan's list of Irish-American economic successes is almost pathetically short. Although Irish-Americans were concentrated in many of the fastest growing American metropolitan areas in the century after the famine, not until the 1950s did their income levels reach the national average, and for generations a disproportionate number lived in poverty.[67]

FAMILY

Irish family ties were strong, but not always enduring. Marriage among the post-famine Irish was often delayed until couples were in their thirties or even forties.[68] Bachelor uncles and spinster aunts, living with a parent or other members of the extended family, were common. In time, many boys became priests and many more girls became nuns. Intermarriage was rare: until well into the twentieth century the Irish in America seemed almost always to seek Irish-born or Irish-American spouses.[69] Once couples were married, large families were still the rule—more than in other immigrant groups.[70]

But many Irish-American families became fatherless; the number of fatherless families was higher than among other immigrant groups. It is not entirely clear why. As Andrew Greeley writes, "Where the missing fathers were is something we do not know;

they may have been dead, they may have been off working on the canals or railroads, they may have deserted the families, or been in jails or hospitals for drunkenness. We have no data to determine the present rate of absent-father families."[71] But the phenomenon was apparent early on. In the 1840s, one scholar writes, "It was almost automatically assumed that an orphan was Irish, and as late as 1914, about half the Irish families on Manhattan's west side were fatherless."[72] Similarly, in Detroit in 1891, about one in four Irish households was headed by a woman—close to the 27 percent among blacks, but well above the 14 percent average. Of applicants to the Detroit Association of Charities, notes historian Oliver Zunz, "58 percent of the women declared their husbands dead; but 25 percent confessed [they] did not know, and another 9 percent declared their husbands still in Detroit or in Wayne County, implicitly implying [sic] desertion. Other responses varied; to some the husband was in Ohio or Ontario; to others he was in a city like Chicago or Grand Rapids; and to yet others he was in prison in Jackson."[73]

Historian Edward Spann describes the results vividly: "Poverty, however, was not the last broken rung on the ladder of misfortune, for with it came the frequent disintegration of the Irish family, resulting from the death, disappearance, or disability of husbands and fathers. One statistic generally overlooked by contemporary social observers was the high ratio of women to men, a striking contrast to the general preponderance of immigrant males both in the city and the nation. In the 1860 census, one-third more Irish females than males were reported, a disproportion which also characterized the black population. The death rate for the Irish males in the United States seems to have been higher than it was for natives and considerably higher than it was for Germans. Other Irishmen disappeared, either temporarily or forever, as they went inland constructing canals and railroads. Among those who remained, poverty intensified family tensions and encouraged male desertions. Absent

fathers, working mothers, crowded living quarters—these led
many juveniles to a life in the streets, frequently to delinquency
and occasionally to crime and prostitution."[74]

RELIGION

One great institution the Irish-Americans created was America's
Roman Catholic Church. In Ireland the Church was almost an
underground institution, disfavored by the state, but deeply
involved in O'Connell's mass political movement and enjoying the
allegiance of the great majority of the people. In the United States
before the 1840s, the Catholic Church was an entirely legal institution, tolerated by the government, uninvolved in politics, but
with very few members, from scattered backgrounds and of no single ethnic identification. The huge waves of post-1846 Irish immigrants changed all that. In a short time the number of American
Catholics quadrupled, and the Church took on a green Irish hue.

The first great leader of the American Irish Catholic Church
was John Hughes, bishop of New York from 1838 until his death
in 1864. Hughes was a man of enormous energy, organizational
ability, and feistiness. "In 1844," Moynihan writes, "when the
good folk of Philadelphia took to burning Catholic churches,
Hughes issued a statement that 'if a single Catholic church were
burned in New York, the city would become a second Moscow.'
None was burned."[75] He called in the Irish-based Sisters of
Mercy, and the St. Vincent de Paul Society came in to serve poor
Irish Catholics.[76] He established doctrinal unity, paid off debts,
tripled the number of churches, created charitable organizations,
and started the building of St. Patrick's, the most famous symbol
of Irish America, located defiantly on the main street of the
Protestant mercantile aristocracy, Fifth Avenue.[77]

Hughes's greatest crusade was in education. In New York
Hughes sought state support for separate Catholic schools

because of the Protestant character of religious instruction. He managed to gain the support of Governor William Seward, a Whig who did not want to see Irish Catholic votes going exclusively to Democrats. But the state legislature—elected mostly from upstate New York, which was settled by Protestant New England Yankees—would not go along, and Hughes resorted to politics. Two historians of New York narrate the story: "Determined to get favorable action, Bishop Hughes decided to impress legislators with the potential power of the city's Irish voters. Under his leadership, for the first and only time in the city's history, a Catholic political party was established to contest the 1842 state legislative race. Ten assemblymen who supported the Hughes school position ran on both the Catholic and the Democratic slates, and they won election. Three nonsupportive Democrats were opposed by Catholic party candidates and were defeated. Although no separate Catholic slate candidates succeeded, Bishop Hughes had made his point: New York's Irish Catholics had enough power to tip the balance of power in citywide elections."[78] But it was a Pyrrhic victory: the legislature barred aid to schools "in which any religious sectarian doctrine or tenet shall be taught," which meant that New York City public schools became secular, while Catholic schools got no public support.[79] In the next three decades, Hughes and his successors built a system of Catholic schools that expanded as rapidly as the public schools, but these latter institutions, despite their Protestant instruction, still remained inexpensive alternatives to parochial schools for most Irish parents.[80]

For a century and more the Catholic hierarchy was predominantly Irish—58 percent of American Catholic bishops from 1789 to 1935 were born in Ireland or had fathers who were,[81] and many more were of Irish ancestry—and the Church itself became an institution insulated from the influence of the Protestant majority. Priests and nuns migrated in the hundreds from Ireland, and the ranks of the priesthood and the convents were overwhelmingly Irish.[82] This strengthened the faith but also fostered a separatism; Irish-Americans in Chicago, Boston, Pittsburgh, and other cities commonly identified their home neighborhoods by parish—St. Pat's or St. Gabe's or OLPH (Our Lady of Perpetual Help).[83] "The dominant American culture," writes journalist Terry Golway, "was more than happy to let Irish Catholics build their own society within a society. In that way, it was thought, the Irish could get along in America—separate, though decidedly not equal."[84] One consequence was that, in the words of Thomas F. O'Dea, the Irish Catholic community "failed to evolve in this country a vital intellectual tradition displaying vigor and creativity in proportion to the numerical strength of American Catholics. It has also failed to produce intellectual and other national leaders in numbers appropriate to its size and resources."[85] The primacy of the Church had other costs as well. "The Catholic Church does not measure its success by the standards of society," writes Moynihan. "In secular terms, it has cost [the Irish] dearly in men and money. A good part of the surplus that might have gone into family property has gone into building the Church. This has almost certainly inhibited the development of the solid middle-class dynasties that produce so many of the important people in America.... The celibacy of the Catholic clergy has also deprived the Irish of the class of ministers' sons which has contributed so notably to the prosperity and distinction of the Protestant world."[86] The greatest strength of the American Irish was in some ways their greatest weakness.

CRIME

"The Irish brought to America a settled tradition of regarding the formal government as illegitimate, and the informal one as bearing the true impress of popular sovereignty," observes Moynihan.[87] They had reason to doubt the legitimacy of the rules of the larger society, and in America "the wild Irish"—the phrase goes back to King Henry II in the twelfth century—had high rates of crime and alcoholism, even while their affinity for hierarchy and politics meant that many of them became cops. As William V. Shannon writes, "The Irish on the eve of emigration lived in an atmosphere of violence. The old rural society long drained by exploitation at the top was shattering under the pounding blow of new economic demands. The coming catastrophe of the great famine was foreshadowed by brief famines in 1822, 1831, 1835, and 1837 and by a cholera epidemic in 1830. Tension reverberated through this sick society. Men got used to lawless ways and rough, direct methods. The Irishman picked up a blunt stick or a shortened pitchfork and 'had at' the head of his enemy with unnaturally reckless abandon. Here in the endemic violence of rural Ireland was the breeding ground for the tough 'bhoys' who in another decade would tear up paving stones and brandish sticks in election-day riots in New York and Philadelphia. Here also was born another Irish type: the fanatic. Men grown used to violence would became the nationalist zealot and the political gunman in his trench coat. In their most familiar guise they became the rebel union leaders in the coalfields of Pennsylvania, the copper mines of Butte, and the sandlots of San Francisco. This was a minority tradition compared to that of the hardworking, conservative farmer and the eloquent lawyer-politician, but it existed and was a long time in dying. An old lady summed it up: 'Ten o'clock in the morning and not a blow shtruck yet!' "[88]

Historian Roger Lane places the Irish experience with crime in perspective: "In terms of social problems in general and crime rates in particular, the Irish were the archetypical white ethnic group of the nineteenth century. No immigrants had a more difficult time than those who fled the famines of the 'hungry 'forties.' No city, until the full onset of industrialism, had jobs enough to absorb the waves of peasants who invaded them over the next several decades. All of the institutions of charity, sanitation, and education were strained by the effort to cope with Irish misery and desperation. So especially were the police. The problem of law and order, as seen by local authorities in many northeastern cities, was specifically an Irish problem throughout these decades, with the newcomers earning a reputation for hard-drinking, aggressive, riotous behavior wherever they settled."[89] Reliable crime statistics are not much available for the nineteenth century, but it is plain that crime rates among Irish-Americans were well above the national average. Lane notes that the rate of indictment for murder in Philadelphia from 1860 to 1873 was 4.7 per 100,000 for those with Irish Catholic names, compared to the citywide average of 2.9,[90] and that murder rates among Irish in the mid-nineteenth century were higher than among blacks.[91] More than half of all arrests in New York in 1859 were of Irish—double their proportion of the population—and more than five times as many Irish immigrants as native-born Americans were convicted in court.[92] By 1860 the Irish accounted for three-quarters of Boston's arrestees and police detainees.[93] The *Chicago Tribune* in 1898 asserted that there were twice as many Irish lawbreakers as from "almost any other inhabitable land on earth."[94] To some extent these figures may represent ethnic discrimination on the part of the still mostly non-Irish police, but the disproportions are so large that there can be no doubt that crime rates among the Irish were far above average.

Irish violence also manifested itself in urban riots. In the May 1849 riot in New York's Astor Place, sparked by the rivalry between British actor William Macready and American Edwin Forrest, ten thousand men took part and around two dozen were killed. Irish gangs—the Bowery Boys and the Dead Rabbits were two with picturesque names—squared off in forced battles; a thousand gang members took part in their July 4, 1857, brawl, in which ten died and eighty were wounded. New York's rudimentary police forces provided little protection. Indeed, in June 1857 two police forces—one commanded by pro-Irish Democratic mayor Fernando Wood, one created by the Republican legislature—faced off in a brawl themselves.[95] The Civil War brought even more violence. The Irish—heavily Democratic and ferociously hostile to the anti-slavery cause—rioted for four days against the military draft in July 1863, burning draft offices and federal property and attacking blacks; at least 105 people died in the worst riot in American history.[96] The gangs did not disappear after the war. "The Bowery Boys and the Dead Rabbits in particular [after the Draft Riots of 1863] grew in size, ferocity, and renown until they were recognized as units of military effectiveness, unstoppable by ordinary means," writes New York City chronicler Luc Sante. "Their conventional battles, which in the early days were still held at Bunker Hill, as if by a formal designation, were bad enough. These battles lasted for days at a time, with the amalgamated gangs massed behind barricades of piled carts and paving stones, fighting with every weapon then available: fists, feet, teeth, bludgeons, brickbats, rocks, knives, pistols, muskets, on several occasions even cannons. More than once, the city had to call out the National Guard or the 27th Regiment to cool things down.... The Bowery Boys ... specialized in supplying bodies to political entities, for poll fixing, poll guarding, repeat voting, and any number of other activities."[97] The boundary between crime and politics was not airtight. In Chicago the violence became an integral part of politics. As Donald Miller writes, "There were street riots, stabbings, and shootings in every Chicago election, and drunken squads of Irishmen packing six-shooters traveled in flatbed wagons from precinct to precinct, assaulting the opposition with bare knuckles, baseball bats, and straight razors."[98]

Irish crime rates began to fall as they were integrated into the industrial workforce[99] and, in Roger Lane's words, developed "the kind of patience needed to stand in line, keep out of trouble, and climb up the predictable white-collar ladder best symbolized by jobs in civil service."[100] But Irish gangs continued to operate in the twentieth century. They were involved in the illegal liquor business during Prohibition in New York and Chicago, though they tended to be elbowed aside, sometimes violently, by Italians. Dion O'Banion was murdered by Al Capone's Chicago gang in 1924, while Owney Madden kept control of Hell's Kitchen and the West Side of Manhattan by cooperating with Italian and Jewish gangsters. In the process he helped the Italians kill Vincent "Mad Dog" Coll, a killer who had started kidnapping higher-up gangsters.[101] Coll was an extreme example of the Irishman as brawler. As T. J. English writes, "From the beginning the saga of the Irish gangster has contained examples of mad behavior, a tendency toward impulsive, counterproductive mayhem that runs like a corrosive wire through the megawatt theatrics of America's brutal gangland history."[102]

"Their failures," Moynihan writes of Irish-Americans, "as they themselves said of their principal one, were 'A good man's weakness.'"[103] He does not have to say what that principal weakness was. Perhaps the biggest quantitative difference separating the Irish from other American ethnic groups was the use and abuse of alcohol. Nineteenth-century statistics are not readily available, but twentieth-century statistics tell the story. In World War I, 10 percent of draftees and volunteers of Irish origin were classed as neuropsychiatric, which in most cases meant alcoholic; for Jews and Italians the figures were 0.5 and 0.4 percent, respectively—one-twentieth or one-twenty-fifth as high. In 1941–1942 the military's rejection rate for alcoholism was 3 percent for Irish, 2.2 percent for blacks, 1.2 percent for Italians, and 0.2 percent for Jews. A twentieth-century study of first admissions for alcoholic psychoses in New York hospitals revealed that the rate per hundred thousand population was 25.6 for Irish, 7.8 for Scandinavians, 4.8 for Italians, 4.3 for English, 3.8 for Germans, and 0.5 for Jews. In other words, the Irish rate was fifty-one times as high as the Jewish rate and five times as high as the Italian rate.[104] In the cities to which the Irish immigrants thronged, alcohol was readily available. In New York, write Frederick Binder and David Reimers, "there seemed to be no end of drinking establishments in the immigrant districts. For the first generation of Irish in particular the saloon was the center of a relatively inexpensive social life, just as the pub had been back home. In 1864 the Sixth Ward [of New York] alone had one drinking establishment for every six people. At Peter Sweeney's saloon, for example, one could gain entry for ten cents and quaff whiskey at three cents a glass. The saloon keeper was a respected figure in his community and by the Civil War had become a key figure in local politics."[105] Of course, many Irish-Americans abstained from alcohol and others partook sparingly. But the stereotype of the heavy-drinking Irishman was widespread in the years from the famine until Prohibition came in 1919.

DISTINCTIVENESS

In her 1904 children's book *Freckles*, Gene Stratton Porter, confident that her readers would know just what she meant, described a boy as having "an Irish face." Today's children—and their parents—are simply puzzled. Characteristic Irish features— freckles, red hair or black hair, blue eyes—can still be seen on Americans with at least some Irish ancestry. But only those with some special interest in ethnicity identify themselves as Irish. Things were very different 100 and 150 years ago. The newly arrived Irish, slow to intermarry with Americans of other ethnic stock, stood out in the crowd. From this flowed consequences, often in the form of ethnic discrimination. Irish immigrants were, statistically, less affluent, less educated, and more prone to crime than other Americans. Many Americans viewed their Catholicism, because of the Church's antirepublican and authoritarian politics and because of relatively fresh memories of religious wars, as a threat to American democracy and American culture. "No Irish need apply," read many signs and help-wanted advertisements. Refusals to rent houses and apartments to Irish led to residential segregation, leaving some neighborhoods— eventually, almost all of the city of Boston—heavily Irish and some neighborhoods almost entirely non-Irish.

At a time when people are often described as "white Europeans," as if that were a homogeneous group, it is easy to forget that a century ago the Irish were considered by many Americans members of a separate and inferior race. As Mike Wallace and Edwin Burrows write, "Just as the English had long characterized their neighboring islanders more harshly than they had Africans, plenty of Anglo New Yorkers routinely used adjectives like 'low-browed,' 'savage,' 'bestial,' 'wild,' and 'simian' to describe the Irish Catholic 'race.'"[106] Thomas Nast, the leading Republican political cartoonist from the 1870s to the 1890s, portrayed Irishmen almost as monkeys and drew Catholic bishops' hats as sharks' jaws.[107] Nast wasn't alone. Andrew Greeley describes the evolution of the Irishman in American cartoons: "In the early nineteenth century Paddy was a rough and uncivilized looking creature, but still distinctly human. By mid-century he was a gorilla, stovepipe hat on his head, a shamrock in his lapel, a vast jug of liquor in one hand and a large club in the other. His face was a mask of simian brutality and stupidity. It was only in the late nineteenth and early twentieth centuries that Paddy began to evolve from an ape to a leprechaun, a figure of gentle fun instead of the crude, rude, filthy monster."[108]

SPORTS AND ENTERTAINMENT

Irish distinctiveness may have led to discrimination, but the success of distinctive Irish figures in sports and entertainment in time gave an Irish cast to American life generally. "The culture of the

Irish was one in which personal charm and fluency with words were highly valued—obviously great assets in politics and in other areas where personality and articulation are important, such as law, show business, the labor movement, journalism, and the priesthood—all areas where the Irish became very successful,"[109] writes Thomas Sowell, who goes on to recount Irish successes: "Many Irish-Americans rose to prominence in sports and entertainment—a pattern to be repeated by later ethnic groups living in poverty and without an intellectual or entrepreneurial tradition. There were idolized actors named Tyrone Power in both the nineteenth and twentieth centuries (father and son), famous singers from John McCormack to Bing Crosby, and sports heroes from John L. Sullivan to John J. McGraw to Knute Rockne and his 'Gipper.' The Irish dominated some sports—such as boxing, baseball, and track—but were not nearly as prominent in swimming or wrestling. The Irish distribution in sports was also a pattern later to be repeated by blacks. In the nineteenth century, it was a foregone conclusion that the heavyweight champion of the world would be Irish—Jack Kilrain, John L. Sullivan, and 'Gentleman Jim' Corbett being the best known. In the twentieth century, Irish-American heavyweight champions included Jack Dempsey and Gene Tunney, and ended with James J. Braddock— whose loss of the title to Joe Louis marked the beginning of ethnic succession in boxing. The early Irish-Americans were so successful in boxing and baseball that non-Irish boxers and ballplayers often took Irish names to help their careers."[110]

In time, Irish popular culture became American popular culture. Irish farces, with simple plots and exaggerated characters, were a staple of the American stage by the 1850s. Dion Boucicault and Victor Herbert, both Irish, became among the best-known writers of drama and operetta in America. Moynihan recounts the importance of Irish entertainment: "Let it be said that the Irish gave style to life in the slums: 'Boys and girls together, me and Mamie Rorke, tripped the light fantastic on the sidewalks of New

York.' They became the playboys of this new Western World. 'None Can Love Like an Irishman' was a favorite song of Lincoln's day. By the turn of the century it had become clear that none could run like them, nor fight like them, nor drink as much, nor sing as well. When it came to diving off the Brooklyn Bridge or winning pennants for the Giants, it took an Irishman. And who could write such bittersweet songs as Victor Herbert? Or enjoy life like 'Diamond Jim' Brady? All was 'bliss and blarney.'... By degrees the Irish style of the gaslight era became less and less Irish, more and more the style of the American city.... When the movies began to fashion a composite picture of the American people, the New York Irishman was projected to the very center of the national image."[111] This was the Irish-American style of George M. Cohan and "I'm a Yankee Doodle Dandy," of James Cagney and Spencer Tracy and Pat O'Brien in the movies, a style that we think of as quintessentially American now but which in its day was widely seen as Irish.

POLITICS

The Irish left their greatest imprint on American life in politics. They brought with them both a sense that the political order of the larger society was unfair and the experience that political organization, electioneering, and mass protests could change that political order.[112] "Most of the Irish arrived in America fresh from the momentous experience of the Catholic Emancipation movement," writes Moynihan. "Daniel O'Connell, [George] Potter wrote, 'was the first modern man to use the mass of a people as a democratic instrument for revolutionary changes by peaceful constitutional methods. He anticipated the coming into power of the people as the decisive political element in modern democratic society.'"[113] O'Connell and his movement gave the Irish a flair for electoral politics that no other immigrant group arrived with. As

William Shannon writes, "In the decades after the Civil War, the Irish developed their characteristic style in American politics. The Irishman as politician is the member of the Irish community most familiar to other Americans. The Irish brought to American politics two advantages other immigrants did not have: a knowledge of the English language and an acquaintance with the dominant Anglo-American culture. In addition to a common language and shared culture, they had gifts of organization and eloquence, a sense of cohesion, and the beginnings of a political tradition in the nationalist agitation in Ireland."[114]

The Irish arrived in large numbers just after Martin Van Buren had organized the Jacksonian Democrats as the first American mass political party; this mostly forgotten, practical-minded New York politico invented the torchlight parade, institutionalized the national party convention, and created what is today the oldest political party in the world.[115] Van Buren's Democrats and Henry Clay's Whigs competed for Irish support in those days when noncitizens could vote.[116] Initially the Irish seemed more inclined to the Democrats, who inherited Thomas Jefferson's impulse toward tolerance of non-Protestants, and to Andrew Jackson, of Protestant Irish descent, who was known to be especially hostile to Britain. Democrats led Irish immigrants straight from the docks to the polls. Yet as we've seen, New York's Whig governor, William Seward, didn't want to forfeit Irish votes and so in 1840 called for state government financing of Catholic schools. That initiative failed, however, and by the 1850s Irish loyalty to the Democratic Party was well established.[117]

Politics was also a way to make a living—the only profession in which it was an asset rather than a drawback to be an immigrant.[118] The Irish saloons became islands of political power, places where information could be exchanged and newcomers could acquire a free lunch or even a job.[119] Frederick Binder and David Reimers describe how New York's Tammany organization worked: "The Irish in New York knew well how to use their saloons and their street gangs for Tammany's causes. In return, Tammany delivered assistance in expediting naturalization; protected saloon keepers from overzealous enforcement of the closing laws; expressed strong anti-nativist and anti-prohibition positions; hosted picnics, balls, river excursions, and other social events; and, most important of all, provided jobs for 'lamplighters, fire wardens, meat inspectors, and policemen.'"[120] By 1855 political connections had helped Irishmen fill the majority of city jobs on sanitation, landfill, and road projects.[121]

The rewards became greater as time went on. As historian Hasia Diner writes, "The Irish began their political career in New York as the pawns of the urban Democratic machine. They exchanged their votes for unskilled jobs, petty licenses, and other relatively low-cost benefits. These 'crumbs' represented the absolutely highest these impoverished newcomers expected. But as they grew in number, they became more American and expected a modest degree of economic mobility, their demands increased, their appetites were whetted, and the Democratic factions responded. The crumbs grew into substantial slices, and by the 1860s, the time of [Boss] Tweed's hegemony, the Irish garnered the most jobs, the best patronage, and increasingly significant positions, even key leadership roles."[122] In 1871, after the downfall of Tweed, who has been called New York's last vulgar Protestant political boss, Tammany got its first Irish leader, Honest John Kelly. In 1886 Richard Croker followed,[123] and in 1902 Charles Murphy began a line of Irish Tammany bosses that remained unbroken for fifty-three years, until the election of Carmine De Sapio.

Similar things happened in other cities. Philadelphia, with its dominant Republican machine, was the one big city where the Irish supported Republicans. In return, Noel Ignatiev notes, the leading Republican boss got "jobs and services for his constituents. Aside from the gas works, he was able to place 'his people' in the custom house, federal construction projects, the U.S. Mint, the federal arsenal, the Eastern State Penitentiary, and the Navy Yard.... He also had influence with private employers, including the giant Baldwin Locomotive Works. As [historian Harry] Silcox puts it, he became 'Philadelphia's best-known Irish employment agency.'"[124] In Chicago, meanwhile, the Irish were a power in the city's Democratic Party by the 1850s, with several council seats and many police and fire department jobs. By 1865, one-third of Chicago's police was Irish, and by 1900 the Irish had six times as many men on the force as the next largest ethnic group.[125]

The Irish did not so much fit into a preexisting structure of big city machine politics; they created it, first by occupying so many of the lower positions, then by becoming party bosses as well. The preference for hierarchy over entrepreneurship, for discipline over independence, apparent in the Irish's success in the Catholic Church and their relative failure as businessmen, was apparent here.[126] As Moynihan explains, Irish peasants "arrived in America with some feeling at least for the possibilities of politics, and they brought with them ... a phenomenally effective capacity for a political bureaucracy. Politics is a risky business. Hence it has ever been the affair of speculators with the nerve to gamble and an impulse to boldness. These are anything but peasant qualities. Certainly they are not the qualities of Irish peasants who, collectively, yield to none in the rigidity of their social structure and their disinclination to adventure. Instead of letting politics transform them, the Irish transformed politics, establishing a political system in New York City that, from a distance, seems like the social system of an Irish village writ large. The Irish village was a place of stable, predictable social relations in which almost everyone had a role to play, under the surveillance of a stern oligarchy of elders, and in which, on the whole, a person's position was likely to improve with time. Transferred to Manhattan, these were the essentials of Tammany Hall."[127]

The Irish machines could not have succeeded but for the fact that Irish-Americans voted as a bloc, a Democratic bloc almost everywhere, with the prominent exception of Philadelphia. From the 1850s to the 1960s, the differences in voting behavior between Yankee Protestants and Irish Catholics in New England were as stark as the differences between whites and blacks in the Deep South today: the first group voted by large margins for Republicans, the second group overwhelmingly—often with near unanimity—for Democrats. The differences were somewhat less wide in New York, Chicago, and other cities, but pronounced nevertheless.

Massachusetts, the heartland of New England Yankees, which did not have large numbers of non-Irish immigrants, provides a particularly vivid example. In 1900 Massachusetts had thirteen congressional districts. Two, both centered in majority-Irish Boston, voted 59 and 67 percent Democratic. Nine of the other eleven districts, with much lower Irish percentages, voted 58 to 69 percent Republican. Only two, centered on heavily Irish Worcester and Lowell but including Protestant Republican towns all around, were marginal. Overall, Republicans led in votes for House candidates, 59 to 40 percent.[128] Over the years the Irish, with their large families, became a larger percentage of the elec- torate, and the Democratic percentage slowly rose. In the 1916 Senate race, the quintessential Yankee Henry Cabot Lodge defeated John F. "Honey Fitz" Fitzgerald, 51 to 45 percent. Some thirty-six years later, when Lodge's and Fitzgerald's grandsons were the candidates, John F. Kennedy beat Henry Cabot Lodge Jr., 51 to 48 percent. In between, the great events that produced sharp changes in voting behavior in most other states—the Depression, the New Deal, World War II, the rise of labor unions—had little effect on voting in Massachusetts; ethnic origin was everything, or almost everything. Since the late 1960s, Massachusetts has become an overwhelmingly Democratic state, but only because the Irish stayed loyal to the party of the Kennedys, while the Yankee elite, following the Ivy League uni- versities, turned left on cultural issues in the years of the Vietnam

War and Watergate. In the past forty years, only when the Republicans nominated a presidential candidate of Irish ancestry, Ronald Reagan, has Massachusetts cast its electoral votes against the Democrats.

Massachusetts is an extreme example. Elsewhere, Irish-American loyalties to the Democratic Party waned: in New York in the 1940s, as James A. Farley challenged his former patron Franklin Roosevelt; in Illinois in the 1950s, as Irish Democrats became Republicans when they moved out of Chicago to the Cook County suburbs and the outer "collar counties"; in the 1960s and 1970s, as Irish attitudes on cultural issues—crime, race, abortion—inclined them to leave their ancestral party. But ethnic loyalty was still strong in 1960 when John F. Kennedy won the votes of 78 percent of Catholics but only 37 percent of white Protestants.

Irish machine politics was never the politics of the civics textbook. The politics of eighteenth- and early-nineteenth-century Ireland was not either. As author Chris McNickle writes, "When they arrived in the United States, the Irish already had a long, if perverse acquaintance with the Anglo-Saxon political system. They had learned from the English about electoral fraud, judicial chicanery, and manipulation of the rules for partisan advantage. They understood politics as the means one group used to secure power for itself, to hold onto it, and to exploit it. Morality had nothing to do with it, nor did any grand ideology. For the Irish, politics differed from other professions only in detail. It was a way to earn a living."[129] Progressive historians are invariably disappointed that the Irish machines did not encourage a populist politics or seek economic redistribution or build class consciousness. New York's Tweed Ring in the 1860s, led by a native Protestant but manned mainly by Irish Catholics, treated control of city government as an opportunity to steal vast sums for its leaders and hand out jobs for its followers.[130] Under Honest John Kelly it did less of the former and more of the latter. In 1886 the Irish machine even supported the free-market capitalist Abram S. Hewitt for mayor over the near-socialist radical Henry George.[131] (The Republican nominee, a young patrician named Theodore Roosevelt, finished third.) Tammany Hall controlled sixty thousand government jobs with a payroll of $90 million a year by the turn of the century,[132] when Tammany leader George Washington Plunkitt propounded his definition of "honest graft" and proclaimed, "I seen my opportunities and I took 'em."[133] Tammany politicians, writes McNickle, "exercised influence over judges and police on behalf of potential voters, they offered families help in the event of eviction or fire, they sponsored summer picnics and social clubs, and on and on."[134]

The record of machine politics differed from city to city. In New York, which was never more than one-third Irish, the Irish leaders of Tammany Hall (which covered only Manhattan and not the four outer boroughs) understood that they could not rely on Irish votes alone. Charles F. Murphy, Tammany leader from 1902 to 1924, was very much aware of the huge floods of Italian and Jewish immigrants who started to arrive in the city in 1890. He knew that while the Italians were politically quiescent, the Jews were hostile to machine politics and attracted to socialism or at least a social democratic welfare state.[135] Murphy picked competent officeholders and adapted smartly to the new voters. Under Murphy-supported mayors, New York City government was able to complete two bridges across the East River in the first decade of the century; Tammany mayor George B. McClellan started the Manhattan Bridge in 1908 and kept a promise to walk across it before leaving office at the end of 1909.[136] After the disastrous Triangle Shirtwaist fire of 1911, Murphy supported workplace safety legislation. He promoted to Assembly and Senate leaders two young politicians, Alfred E. Smith and Robert Wagner, who later as governor and senator, respectively, would be, next to Franklin Roosevelt, the most effective advocates of welfare state measures. But after the death of the stern Murphy, New York machine leadership deteriorated. Mayors Jimmy

Walker ("P. T. Barnum in a speakeasy: predatory, not evil," writes Moynihan)[137] and William O'Dwyer were ousted for corruption; the Republican New Dealer Fiorello LaGuardia held the mayor's office for twelve years in between.

Boston, with an Irish majority, had a very different politics. Here the fights were not between an Irish-led Democratic machine and various combinations of Republicans and Socialists but between different Irish leaders, each with his own faction. The most colorful and enduring was James Michael Curley, whose political career spanned the years 1898 to 1949. He went to jail twice, once for taking a civil service exam for a constituent ("He did it for a friend!").[138] His goal was to provide public jobs for Irish constituents whose incomes continued to lag far behind the norm. He and other Irish politicians succeeded in loading up the public payroll to the point that Boston's property taxes reached the 10 percent level by the 1950s, which effectively squelched economic growth there. Curley claimed credit for some reforms—cutting workweeks, expanding workmen's compensation[139]—but his achievements over a long career were meager. As William V. Shannon writes, Curley "never transcended the boundaries. He exploited the sufferings and the inexperience, the warm sentiment, the fears, and the prejudices of his own people to perpetuate his personal power. He solved nothing; he moved toward no larger understanding; he opened no new lines of communication.... He did all this with wit and panache, but he nevertheless committed two mortal sins against the public good: his bad example debased the moral tone of political life in a great city for a generation, and his words distorted the people's understanding of reality."[140] This was predatory politics, the looting of the private sector by the public sector.

Similar were the effects of Frank Hague, the longtime (1917–1949) boss and mayor of Jersey City, New Jersey. "I am the law," Hague proclaimed. He cast Hudson County's votes as a bloc, electing governors and senators; he levied high taxes on industries and cracked down on crime and unions. "Most local residents who recall Hague and his era do so with nostalgia and deep affection," writes local historian Bob Leach, quoting a senior citizen who said, "Hague took care of himself, but he took care of the people too. When Hague was in charge, no family got put out on the street because they couldn't pay the rent, and nobody froze for want of coal in the winter and, if you needed a doctor, the Medical Center had the best of them—all free—and you could walk the streets at night like it was broad daylight."[141] But Hague's high parasitic taxes, like Curley's, stifled economic growth in his city and prevented the job-creating private-sector development that finally, a half century later, made Jersey City and Boston economically vibrant again.

Chicago was more like New York. By the turn of the century it had an Irish-run Democratic machine that levied taxes to give its Irish followers jobs. Aldermen in Chicago got bribes for themselves and jobs for faithful constituents from streetcar, gas, electric, and phone companies that wanted franchises to operate in their wards.[142] This took political skill: as in New York, the Irish weren't a clear majority. Donald Miller observes that, although the Irish "were a numerical majority in only a handful of wards and were outnumbered by Germans by more than two-to-one in the city in 1890, almost three of four members of Chicago's Democratic committee and 24 of the 28 most powerful ward bosses were Irish. The result was a Hibernization of the public payroll."[143] And Chicago's Democrats continued to face competition. "Big Bill" Thompson, the famous mayor who in the 1920s promised to "punch King George in the snoot" if he came to Chicago, was a Republican. The Democratic machine consolidated control under Thompson's successor, Anton Cermak, a Bohemian (i.e., Czech), and Ed Kelly, who became mayor after Cermak was shot in 1933. Kelly admitted an income of $724,000 in the 1920s, when he was being paid $15,000 a year as an employee of the Sanitary Commission, and paid a fine of

$105,000; in 1935 Interior Secretary Harold Ickes wrote in his diary of a construction project, "I also told the President that any funds given Kelly would be subject to 20 percent for graft and he said he was afraid that was true."[144] Machine control did not, however, reach a peak until the time of Richard J. Daley, mayor from 1955 until his death in 1976. Daley's machine was multi-ethnic and multiracial, but still disproportionately Irish. He was never personally corrupt, but he practiced patronage politics until a 1973 court ruling outlawed it. He undertook major projects like the building of O'Hare Airport (named for a local war hero) that maintained Chicago as a business center.[145]

The Irish-led political machines served a useful function: they regulated and kept peace among the hundreds of thousands of immigrants and low-wage workers who thronged to the great American cities from the 1840s to the 1940s. As Moynihan puts it, "The Irish leaders did for the Protestant establishment what it could not do for itself, and could not do without."[146] Great cities in Europe had revolutions; great cities in the United States had political machines. Of course, articulate elites—from New York mayor Philip Hone and diarist George Templeton Strong in the 1830s, to Lincoln Steffens and other Progressive era muckrakers in the 1900s, to New York and Chicago reform Democrats in the 1960s—looked at Irish machine politics and saw nothing but fraud and corruption. Such elites never sanctioned and usually criticized vociferously ethnic loyalties in voting and ethnic preferences in public jobs as well as in private jobs subject to machine influence—for that is what patronage hiring amounted to. At their worst—in Boston or Jersey City—Irish machines produced predatory government, which took so much out of the private sector that it withered and, in a country with great economic growth, produced no jobs or chance at wealth for the machine's constituents. At their best the machines built great public works—the East River bridges, O'Hare Airport—that promoted economic growth and creativity. At their worst the machines tolerated and facilitated organized crime. At their best they promoted the domestic order that people need to make a living and strengthen their communities. At their worst they practiced electoral fraud. At their best they helped to stifle the impulses to totalitarianism that prevailed in great cities in Europe.

But one failure seldom mentioned by their critics is that the machines did so little for, and arguably held back the progress of, the Irish-Americans in whose behalf and with whose votes they ruled. As Moynihan puts it, "The Irish were immensely successful in politics. They ran the city [New York]. But the very parochialism and bureaucracy that enabled them to succeed in politics prevented them from doing much with government. In all those 60 or 70 years when they could have done almost anything they wanted in politics, they did very little.... In a sense, the Irish did not know what to do with power once they got it.... They never thought of politics as an instrument of social change—their kind of politics involved the processes of a society that was not changing."[147] And while producing no social change through the public sector, they also retarded the upward mobility of their constituency in the private sector. Continues Moynihan, "The small potatoes of political success have become even less nourishing over the years. Swarms of Irish descended on the city government after the Civil War and began successions of low-grade civil servants. Here, as with the top-rank politicians, there was little cumulative improvement from one generation to the next. The economic rewards in America over the past century have gone to entrepreneurs, not to *fonctionnaires*, and hence, in that measure, not to the Irish of New York."[148]

CONVERGENCE

Well into the twentieth century, Irish-Americans lagged behind the national average in income and wealth. For many, ethnic discrimination still seemed to be the cause, and discrimination was certainly visible. "No Irish Need Apply" signs were no longer much seen, but there undoubtedly were employers who would not hire Irish. Housing discrimination against the Irish was nowhere near as systematic and total as it was against blacks, but there were neighborhoods in which Americans with Irish names found it difficult to buy a house or rent an apartment. Law firms, banks, elite clubs—all discriminated against the Irish; it was his failure to get into clubs that led Joseph Kennedy to leave Boston and move to New York in 1927. The memory of past discrimination remained bright; as Kerby Miller writes, "American nativism, reinforcing a legacy of colonialism and social inferiority, made most Irish Catholic emigrants almost morbidly sensitive."[149]

But these memories were also an obstacle to getting ahead in twentieth-century America, which, after all, was by no means as fundamentally unfair as nineteenth-century Ireland. The prevalent attitude that the larger society was illegitimate produced high crime rates and predatory political machines that worked against upward mobility and economic growth. It also produced low levels of educational achievement, which sharply limited opportunity. It was fortunate, though it was irritating to many Irish-Americans, that the articulate elite of the larger society never sanctioned Irish transgressions of the rules. Crime was never excused as the inevitable product of an unjust society; alcohol use and abuse was officially castigated by the enactment of Prohibition; political machines always operated under a cloud of disapproval. Over generations this had an effect on opinion and behavior. William V. Shannon writes, "The Irish among other immigrants had the attitude typical of those who comprise a client group and not a ruling group. For a long period, they were people who had stature without status, power without responsibility. Only gradually did the social discipline grow to match the power, and only when that happened did the majority detach themselves from the values of the political machine."[150]

Ethnic loyalty in voting came to be regarded as illegitimate; ticket-balancers usually felt obliged to claim they were making decisions on merit, not ethnicity. "I always vote for all the good Irish names," one Boston lady told me in the early 1960s; that was not something most people would admit in public.

Irish-Americans, like other immigrants and their offspring, had one bit of good fortune: they were concentrated in places with above-average economic growth. Immigrants, even those like the Irish who are torn by disaster from the old country, usually avoid areas of economic stagnation and head for places that are economically vibrant, and by their own hard work make them more economically vibrant still. The great cities to which most Irish immigrants came and where most of their descendants remained proved in the century from 1830 to 1930 to be the focus of America's astonishing economic growth, and in time the Irish partook of its rewards. Even if they were slower to rise economically than English, German, and Jewish immigrants, they did eventually rise. Though precise data are lacking, it appears that by the end of the 1950s Irish Catholic immigrants and their descendants had equaled other Americans in occupational distribution and surpassed some in income and education.[151] And, though once again precise data are lacking, by the 1950s the once "wild Irish" now had disproportionately low crime rates. Intermarriage with non-Irish, rare as late as 1920, when three-quarters of Irish married Irish, became much more common, and most distinctively Irish neighborhoods disappeared after 1920.[152] Even the demographic characteristics of as late as 1960—delayed marriage and high rates of both celibacy and fertility[153]—had largely disappeared by the end of the century.

But one grievance remained: in the political process, Irish Catholics in the 1950s still sensed that they were not considered fully American. In 1928 the Democratic Party nominated Al Smith for president. Smith had been the governor of the largest and richest state, New York, for eight years; he was by common consent the outstanding state governor of his generation. The product of a political machine, he was smart and honest. But he was also a Roman Catholic and, as such, suspect to many American Protestants, who regarded the Catholic Church as a subversive foreign power commanding the loyalty of its followers over allegiance to their country. To Smith this was nonsense, but it was an attitude deeply rooted in British and American history. Smith lost by a wide margin to Herbert Hoover, and lost southern states—Virginia, North Carolina, Tennessee, Florida, Texas—that ordinarily went heavily Democratic. His defeat was taken as an indication that Americans would not elect a Catholic as president. Less noticed at the time was the fact that Smith's Catholicism enabled him to carry heretofore Republican Massachusetts and Rhode Island; as Samuel Lubell pointed out, he converted million-plus Republican majorities in the counties containing the nation's twelve largest cities to a Democratic majority. Lubell wrote, "While Hoover was carrying more than 200 southern counties which had never gone Republican before, Smith was swinging 122 northern counties out of the G.O.P. column."[154]

For thirty years after Smith's defeat, no party seriously considered nominating a Catholic. Then came John F. Kennedy. Kennedy was the grandson of a mayor of Boston, James M. Curley's rival John F. Fitzgerald, and the son of Joseph P. Kennedy, the wealthy movie mogul and Wall Street speculator, first head of the Securities and Exchange Commission and ambassador to Great Britain, who once had presidential ambitions himself. In a family conference after the 1956 election, Joseph Kennedy batted down his son's argument that his Catholicism meant he could not be elected president. "Just remember, this country is not a private preserve for Protestants. There's a whole new generation out there and it's filled with the sons and daughters of immigrants from all over the world and those people are going to be mighty proud that one of their own is running for president. And that pride will be your spur, it will give your campaign an intensity we've never seen in public life."[155]

And so it was. But even then, Kennedy had to convince voters he was not just a sectarian or ethnic candidate. It helped that the young Senator Kennedy, with his Harvard degree and Pulitzer Prize, with the demeanor of a British aristocrat (one of his sisters married the heir to the duke of Devonshire), was not at all the stereotypical Irishman. Still, Kennedy's candidacy evoked strong feelings from Catholics and anti-Catholics; in an election that produced the highest voter turnout since 1908, 78 percent of Catholics voted for Kennedy, while 63 percent of white Protestants voted for his Republican opponent, Richard Nixon. Kennedy's victory margin was narrow, but he proved to be exceedingly popular. His job approval rating hovered around 70 percent (except among white southerners after he endorsed the civil rights bill in May 1963). His assassination in November 1963 shocked the nation, which watched in dazed silence the Catholic funeral ceremony.

Kennedy's election and success as president settled the question of whether Catholics were truly Americans. It was also a moment when the American Catholic Church, long dominated by the Irish, suddenly became a less distinctive institution. In those same years, Catholics abandoned the Latin Mass and meatless Fridays, vocations of priests and nuns dropped abruptly, and, with the advent of the birth control pill, Catholics stopped producing the large families that were so common in the 1950s (in that decade Catholics accounted for 38 percent of America's population increase).[156] Politically, the Irish, starting in the late 1960s, became increasingly Republican—in proportions similar to that of the electorate as a whole. The Irish, still distinctive on St. Patrick's Day, had become interwoven into the fabric of American life. "Their adjustment and that of their descendants," a scholar wrote in 1980, "is today almost complete."[157] It took 120 years.

CHAPTER 2

BLACKS

THE OLD COUNTRY

I t is still visible to a traveler in the Mississippi Delta or the Black Belt of Alabama who turns off the main highway and drives away from the center of the county seat. At one edge of town below the railroad tracks or in the farm fields sit the ramshackle, unpainted wood cabins, the occasional country store, the proud but tiny churches and their small graveyards. Such are the visible remains of the segregated rural South, where nearly three out of every four black Americans lived in the 1930s. Many of these rural enclaves have been almost entirely depopulated since then: Greene County, Alabama, with 19,000 people in 1940, has under 10,000 today; Tunica County, Mississippi, often ranked the poorest in the nation, fell from 22,000 in 1940 to 8,000 in the 1990s. Abandoned cabins and the empty stores are evidence of the greatest internal migration in American history, of southern blacks to northern cities in the years from 1940 to 1965. In the seventy-five years before that, only 1 million blacks (and 1 million whites) moved from South to North, even while 27 million Europeans crossed the Atlantic Ocean and even though wage rates were twice as high in the North as in the South.[1] To cross the border from South to North, Americans did not need to board a steamer, survive the scrutiny of officials at Ellis Island, or learn a new language. If economic incentives had been the only factor, many more southerners, black and white, would have moved. But even after seventy-five years the Civil War was still such a living, burning memory that to move across the invisible line that divided North from South was in many people's minds like moving to another country.[2]

The racially segregated South of 1940 was, in very many ways, another country, set apart from the rest of America, and one about which northern whites remained mostly ignorant. When the pioneering sociologist John Dollard published *Caste and Class in a Southern Town* in 1937, the picture he painted of "Southerntown" (actually Indianola, Mississippi) was as remote and unfamiliar to most of his readers as Margaret Mead's less accurate portrait of Samoa. Dollard showed how blacks were expected to use "Mr." or "Mrs." to address white people, while they were always addressed by their first names. He described how blacks were not allowed to vote or express political opinions and how southern whites regarded the prohibition on sexual contact between black men and white women as centrally important. Schools and public libraries were racially segregated by law in every southern state; blacks were required to sit in the back of the bus or, if seats were all taken there, to stand; hotels and restaurants and lunch counters and drinking fountains were segregated, as were hospitals.[3] Blacks were not allowed to come into white people's houses through the front door. Whites never shook hands with blacks. And Dollard described how the failure to follow these rules was often punished with physical violence.

Black-on-black crime, meanwhile, was often ignored or condoned by the authorities. "All white families expend a large amount of time, money, and emotion in preventing the criminals they employ from receiving their legal deserts," wrote the planter William Alexander Percy in 1941.[4] But black crimes against whites were punished ferociously by the law and sometimes by the lynch mob. Ten lynchings were recorded in the years from 1931 to 1940, and they had been much more frequent (104 from 1891 to 1900) in the recent and vividly remembered past.[5] In 1937 an anti-lynching bill passed the House of Representatives but got nowhere in the Senate; President Franklin Roosevelt refused to support it. Blacks and whites, in Dollard's view, were separate castes, with separate classes within each caste. "Caste has replaced slavery as a means of maintaining the essence of the old status order in the South," Dollard wrote. "It defines an inferior and a superior group and regulates the behavior of members of each group."[6]

If southern blacks were legally barred from the political arena, they were also largely barred from the economic marketplace. Some blacks did own farms, but these were typically small and unproductive, and often tied down by unpayable debt. Seven-eighths of black farmers in 1940 worked as field hands, tenants, or sharecroppers. Their earnings, if any, were pathetically low and left them economically dependent on whites. "Sharecroppers rented the land they cultivated," write Stephan and Abigail Thernstrom in their magisterial *America in Black and White*, "but lacked the cash to pay the rent in advance or to obtain food, clothing, and other necessities. In return for providing these, the landlord took a share of the crop when it was harvested. What was due the landlord at year's end was often more than the crop was worth, so that the cropper ended up another year older and deeper in debt."[7] Thus many southern blacks lived almost outside the cash economy, with no experience of the economic marketplace. As late as 1956, Martin Luther King Jr. met sharecroppers on an Alabama plantation who had never seen United States currency.[8]

Under these circumstances it is not surprising that blacks had low levels of education. The Supreme Court had ruled in 1896 that states could have racially segregated schools, provided they were "separate but equal." In practice they were separate but anything but equal. The average southern black adult in 1940 had spent only five years in school, three and one-half less than the average southern white. In 1920, 23 percent of southern blacks were illiterate, and two decades later, one out of every nine was still illiterate.[9] Southern states, dominated by planters who wanted docile field workers, spent three to seven times as much on schooling for whites as for blacks; one out of three teachers of southern blacks did not have a high school diploma. "Incredible as it may seem, in 1940 the Mississippi state Senate debated a proposal to purge all references to voting, elections, and democracy in civics texts used in the black public schools," the Thernstroms write. "It was defeated by a slim margin."[10]

The southern system of segregation and sharecropping bore down particularly hard on men who were addressed by whites as "boy," prevented from making a good living, and subject to violence—often death—if they were thought to show any disrespect to a white woman. The result was that sharecropper communities were in practice matriarchies. In a study of sharecroppers in rural Georgia in the 1930s, sociologist Charles S. Johnson found that one-quarter of 612 black families were headed by single women, and that many of the marriages were common law. "There is more illegitimacy among the Negro group and consequently more children dependent on one parent," he wrote. Anthropologist Hortense Powdermaker, who worked in Indianola, Mississippi, in the 1930s, wrote that "the typical Negro family throughout the South is matriarchal and elastic." "In the lower-class Negro family the woman plays a more important role than in the usual American family," wrote John Dollard. "Her economic independence puts her in a position to challenge the assumption of the strict patriarchal position by the Negro man."[11] Gunnar Myrdal, who traveled throughout the South in researching his 1944 best-seller *American Dilemma*, reported that 16 percent of births to blacks were illegitimate and argued that "the census information on the marital status of Negroes is especially inaccurate, since unmarried couples are inclined to report themselves as married, and women who have never married but who have children are inclined to report themselves as widowed."[12]

There was a small professional class among southern blacks—in Dollard's terms, a middle class in the second caste. "Preach, teach, or farm"—those were considered the only available choices for southern blacks. Especially important were the preachers, who were very often the effective leaders of the black communities. Trained in seminaries almost completely separated from the white society, depending for their livelihood on building congregations, they could communicate with their congregations at services mostly out of the hearing of white leaders. "The Negro church," writes Taylor Branch in his Pulitzer Prize–winning *Parting the Waters*, "served not only as a place of worship but also as a bulletin board to a people who owned no organs of communication, a credit union to those without banks, and even a kind of people's court."[13] The black ministry, like the Irish priesthood, channeled many talented men from commerce to the clergy; but unlike Irish priests, black ministers had families and built dynasties, like Martin Luther King's. Ministers would lead the civil rights movement in the South and would wield great political influence in the North.

Back in 1940 black ministers probably seldom dared criticize the South's caste system explicitly. But southern blacks did not need to be educated to know that every aspect of this system, from segregation to sharecropping, was fundamentally unfair. They knew that white southern society maintained these rules through force, violence, something akin to terror. As with Irish-Americans, that habit of mind—a sense that one had no obligation to obey the rules of a fundamentally unfair larger society—was deeply imprinted. It was a part of the culture in the sense used by sociologist Orlando Patterson, "a repertoire of socially transmitted and intra-generational ideas about how to live and make judgments, both in general terms and in regard to specific domains of life."[14] But at the time there seemed to be little one could do to change the southern system. As Stephan and Abigail Thernstrom write, "No one in the 1930s predicted the remarkable change in the status of black Americans about to take place."[15]

Yet for some there was living memory of a time when a better system had seemed possible, the years of Reconstruction after the Civil War. Slavery had been ended and blacks, protected by the U.S. Army, had the right to vote. After the federal troops had withdrawn in 1877, as historian C. Vann Woodward has shown, it took two decades for the system of legal segregation to be fully developed.[16] Blacks who voted—in northern cities and in scattered parts of the South—remained loyal to the Republicans, the party of Abraham Lincoln, until the 1930s; they voted for Herbert Hoover over Franklin D. Roosevelt in the Depression year of 1932 with the highest percentage margin of any demographic group.[17]

The possibilities for change through electoral politics seemed limited, however. In no election from 1900 to 1926 was a black elected to the House of Representatives. In 1928 Oscar DePriest became the first black elected in the twentieth century, from a district on the South Side of Chicago with many members of the black middle class and recent migrants from the South. DePriest was a Republican, and this was a heavily Republican district. Even so, DePriest's percentage in 1928 was 20 percent lower than his predecessor's had been in 1926; evidently many white Republicans were unwilling to vote for a black. In 1934, as blacks shifted from the party of Lincoln to the party of Franklin Roosevelt and his New Deal, DePriest was defeated by another black, Democrat Arthur Mitchell. New York, with its large black community in central Harlem, did not elect a black until 1944. The district lines in effect until then, drawn under the 1910 census, placed Harlem in districts dominated by other neighborhoods, and not until new lines were drawn did a Harlem-dominated district elect the Reverend Adam Clayton Powell Jr.

Far more effective in the 1940s than one or two junior congressmen was the one black public figure with a national constituency, A. Philip Randolph, the founder and president of the all-black Brotherhood of Sleeping Car Porters. As war loomed, Randolph started organizing a protest march on Washington scheduled for June 1941 to demand integration of the armed forces and assurance that blacks would not be barred from war industry jobs. "In the interest of national unity," he said, he called for "the abrogation of every law which makes a distinction in treatment between citizens based on religion, creed, color, or national origin."[18] President Roosevelt feared that the march would produce violence—race riots in the years after World War I had resulted in many deaths—and that racial violence would besmirch America's reputation in the struggle against Nazi Germany and Japan. Roosevelt begged Randolph to call off the march, but Randolph insisted on a ban on racial discrimination in defense industries and government. In the end, Roosevelt created a Fair Employment Practices Committee (FEPC) by executive order and Randolph cancelled the march. The FEPC accomplished little, and Randolph accepted less than his initial demands. But he showed that blacks could achieve political goals by the threat of mass action, and he got the government to endorse the principle of equal treatment for blacks—both of which would be of enormous import in the years after the war.[19]

CRISIS

The movement of blacks from the rural South to the urban North in the quarter century from 1940 to 1965 was the largest internal migration in American history. It dwarfed the previous movement of blacks from South to North: between 1865 and 1940, about 1.7 million blacks moved north, whereas between 1940 and 1965, about 4.4 million did.[20] Migration in the years before 1940 was inhibited by laws the southern states passed starting in the 1880s "limiting the free movement of Negro workers and tenants and heavily taxing all labor agents sent south to 'entice' them away."[21] "In some places," writes author Nicholas Lemann, "the police would arrest black people for vagrancy if they were found in the vicinity of the train station, or even pull them off of trains and put them in jail. There was a great deal of local propagandizing against migration by planters, politicians, black preachers in the hire of whites, and the press."[22] This was not out of any affection for blacks but because white planters could not harvest their cotton and other crops without cheap black labor. Southern blacks knew that racial discrimination existed in the North and had no reason to think that in ordinary times they would have an easy time finding jobs or housing there. (Significantly, migration accelerated during World War I, when the tight war labor market induced many northern employers to hire blacks. In 1930, 79 percent of American blacks still lived in the South, mostly in the rural South; in 1940, the figure was 77 percent.[23] By 1965, the figure was 54 percent, a number that has changed only marginally since.)

What then prompted the great migration that began around 1940? First, government action—the minimum wages promoted by the 1933 National Recovery Act and the 1938 minimum wage law—raised the cost of black labor. New Deal farm laws encouraged landowners to switch from sharecroppers to wage labor.[24] Southern politicians, however, worked to exempt farm workers, and southern planters were willing to evade any law that did apply. Moreover, war industries increased the demand for labor beginning in 1940, and such jobs were covered by the new FEPC. Also, the big CIO (Congress of Industrial Organizations) unions that organized the auto and steel industries between 1937 and 1941, unlike most older unions, opposed racial discrimination.

But the major cause of the great 1940–1965 migration was a technological development, the mechanical cotton picker.[25] The first practical cotton picker was introduced in 1944. A field worker could pick twenty pounds of cotton an hour; the cotton picker could pick a thousand pounds. This machine, which could do the work of fifty people, was revolutionary. Lemann reports that one planter's accounting showed that "picking a bale of cotton by machine cost him $5.26, and picking it by hand cost him $39.41."[26] Suddenly, in the years after World War II, southern planters who had worked for years to keep blacks from migrating north were now urging them to do so. In some cases, Mississippi Delta planters put whole sharecropper families on the Illinois Central with one-way tickets to Chicago; by the 1950s the Mississippi Citizens Council was making standing offers of free one-way passage to the North.[27]

THE NEW COUNTRY

The great migration that began during World War II swelled in size in the years after the war. Southern blacks liked much of what they found in Chicago, New York, Detroit, and other northern cities. There were low-skill jobs aplenty during the war and, thanks to the unexpected postwar boom, afterwards.[28] In the 1950s the income of a typical black family in the North was about twice as high as in the South—93 percent more in 1953, 119 percent more in 1959.[29] And refreshingly absent was "the elaborate code of racial etiquette" that was enforced, ultimately by violence, in the South. "Whites did not habitually refer to black men by their first names or as 'boy' or 'uncle,'" write Stephan and Abigail Thernstrom. "The notion that blacks should only enter white homes by the back door was unheard of. For members of the two races to dine together was not taboo, nor was the simple act of shaking hands. Black people were not automatically at the back of any line that formed. [Novelist] Richard Wright at first found it startling to stop at a busy newsstand and to find that he was able to buy a paper before all the whites crowding around it were served."[30]

Patterns of migration followed the railroads. From Mississippi, blacks headed straight north on the Illinois Central or the parallel U.S. 51 to Chicago. From Alabama, blacks headed up the Louisville & Nashville to Detroit. From coastal South Carolina, North Carolina, and Virginia, blacks headed up the Atlantic Coast Line to New York and Philadelphia. The numbers were huge. One-quarter of southern blacks ages twenty to twenty-four migrated north in the 1940s, and another quarter went in the 1950s. More than a third of young blacks in the Deep South states of South Carolina, Georgia, Alabama, and Mississippi headed north in the 1940s.[31] Chicago's black population increased from 278,000 in 1940 to 492,000 in 1950 and 813,000 in 1960.[32] New York's black population increased from 458,000 in 1940 to 748,000 in 1950 and 1,088,000 in 1960.[33] The ten largest cities in 1940 had a total black population of 1,646,000; by 1960 the black population in those cities was 4,205,000.[34]

The migration, once started, accelerated as farm jobs disappeared in the rural South and as southerners violently resisted the civil rights movement. Nicholas Lemann describes this northward movement vividly: "For a time, in the late 1950s and early 1960s, it seemed as if the whole black society of Clarksdale and the Mississippi Delta had transferred itself to Chicago. Everybody was either living in Chicago, or back and forth from Chicago, or occasionally visiting Chicago. Certain venues in Chicago were known to be gathering places for Clarksdalians—taverns on the South Side, kitchenette apartment buildings, weekly-rate residential hotels on the Near West Side. Children would be sent up for the summer to stay with relatives and get jobs that paid much better than chopping cotton on the plantations back home."[35] Sometimes this straddling of two worlds could lead to tragedy.

Emmett Till, a fourteen-year-old raised in Chicago, visited relatives in Mississippi in 1955 and there reportedly "wolf-whistled"
at a white woman. He was murdered by two white men who,
when they were tried for the crime, watched the proceedings con-
temptuously and were quickly acquitted by the all-white jury.[36]

One result of this vast movement was rapid neighborhood
change, as it was called. Not atypical was Chicago's West Side
neighborhood of Lawndale, which was 13 percent black in 1950
and 91 percent black ten years later.[37] Ethnic neighborhoods
were the norm in the big cities of the North. A hundred years
before, neighborhoods changed from native to Irish almost
overnight, and new immigrant groups tended to cluster in streets
and neighborhoods inhabited largely, though not entirely, by
others from the old country. The greater physical distinctiveness
of blacks and the norm of racial segregation in housing—it was
required for Federal Home Administration loans and recognized
by newspaper classified sections, which had separate listings for
"Apartments, Colored"—meant that the appearance of even a
few blacks in a neighborhood sometimes resulted in panic selling
by whites. During World War II, most blacks in cities like
Detroit packed into small, preexisting black neighborhoods,[38]
but after the war they, like whites, sought housing with more
room. Blacks moving into white neighborhoods were often
greeted with hostility and sometimes even with violence. There
were charges that unscrupulous real estate agents would move a
black family into a neighborhood and then would try to panic
white homeowners into selling at low prices.[39] It is not clear how
true these stories are; what is undisputed is that most whites did
not want to live in neighborhoods with many black residents and
that the large influx of blacks inevitably meant that many neighborhoods transformed from all-white to mostly or all-black.
Large black ghettoes would have developed in the northern cities
even if local governments and real estate industries had tried to
prevent this result.

Unfortunately, many black rural migrants, cast out of the South by economic necessity, were unprepared for city life. Sociologist Charles S. Johnson, in his pioneering 1930s study of sharecroppers, warned that sharecroppers were living "outside the dominant culture of American society" and predicted that "the very fact of this cultural difference presents the danger of social disorganization in any sudden attempt to introduce new modes of living."[40] As Richard Wright put it in the 1940s, "Perhaps never in history has a more utterly unprepared folk wanted to go to the city; we were barely born as a folk when we headed for the tall and sprawling centers of steel and stone. We, who were landless upon the land; we, who barely managed to live in family groups; we, who needed the ritual and guidance of institutions to hold our atomized lives together in lines of purpose; we, who had known only relationships to people and not relationships to things; we, who had had our personalities blasted with two hundred years of slavery and had been turned loose to shift for ourselves—we were such a folk as this when we moved into a world that was destined to test all we were, that threw us into the scales of competition to weigh our mettle."[41] Sharecroppers did improve their economic circumstances by moving north, however, and there is evidence that it was the more educated and enterprising children of the Delta and the Black Belt who went north.[42]

RELIGION

As in the rural South, the church in the urban North was the one institution that blacks could control, free from white interference or dictates. By many measures, blacks have been the most religious of any American group. Whereas the Irish accepted the hierarchical structure of the Roman Catholic Church, blacks have created dozens of denominations and thousands of individual churches. Even before the great northward migration began around 1940, these churches, often started by charismatic, entrepreneurial individuals, proliferated in great numbers. "Harlem is perhaps overchurched," wrote W. E. B. DuBois in the 1920s, when an investigator found 140 black churches in a 150-block area of Harlem. Historian Gilbert Osofsky writes, "Only about a third—54—of Harlem's churches were housed in regular church buildings—and these included some of the most magnificent and costly church edifices in New York. The rest held services in stores and homes and appealed to Harlem's least educated people. 'Jack-leg preachers,' 'cotton-field preachers,' as these critics called them, hung out their poorly printed signboards and 'preached Jesus' to all who wanted to listen. One self-appointed pastor held meetings in the front room of his home and rented chairs from the local undertaker to seat his small congregation."[43] In time there grew up, as Nathan Glazer described them in the early 1960s, "the large institutional churches, in well-equipped buildings, with various group activities, with associated social services, with a large membership and a prominent minister. These churches, which elsewhere in America, for most groups, are fifth wheels, are in colored America, and in colored New York, in the center of things. And they play a role in politics that the churches of no other group can aspire to, or would dare to."[44] It was just such an institution, the Abyssinian Baptist Church, built from the savings of modest-income and poor congregants, that produced Adam Clayton Powell Jr., the first black congressman from New York.

One example of the entrepreneurial preachers who often started black churches was Chicago's Moses Cross. Author Alan Ehrenhalt tells his story: "Born in Mississippi, he had opened his first church in an empty store on the South Side [of Chicago] in 1941, preaching to a flock that consisted of his wife, his 12 children, and virtually no one else. Later he moved the church into an abandoned factory. By 1956, he had 200 members, a vibrato

Hammond organ, a senior choir, a gospel chorus, and a sewing circle. The following year, he bought a four-story building and set up a sanctuary seating 300 people, a banquet hall for 250, and a youth center and library upstairs."[45] "Of all the Bronzeville institutions of the 1950s," Ehrenhalt writes, "the churches were the most uniformly successful and self-reliant." Ministers were "figures of authority and respect" and "played a role more important than the businessman, the newspaper editor, even the machine boss. They were the indispensable coordinators of the community. They were into everything, acquainted with everybody, able to make connections and contacts between one set of institutions and another. 'I am a part of every organization in the Baptist Church,' one minister [said]. 'I am secretary of the Apex Funeral Parlor, Incorporated, and I own a half-interest in the business and the funeral cars. I am a Mason and also the sponsor of a Boy Scout troop. I own a three-flat building and a vacant lot. I also have a two-car garage.' More than virtually anyone in Bronzeville, the pastors were free agents, beholden to no larger force or interest."[46]

SPORTS AND ENTERTAINMENT

Blacks made great contributions to popular culture and entertainment, even before the great northward migration. Sports, with their strict meritocracy, were a venue for black talents. In 1908 Jack Johnson became the first black heavyweight champion boxer, replacing a run of Irishmen. He was widely unpopular, and fans looked for a "great white hope" to defeat him. In the 1930s Joe Louis became a much more popular heavyweight champion, partly because he beat the pride of Nazi Germany, Max Schmeling, and also because of his humble manner. Another superb black athlete, sprinter Jesse Owens, won four gold medals at the 1936 Olympics in Berlin, to the consternation of Adolf

Hitler. It was not until 1947, however, that major league baseball was integrated, when Brooklyn Dodgers president Branch Rickey put Jackie Robinson in the infield; other black baseball stars soon followed, but some—like the ancient pitcher Satchel Paige—played their best years in the Negro Leagues. Professional football was integrated before baseball, but it was not nearly so popular as it later became. Professional basketball integrated just a few years after Robinson joined the Dodgers; in the coming decades, many of the players who drove that sport to new heights of popularity were black. Black athletes drew fans from all races, though some bigots remained: Hank Aaron was the target of much hate mail when he threatened and eclipsed Babe Ruth's career home run record. The 1990s witnessed two interesting phenomena: Michael Jordan became the biggest star in basketball history, and Tiger Woods—of black, white, and Thai descent—began a career in golf that seemed likely to be the greatest ever.

If black athletes excelled at, and in some cases transformed, sports that had been created earlier, black musicians created new art forms of their own. The foremost was jazz, music influenced by the blues of the Mississippi Delta and by Beale Street in Memphis and Bourbon Street in New Orleans. Jazz musicians like Louis Armstrong emerged as national stars in the 1920s, and jazz became widely recognized as the first great American art form. Rhythm and blues continued with mainly a black audience, but the sudden popularity of rock and roll and Elvis Presley, who was heavily influenced by black musicians, moved it toward the mainstream in the 1950s and 1960s. The Motown sound topped the popular charts often in the 1960s and 1970s. More recently, as the music market has segmented, other forms—rap, hip-hop—have grown widely popular. It is impossible to imagine American popular music without the contributions of black musicians; in this one area blacks early on became interwoven into the American fabric.

WORK

The great northward migration produced huge and steady economic gains for blacks. For a decade before the Second World
War, America had built almost no new factories or office buildings; suddenly, the war increased the demand for both skilled and
unskilled labor. That demand continued unabated in the postwar
years, when central cities reached their all-time high as a percentage of national population and when labor unions reached
their all-time high as a percentage of the workforce. The
Thernstroms set out the stark figures: "Between 1940 and 1950
the earnings of the average black man, in real dollars adjusted for
inflation, went up a stunning 75 percent. They increased another
45 percent in the 1950s. In 1960 African-American men earned,
on the average, a staggering two and a half times what they had
earned on the eve of World War II. Their incomes rose from
$6,648 a year (in 1995 dollars) in 1940 to $16,851 twenty years
later. Black women matched these gains almost precisely. In 1960
their incomes were 2.3 times as high as they had been in 1940."[47]
Indeed, black migrants from the South, after a short adjustment
period, did better economically than northern-born blacks and of
course did far better than they had been doing in the South.[48] In
percentage terms the income gains were much greater than those
of non-blacks. And these gains were made before the civil rights
revolution and the passage of the Civil Rights Acts, before the
government's antipoverty programs of the 1960s and the affirmative action programs of the 1970s.

Thus blacks made great strides despite barriers that put many
occupations off-limits and despite most black adults' low levels of
education. And the gains were not just in income. Black life
expectancy increased from 53.1 years in 1940 to 63.6 years in
1960. Homeownership increased from 23 percent of blacks in
1940 to 38 percent in 1960.[49] To be sure, blacks at the end of that
period remained significantly below whites in income, life

expectancy, and homeownership, but the gaps in each case had sharply narrowed. Like immigrant groups who worked at subsistence farming in the old country and moved to blue-collar jobs in America, the black migrants from the rural South did not reach paradise, but they made substantial economic gains by moving and working hard at jobs that a growing private-sector economy made available.

For some, that progress became more difficult in the 1960s. As wages and labor costs increased, businesses invested in new equipment that eliminated many lesser-skilled jobs. It was apparent first in New York. In the early 1960s Nathan Glazer, discussing "the problem of the Negro man" in New York, wrote, "He has mostly depended in New York on unskilled labor and services. We are dispensing with unskilled labor by new machines, better organization, poorer maintenance, and simply learning to just do without. Just as the southern Negro agricultural laborer has been displaced by machinery, so too the Negro urban unskilled laborer is being displaced."[50] In 1965 Daniel Patrick Moynihan, then assistant secretary of labor, wrote, "From 1951 to 1963, the level of Negro male unemployment was on a long-run rising trend, while at the same time following the short-run ups and downs of the business cycle.... In 1963, a prosperous year, 29.2 percent of all Negro men in the labor force were unemployed at some time during the year. Almost half of these men were out of work 15 weeks or more."[51] This was one of the results of the move to the North. The Thernstroms note, "Desperate black men in the Depression years [in the South] could usually find someone to take them on as a farmhand," although "the jobs were so unattractive that classifying those who held them as 'employed' seems overly generous."[52] But in the North a man laid off a job in a factory was not likely to find casual agricultural work.

One thing the migrating blacks did very little was start businesses. The entrepreneurial impulse that found such vivid expression in the creation of black churches was seldom apparent in the private economic sphere. As Shelby Steele writes, "In black communities the most obvious entrepreneurial opportunities are routinely ignored."[53] The caste system of the South gave blacks little opportunity to own businesses and, in many cases, kept them out of the cash economy entirely. Even more important, Glazer argued, was "the failure of Negroes to develop a pattern of savings."[54] Slavery and sharecropping gave an individual no real chance of accumulating capital on his own but promised that he would be taken care of if destitute. Barriers to entrepreneurship—the difficulty of saving and of getting loans from banks—confronted every poor ethnic group, but blacks have proved particularly disinclined to start businesses of their own, preferring the apparent security of large organizations—large manufacturing corporations; labor unions; federal, state, and local government—to the hazards of running one's own business. The most striking exceptions, the corporations started by a few businessmen like Reginald Lewis and Robert Johnson, have received financing from much larger corporations. In heavily black neighborhoods, small stores typically have been owned and operated by others—at first Jews, more recently Koreans, Arabs, and other recently arrived ethnic groups—a fact that often has led to racial tension and violence.

Nevertheless, for all the difficulties, most blacks continued to make economic gains from the 1960s to the 1990s. The percentage of black men holding white-collar jobs rose from 5 percent in 1940 to 22 percent in 1970 and 32 percent in 1990; for black women the rise was even greater, to 59 percent in 1990.[55] As the Thernstroms show, the number of black professionals rose prodigiously between 1940 and 1970 and again between 1970 and 1990 (though not at any faster pace in the latter decades, despite the institution of affirmative action programs including racial quotas and preferences).[56] Black men's incomes as a percentage of whites' increased from 41 percent in 1940 to 59 percent in 1970 and 67 percent in 1990; black women's incomes as a percentage of whites' rose even more, to 89 percent in 1990. In 1940 only 1 percent of black families had what the Thernstroms define as middle-class incomes—double the poverty line. In 1970, 39 percent did, and in 1990 that number rose to 49 percent, compared to 75 percent among whites. The income gap among married-couple families grew even narrower. By 1995 the median income of black married-couple families was 87 percent that of whites.[57] This suggests that racial discrimination is a diminishing factor in holding down blacks' incomes.

"There is considerable evidence," Moynihan wrote in 1965, "that the Negro community is in fact dividing between a stable middle-class group that is steadily growing stronger and more successful, and an increasingly disorganized and disadvantaged lower-class group."[58] So it has been. The number of black professionals rose from 105,000 in 1940 (nearly two-thirds of them teachers) to 395,000 in 1970 and 934,000 in 1990.[59] The proportion of blacks identifying themselves as "middle class" rose from 12 percent in 1949 to 22 percent in 1976–1978 to 44 percent in 1994. "The black middle class," write the Thernstroms, "is now proportionally as large as the white middle class was at the end of Dwight Eisenhower's second term, a time when American society as a whole was usually described as being predominantly middle class."[60] By the 1990s large, stable, middle- to high-income black communities emerged in many metropolitan areas—in the Prince George's County suburbs of Washington and the DeKalb County suburbs of Atlanta, in the borough of Queens in New York and Fox Hills in Los Angeles, in the southern suburbs of Cook County, Illinois, and Oakland County, Michigan.

FAMILY

Unfortunately, not all blacks have moved ahead at this rate because of another factor, one of great social import—the declining percentage of black families headed by married couples. In 1995 black female-headed families had median incomes that were only 61 percent of whites', and 47 percent of black families were female-headed, as compared to 14 percent of white families.[61] A turning point seems to have come around 1960, not long before the conclusion of the great northward migration. At that point 67 percent of black children lived in two-parent families, well below the 91 percent among whites but still a clear majority.[62] Some of the difference represented the sharecropper heritage. "The typical Negro family throughout the South is matriarchal and elastic," wrote the pioneering sociologist Hortense Powdermaker, and "the personnel of these matriarchal families is variable and even casual," including illegitimate children.[63] Other scholars came to similar conclusions in the 1930s and 1940s.

But the similar pattern in northern cities was not spotlighted until 1963, when Nathan Glazer wrote in *Beyond the Melting Pot*, "There were in 1960 in the New York metropolitan area 353,000 Negro families; a quarter were headed by women. In contrast, less than one-tenth of the white households were headed by women. The rate of illegitimacy among Negroes is about fourteen to fifteen times that among whites."[64] In 1965 Glazer's coauthor, Daniel Patrick Moynihan, as assistant secretary of labor, wrote a report on "The Negro Family." Moynihan observed that 21 percent of black families were headed by females in 1960, up from 18 percent in 1950, and that the percentage of black births to unwed mothers had risen from 17 percent in 1940 to 24 percent in 1963.[65] This reversion to the loose family structure common in sharecropper communities came in spite of blacks' steady upward progress from the dreadful economic circumstances of sharecropping. Subtitling his report "The Case for National Action," Moynihan hoped that the antipoverty programs then being developed could reverse the trend. He noted that the breakdown of the black family had resulted in a "startling increase" in welfare dependency in a time of general economic growth.[66] But the report was controversial—

Moynihan was accused of "blaming the victim" and of seeking to impose middle-class standards on those who should be encouraged to become liberated from them.[67]

The trend Moynihan pointed to vastly accelerated after 1965. Evidently the northward migration that improved blacks' economic status had helped weaken family ties. The percentage of births out of wedlock among blacks rose from 22 percent in 1960 to 38 percent in 1970, 55 percent in 1980, and 70 percent in 1995.[68] The number has reached 80 percent in some central cities. A similar trend is apparent among whites, among whom out-of-wedlock births increased from 2 percent in 1960 to 25 percent in 1995, but that still means that three of four white babies are born to married parents while only three in ten black babies are. "A social pattern with devastating economic consequences has become the norm in the black community, while it is still a deviant pattern among whites," the Thernstroms conclude. "To be born out of wedlock is a ticket to an impoverished childhood."[69] Single motherhood has meant that black women are much more likely than white women to have incomes below the poverty line, even when they have jobs, and female-headed families are by definition unable in almost all cases to increase family incomes as most Americans have—by becoming two-earner families.

EDUCATION

Black educational levels rose sharply in the 1940s and 1950s, from the abysmal levels of the rural South. But blacks formed a disproportionately low number of those excelling in northern public schools,[70] and as schools became predominantly black, the levels of achievement slumped sharply. Black test scores and academic performance have increased somewhat over the years, but the results are still disappointing. In 1995 black students still trailed far behind whites and Asians on standardized tests. The mean College Board SAT verbal score among blacks was 356, far below the 448 of whites; on the math SAT blacks scored 388, whites 498. Only 2 percent of blacks scored 600 or higher on the verbal SAT, compared to 10 percent of whites and Asians; 2 percent of blacks scored 650 or higher on the math SAT, compared to 13 percent of whites and 26 percent of Asians.[71]

Many blacks and other critics have charged that such disappointing results occur because white politicians have neglected black schools. There has certainly been some evidence for this—notably the huge class sizes in Chicago's South Side and West Side public schools in the 1960s. But increasingly it has been blacks who have been administering central city school districts and above-average-income suburban districts where blacks are a majority or large minority, such as Prince George's County, Maryland, DeKalb County, Georgia, and Shaker Heights, Ohio. Another barrier to black achievement has surely been the habit of mind developed in the rural South that cast doubt on the idea that there was any reliable connection between effort and reward. As historian Roger Lane writes, "It is clear to a historian that some widely transmitted values, attitudes, or priorities now combine to keep many ghetto-dwellers from entering the economic mainstream."[72] Also, black churches produced few equivalents of the Catholic schools, whose strong discipline and promotion of traditional virtues helped to shape so many Irish Catholic children. Unfortunately, as the 1960s melted into the 1970s, most blacks found their children in public school systems run by people who abhorred rote memorization and drill, insisted that there was no need to learn basic rules of English and mathematics, and were content to provide social promotions to pupils who learned very little but did not cause major trouble.

In addition, the prevalence of crime in and around the schools made learning difficult. Court-generated rules designed to protect putatively innocent students from "abusive practices by school guards" and insisting on courtroom-style due process for school discipline made it very hard to maintain orderly and productive classrooms. The problem has gotten worse: black student achievement scores increased from 1971 to 1988, then started to decline. "Mounting levels of school violence and disorder could in part account for the reversal of black educational progress in the last decade," wrote the Thernstroms in 1997. "Is it just a coincidence that the crack cocaine epidemic, the spectacular rise in the homicide rate for young black males, and the reversal of progress in educational achievement all began in the latter half of the 1980s? Even if it is a coincidence, it still seems safe to say that children can't learn in chaotic and dangerous school environments."[73]

Another factor holding back blacks in schools has been an attitude linguist John McWhorter identifies as "anti-intellectualism." Encouraged to think of themselves as victims, prone to see themselves as separated from the larger white society, black youngsters, he argues, tend to regard studying as "acting white" and show little curiosity about subjects they don't already know about.[74] Using his own experience as a college teacher, as well as statistics and other reports, he concludes that "the sad but simple fact is that while there are some excellent black students, on the average black students do not try as hard as other students."[75]

One reason is that racial quotas and preferences in college admissions reduce the incentive for blacks to achieve. McWhorter admits that in high school he "quite deliberately refrained from working to my highest potential because I knew I would be accepted to even top universities without doing so."[76] He goes on: "Imagine telling a Martian who expressed an interest in American education policy: 'We allow whites in only if they have a GPA of 3.7 and an SAT of 1300 or above. We let blacks in with a GPA of 3.0 and an SAT of 900. Now, what we have been pondering for years now is why black students continue to submit higher grades and scores than this so rarely.' Well, mercy me—what a perplexing problem!"[77] Even in an ideal setting blacks have been low

achievers. For instance, black students in middle-class Prince
George's County, reported the *Washington Post*, have lower grades
and test scores than white students from families of similar
income and educational achievement.[78] In Shaker Heights, Ohio,
a high-income, integrated suburb of Cleveland, black high school
students constituted just 7 percent of the top fifth of the class and
90 percent of the bottom fifth, even though most come from two-
parent, professional-income families.[79] This is not just a local
problem. In 1995 the mean SAT score for blacks from families
making more than $50,000 was 849, 20 points lower than that for
whites from families making less than $10,000.[80]

Even blacks who reject McWhorter's opposition to racial quotas and preferences have recognized the problem. The notion that
doing well in school was "acting white" was widespread enough
that in 1987 newspaper columnist Carl Rowan started a Project
Excellence program to give scholarships to high-achieving black
students.[81]

Blacks are not the only ethnic group among which learning has
been discouraged. Reporter Pete Hamill recalls that, when he was
growing up in a working-class Irish neighborhood in Brooklyn in
the 1940s and 1950s, he was scorned for getting top grades.
"There was an assumption that if you got good grades you must
be soft, a sissy, or an AK—ass kisser. This was part of the most
sickening aspect of Irish-American life in those days: the assumption that if you rose above an acceptable level of mediocrity, you
were guilty of the sin of pride.... It was arrogant, a sin of pride, to
conceive of a life beyond the certainties, rhythms, and traditions of
the Neighborhood.... Who did I think I was? Forget these kid's
dreams, I told myself, give 'em up. Do what everybody else does:
drop out of high school, go to work, join the army or navy, get
married, settle down, have children."[82] Such attitudes, and the
practice of encouraging talented students to enter the celibate
clergy, were undoubtedly a factor in preventing the Irish from
moving up rapidly.

Among blacks, the progress in educational achievement has been great but now seems stalled. The percentage of blacks with high school diplomas shot up from 20 percent of black adults in 1960 to 74 percent in 1995 (and 86 percent of blacks age twenty-five to twenty-nine, just below the 87 percent of whites).[83] But a high school diploma in many cases is simply evidence that the student showed up. Many black high school graduates are unprepared for college, in need of remedial reading and math courses. By 1995, 37 percent of adult blacks had attended college, not very far below the 49 percent of whites, but only 13 percent were college graduates, about half the 24 percent among whites—after a quarter century of racial quotas and preferences.[84]

CRIME

The uncomfortable fact is that, over the past half century, crime rates have been much higher among blacks than among any other demographic group in America. This is perhaps what one must expect for a group that has had very good reason to regard the larger society as fundamentally unfair and to believe itself to be under no obligation to obey that society's rules. In the grim ghetto neighborhoods of so many central cities, with their empty storefronts and burnt-out houses, one can see the results of this high rate of crime. There is, moreover, perhaps a resemblance to the sharecropper communities of sixty years ago, which, Nicholas Lemann writes, "had an extremely high rate of violent crime: in 1933, the six states with the highest murder rates were all in the South, and most of the murders were black-on-black. Sexually transmitted disease and substance abuse were nationally known as special problems of the black rural South; home-brew whiskey was much more physically perilous than crack cocaine is today, if less addictive, and David Cohn reported that blacks were using cocaine in the towns of the Delta before World War II."[85] Lemann's story of Ruby Harper or Leon Dash's story of Rosa Lee Cunningham, in his 1996 book *Rosa Lee*, shows how specific individuals—black women from sharecropper families in the Mississippi Delta and eastern North Carolina—transmit habits of mind to their children and grandchildren that produce generations of welfare dependency, drug addiction, and criminal behavior.

But the picture is more complicated than a simple transference of sharecropper criminality to northern cities. David Whitman has shown that black northward migrants were less likely to commit crimes and more likely to succeed economically than the northern-born blacks they lived with.[86] Nor did black crime rates in the big northern cities spike sharply upward in the 1940s and early 1950s.[87] In those years crime in black neighborhoods generally took the form of petty vice, hustling, and illegal gambling. The numbers game—"policy wheels" in Chicago—was a black-run illegal business that politicians protected and police tolerated;[88] when Chicago mayor Martin Kennelly sent in police to arrest policy wheel operators, Congressman William Dawson, the city's leading black politician, objected strenuously and opposed Kennelly's renomination.[89] But the hustlers who ran the numbers game had their own ethic: if you reported to them that some property had been stolen, they might well have it back for you the next day.[90] In the early postwar ghetto, crime was, in a sense, under control—as it was in the larger society, for in the 1930s and the 1940s America had what we now regard as very low rates of crime generally.

Crime rates inched up in the 1950s and then increased sharply in the 1960s, in years in which blacks were becoming increasingly numerous and visible in large cities. Historian Roger Lane points out that in one fairly typical northern city, Philadelphia, the homicide rate among whites increased more than 50 percent from the early 1950s to the mid-1970s, from 1.8 per 100,000 population to 2.8; the black homicide rate "shot up more than two and one-half times in the same period, to 64.2 per 100,000, or fully 23 times higher than the white rate."[91] Overall, the number of violent crimes in the United States roughly doubled between 1957 and 1965, then roughly tripled between 1965 and 1975.[92] From then until about 1993, it remained on a high plateau, fluctuating upward and downward sometimes, in tandem not with the business cycle but with other developments: the crack cocaine epidemic produced a rate of 732 violent crimes per 100,000 people in 1990, more than triple the rate of 200 in 1965.[93]

Blacks were committing a hugely disproportionate number of these crimes. Since the 1950s, about 30 percent of people arrested have been blacks, and about 45 percent of prison inmates have been blacks.[94] It could be argued that blacks are arrested and imprisoned for long periods more often than deserved and that racial discrimination therefore makes it appear that blacks commit more crimes than in fact they do. But even after we apply any reasonable discount to these figures, it seems clear that blacks—and we are talking primarily of young males here, as is the case with any ethnic group—commit several times as many serious crimes per capita as other Americans. As Michael Tonry, a scholar sympathetic to claims that the criminal process treats blacks discriminatorily, concluded in 1995, "For nearly a decade there has been a near consensus among scholars and policy analysts that most of the black punishment disproportions result not from racial bias or discrimination within the system but from patterns of black offending and of blacks' criminal records."[95] For crimes other than murder, by 1995 blacks were the victims at a rate one-third more than whites.[96] By 1993 the rate of black murderers and murder victims among males age fourteen to twenty-four was eight to ten *times* higher than among whites.[97]

These crimes were largely the product of a criminal underclass of young black males that began developing in the same years when, as Moynihan noticed, fatherlessness was increasing in the black community. Gangs formed by black youths came to dominate the lives, and at night control the streets, of large urban ghettoes. Lemann describes the process in Chicago: "young black men who had been born in the South during the 1940s and brought to Chicago in early childhood, and who were teenagers during the mid-1960s, produced most of the celebrities of the gang world, the people who masterminded the transformation of scattered groups of street fighters into large criminal organizations that were armed, murderous, prosperous from drug dealing and other illegal businesses, and firmly in control (after dark, at least) of Mayor Daley's new high-rise housing projects."[98] These gangs were a far cry from the policy wheel operators William Dawson protected. Unlike the numbers runners, they had no positive interaction with the working people in the community, no connection with the constructive life of ordinary citizens; they were purely predatory. Their home turf—the housing project— was very different by the 1960s from the immediate postwar years. Stable families and tenants with good incomes tended to leave the projects as better housing became available elsewhere and as court decisions, starting in 1967, limited the ability of housing authorities to evict tenants for criminal and other misbehavior.[99] Increasingly, public housing was occupied by very low-income single mothers and was controlled by criminal gangs.

Not long after the rise of the gangs came the riots of the 1960s. Previous race riots had occurred in or just after wartime, in Chicago in 1919, Tulsa in 1922, and Detroit in 1943, and in most cases white mobs, unhindered by sympathetic police, had attacked blacks. The 1960s riots were different: the violence was committed by blacks and consisted mainly of looting and destruction of property in mostly black neighborhoods, which the outnumbered police were for days unable to prevent. The first of these to receive nationwide notice was the Watts riot in Los Angeles in August 1965; then came Newark and Detroit in July 1967; then riots in Washington and many other cities after the murder of Martin Luther King Jr. in April 1968. Some hailed these riots as revolts against poverty and oppressive racism, yet two of the most destructive riots occurred in cities where unemployment was low, blacks had incomes close to those of whites, and rates of black home-ownership were high.[100] Riots seemed to occur when and where many people suddenly came to believe that looting and destruction would go unpunished. Speculation that there would be a riot was, it seemed, more the cause of rioting than long-suppressed rage or a desire to overthrow white society. Detroit rioted a week after Newark, amid speculation about which city would have a riot next; the April 1968 riots came when it was widely predicted that blacks would riot after the murder of Martin Luther King Jr. There were no major riots in the South, the Thernstroms point out, where the police were likely to respond more forcefully than in the North. Riots continued for days in Los Angeles, Newark, Detroit, and other cities where police were forbidden to use force to stop them. In Detroit, rioting continued while Mayor Jerome Cavanagh declined to call in the National Guard (he was afraid poorly trained guardsmen would shoot innocent people, which they did) and while he and Governor George Romney tried to persuade a reluctant President Lyndon Johnson to send in federal troops.* The rioting stopped a few days after seven thousand federal troops were sent in. In contrast, the rioting in Los Angeles in 1992, which followed the acquittal of the police officers who beat Rodney King, stopped after eighteen hours when Governor Pete Wilson and President George Bush quickly announced they were sending in twenty-five thousand federal troops.

Riots and rising crime rates helped empty out the central cities. In the two decades after the riots, from 1970 to 1990, Detroit fell in population from 1,514,000 to 1,027,000, Newark dropped from 381,000 to 275,000, and Washington fell from 756,000 to 606,000—losing one-third, one-fourth, and one-fifth of their populations, respectively. Several other central cities—

---

* As a summer intern in Mayor Cavanagh's office, I witnessed much of the high-level response to the riot, including meetings between Cavanagh and Romney.

notably Cleveland and St. Louis—lost population at similar rates. Crime helped to destroy property values, especially the values of homes owned by law-abiding blacks. Since housing values constitute most of the wealth accumulated by ordinary people over a lifetime, crime was in effect a nearly confiscatory tax on the wealth of millions of hardworking American blacks. Yet the habits of mind blacks brought from the South and the often brutal and insensitive conduct of northern policemen made many blacks reluctant to cooperate with the police in stopping crime and led many otherwise law-abiding blacks to participate in the looting. The habit of mind that regarded the larger society as so fundamentally unfair as to leave one under no obligation to obey its rules proved severely dysfunctional.

Crime rates among the Irish immigrants who started arriving in the 1840s remained extremely high for several decades and then dropped by the 1880s as the Irish submitted to the discipline of public and Catholic schools and of industrial employers.[101] Among blacks, crime rates did not diminish until the early 1990s; the public schools did not exert strong discipline in the twentieth century as they had in the nineteenth, and, as scholar William Julius Wilson has shown, low-skill, high-paying unionized industrial jobs became largely unavailable in the central cities after 1970. Then, in the early 1990s, crime rates, generally and among blacks, plummeted sharply. From its 1991 peak, the violent crime rate had by 1997 declined 17 percent and has declined further since; the rate for murder, for which the statistics are most reliable, declined 31 percent in those years.[102] In other words, crime has been declining on almost as steep a curve as that on which it increased during the awful decade from 1965 to 1975. No one is quite sure why this has happened. More sophisticated and aggressive policing, on the model pioneered by New York mayor Rudolph Giuliani and his police commissioners, William Bratton and Howard Safir, certainly played a part. In fact, for several years New York City alone accounted for most of the drop in national crime rates, and other cities began to copy the Giuliani crime-fighting program. Interestingly, black voters have reacted angrily to Giuliani and his policies, focusing on a few highly publicized and aggressively demagogued incidents of police abuse and ignoring the fact that shootings and misconduct by police were sharply reduced during his tenure—and the fact that black neighborhoods became significantly safer and housing values much higher as a result of lowered crime rates.

But police tactics alone probably cannot account for the entire drop in crime. Another cause has been starkly different behaviors by those—especially young black males—who were most likely to commit crimes in the past. It is possible that we were seeing in the 1990s what Americans of the 1880s saw: a change in habits of mind of what had been the most crime-prone segment of the population. The fact is that the latest age cohort of young black males is strikingly less likely to commit crime than the three or four age cohorts that came before. For three decades we have seen a sharp dichotomy between two trends among black Americans—the trend toward an increasingly large, self-confident, highly competent black middle class and the continuing prevalence of a vast criminal underclass. Now, perhaps, the dichotomy is being resolved: the middle class continues to grow, while the criminal underclass is diminishing and may be withering away. It happened before, with the Irish, and it may be happening again today, so that in time it may be only a few historically minded Americans who will remember that blacks once were much more likely than their fellow citizens to commit, and to be victims of, violent crimes.

DISTINCTIVENESS

Of all the immigrant and ethnic groups in the United States, blacks seem the most physically distinctive. In addition, there is the American tradition, established first in the segregated South and now adhered to by leaders of black organizations who want to claim as large a constituency as possible, that anyone with any African ancestors—anyone with "one drop" of African blood—is black. Without giving it a thought, most Americans will identify even a light-complected person of partial African ancestry as black, yet they will identify a deeply tanned, darker-complected person of European ancestry as white. This distinctiveness has made it difficult, indeed usually impossible, for anyone of black ancestry to escape the negative consequences of being black, consequences that in the segregated South were all-encompassing and that are still significant today.

One of those consequences is that blacks are often stopped by police or security guards for no other reason than that they are black; they are subjected to interrogation, arrest, or demeaning comments. Sometimes the only offense seems to be, in an oft-used phrase, DWB—"driving while black." This results sometimes from "racial profiling" by law enforcement officials, which, as a result of incidents in New Jersey, came under harsh political attack in 2000. It is easy to understand why a respectable citizen would feel irritated or infuriated when confronted by a police officer for no good reason and subjected to possibly humiliating or offensive questioning. At the same time, it is also obvious that the reason for such racial profiling, whether officially sanctioned or simply the result of informal decision making, is that blacks are significantly more likely than other Americans to commit crimes. So long as that is the case, and even if police officers and others grow more sensitive in assessing whether particular blacks are behaving unlawfully, these consequences of black distinctiveness are likely to persist.

But it is useful to remember that other, admittedly less physically distinctive ethnic groups have come to be regarded as less distinctive over the years. The Irish, for example, were often singled out with negative consequences one hundred years ago; that happens very seldom today. Physical traits that one generation regards as defining can be regarded as simply different by another. Babies do not distinguish between people of African and European descent; they recognize only other human beings. They have to be taught to differentiate between blacks and whites. Is it too much to hope that in one hundred years Americans will not regard the physical distinctiveness of black Americans as a warrant for treating people differently?

Certainly by that time the physical distinctiveness of blacks will be reduced by intermarriage. And perhaps also by technology, says sociologist Orlando Patterson. "Science is likely to create dramatic new methods of changing hair texture and skin color," he writes. "In a world dominated by mass culture, many will embrace changes that enhance their individuality. Once dramatically manipulable by human action, 'race' will lose its social significance." W. E. B. DuBois predicted that the twentieth century would be the century of the color line, and in many ways it was. But, writes Patterson, "his modern-day disciples, who insist the color line will define the next 100 years as well, are altogether wrong. The racial divide that has plagued America since its founding is fading fast—made obsolete by migratory, sociological, and biotechnological developments that are already under way. By the middle of the twenty-first century, America will have problems aplenty. But no racial problem whatsoever."[103]

POLITICS

The migration from rural South to urban North was a migration from an old country where blacks had no political rights or leverage at all to a promised land where they had political rights and where over time they developed great political leverage and, in some cases, political power. As Stephan and Abigail Thernstrom write, "The radical difference between North and South was equally evident in the realm of politics. Black people could run for office, and they were actually encouraged to vote. Not because politicians were passionately committed to egalitarian ideals, but because they were realists and knew how to count. As *Black Metropolis*, the classic sociological account of black life in a northern city, put it, Chicago's politicians realized that 'the Negro had a commodity in which they were interested—the vote.'"[104] Indeed, in the 1940s and 1950s the two major parties competed vigorously for the votes of black Americans, who at the time appeared to have no settled partisan preference. Blacks also brought from the South a faith that participation in politics could change their second-caste status—otherwise, why did white southerners fight so hard against allowing them to vote?

At the beginning of the northward migration, the memory was still vivid of the time when blacks had an overwhelming preference for the Republican Party. Then the New Deal converted many blacks to the Democratic Party.[105] Many but not all. In Louisville and Richmond, border cities where blacks had long been allowed to vote, they stayed faithful Republicans for many years; in the large cities of the North, blacks cast lower percentages for Democratic candidates than many white ethnic groups up through and including the election of 1960. It is interesting that the New Dealers who most prominently favored civil rights for blacks—Harold Ickes, Eleanor Roosevelt, and Henry Wallace—were all former Republicans. In the 1948 election, when blacks were only about 3 percent of the national electorate (since most blacks still lived in southern states where they could not vote), three of the four presidential candidates vied to be the strongest supporter of civil rights—Harry Truman, who did not particularly like blacks but who thought they should be treated equally and had voted for the anti-lynching law in the Senate; Thomas E. Dewey, an ancestral Republican who genuinely favored equal rights; and the Progressive Party's Henry Wallace, whose Communist allies always proclaimed their devotion to civil rights. But it must be added that the target of their civil rights appeals was not so much black voters as it was Jewish voters, who were more numerous nationally and who were concentrated, more than blacks were, in the pivotal big northern states whose electoral votes were most in doubt. Both presidential nominees in 1952 were more lukewarm to civil rights: Dwight Eisenhower had not been uncomfortable commanding a racially segregated military in World War II and sent federal troops in to enforce desegregation in Little Rock in 1957 only with great reluctance; Adlai Stevenson shared the view of many of his southern admirers that it was best to hope for quiet progress in racial relations rather than stir up the hatreds of (and perhaps lose the votes of) southern whites. Prominent blacks favored both parties in the 1950s and early 1960s. In 1956 Congressman Adam Clayton Powell Jr. endorsed Eisenhower for reelection. Jackie Robinson, a strong supporter of New York governor Nelson Rockefeller, favored Richard Nixon in 1960. Martin Luther King Sr. endorsed Nixon in 1960 and switched only after Robert Kennedy placed a phone call to Coretta Scott King after his son had been imprisoned in Georgia. John Kennedy carried the black vote by 63 to 37 percent, a handsome margin but far less than his 78 to 22 percent margin among Catholics.

In 1964 black voters became almost unanimously Democratic. The precipitating event was the Civil Rights Act endorsed by Kennedy in May 1963 and passed with the strong support of Lyndon Johnson in July 1964. Ironically, a higher percentage of congressional Republicans than of Democrats voted for the bill; almost all of its opponents were white southern Democrats, at a time when few Republicans were elected from the South. But Republican Party nominee Barry Goldwater opposed the bill on the grounds that its public accommodations section violated people's right to do business with whom they pleased. Goldwater was perhaps one of the least racist politicians in the nation; years before, he had integrated the workforce in his department store in Phoenix. But his stand on the Civil Rights Act and his support from white southerners (he carried the still almost entirely white electorates in South Carolina, Georgia, Alabama, Mississippi, and Louisiana, as well as his native Arizona) convinced blacks that the Republican Party was irredeemably hostile to blacks. His and his party's opposition to the big government policies of Johnson's Great Society strengthened that view, and for the next thirty-five years blacks voted 85 to 90 percent for Democratic candidates for president and almost all other offices.

This switch came just at the end of the great northward migration. Suddenly there was a large, almost entirely Democratic constituency in the big states of the North—New York, Pennsylvania, Ohio, Michigan, Illinois. Yet there were only a few black elected officials in those or other states. The Congress that assembled and enacted the Great Society legislation in 1965 had only six black members—Adam Clayton Powell Jr. of New York, William Dawson of Chicago, Robert Nix of Philadelphia, Charles Diggs and John Conyers of Detroit, and Augustus Hawkins of Los Angeles. No central city had elected a black mayor. There were relatively few black state legislators or big city council members. Within a few years that changed, however. In 1966 and 1972, Edward Brooke was elected as a Republican senator from Massachusetts, which had only a small black population. In 1974, ten years after the Johnson-Goldwater election, sixteen blacks were elected to the House of Representatives—including Ronald Dellums and Andrew Young, first elected in white-majority districts in California and Georgia in 1970 and 1972, respectively.* Black mayors were elected in large numbers: Richard Hatcher of Gary and Carl Stokes of Cleveland in 1967, Tom Bradley of (white-majority) Los Angeles and Kenneth Gibson of Newark in 1969, Coleman Young of Detroit in 1973. From 1967 to 1993

---

* The others were Yvonne Burke and Augustus Hawkins of California, Ralph Metcalfe and Cardiss Collins of Illinois, Parren Mitchell of Maryland, John Conyers and Charles Diggs of Michigan, Bill Clay of Missouri, Shirley Chisholm and Charles Rangel of New York, Louis Stokes of Ohio, Robert Nix of Philadelphia, Harold Ford of Tennessee, and Barbara Jordan of Texas.

blacks were elected mayor in eighty-seven cities with a population above 50,000; interestingly, two-thirds of those cities did not have black majorities.[106]

Black political organizations sprang into existence in most big cities in the 1960s. But they did not resemble the Irish-dominated political machines created in the nineteenth or early twentieth centuries. The Irish developed elaborate hierarchies resembling those of the Roman Catholic Church; faithful machine operatives were rewarded with patronage jobs and could expect to move slowly up the ladder after years of service. Black political organizations resembled more the black churches, whose entrepreneurial preachers assembled congregations in different ways and provided a variety of services.

Successful black politicians came from diverse backgrounds and built constituencies in many different ways. Some came from roles large and small in the civil rights movement—Andrew Young of Atlanta and Marion Barry of Washington. Some were old-line left-wingers in the labor movement—Coleman Young of Detroit and Bill Clay of St. Louis. Some relied for their greatest support on those for whom they obtained generous contracts—Maynard Jackson of Atlanta and the group around Charles Rangel and Percy Sutton in New York. Others were former machine loyalists who turned rebel—Ralph Metcalfe and Harold Washington of Chicago. Others were former welfare state administrators—Walter Washington of Washington and Wilson Goode of Philadelphia. Some were young Ivy League graduates whose talents made them local celebrities—Kurt Schmoke of Baltimore. Their campaigns relied heavily on near-unanimous support from black voters, but, as noted, many were first elected mayor when their cities did not have black majorities.

Like black voters, the overwhelming majority of black politicians were Democrats—and almost all were left-wing Democrats. Edward Brooke, defeated for reelection in 1978, left no political heirs. Only two black Republicans have been elected to

Congress since the 1960s, both from districts with relatively few black voters—Gary Franks of Connecticut and J. C. Watts of Oklahoma. Almost all the black mayors and congressmen backed policies similar to those of the white liberal mayors of the late 1960s and early 1970s: vast government spending, made possible by higher tax rates and aggressive pursuit of federal funds, for programs intended to curb poverty; increasing the number of black police and curbing what they considered police brutality. To this they added support of the racial quotas and preferences developed in the 1970s, especially set-asides for minority contractors and quota-hiring of police and other public employees. Few mayors had direct responsibility for public schools, but black mayors and members of Congress opposed measures to end court-ordered school busing.

These black politicians, unlike their Irish counterparts of a half century or century before, thought of politics and government as instruments of social change. Federal government action had ended legal segregation in the South; it seemed logical to look to the federal government to end poverty and discrimination in the North. If blacks continued to lag behind in the private economy after the passage of the civil rights acts, then the solution was economic redistribution by the federal government. Shortly before his death, Martin Luther King Jr. proclaimed that "socialism" was required to ensure racial justice, and in 1968 Congressman John Conyers introduced a bill, drafted by the *Yale Law Journal*, calling for a negative income tax to guarantee an income of $15,000—a solid middle-class income at the time.

In its March 1968 report, the President's National Advisory Commission on Civil Disorders (the Kerner Commission), formed in response to the urban riots of 1967, endorsed massive government spending. "Our nation is moving toward two societies, one black, one white—separate and unequal," the report announced. It called for government programs, including a guaranteed annual income, that "will require unprecedented levels of funding and performance." But the Kerner Report was wrong on its facts and wrong, most people would say after the history of the last third of the twentieth century, in its call for an ever bigger government. Embedded in the Kerner Report were assumptions that proved to be far wide of the mark. The report assumed that the northward migration of blacks from the South would continue indefinitely. In fact, it had stopped around 1965, as the Civil Rights Act made the South more hospitable to blacks and more attractive to investors, and as the economic growth of the Sun Belt began. The Kerner Report also assumed that almost all the big cities in the North would soon have black-majority populations. But without black migration, that never came to pass. Of the twenty largest cities in 1960, one in 1968 had a black majority (Washington) and four were more than 40 percent black (Detroit, Baltimore, St. Louis, New Orleans). But only those and one other city, Cleveland, had black majorities in 2000, and in Cleveland and St. Louis blacks were barely a majority (51 percent). Meanwhile, the black percentage in Washington declined substantially, from 72 percent in 1970 to 61 percent in 1999.[108]

The Kerner Commission devoted a separate chapter to arguing that blacks could not be expected to move up through the private sector because it was no longer producing large numbers of low-wage jobs. It was wrong again. Over the next third of a century the private sector produced more than 20 million low-income jobs, very many of which were filled by immigrants from Latin America and Asia. These immigrants by their hard work disproved the thesis that not enough job opportunities were available for members of minorities. At the same time, the Kerner Report ignored the enormous increases in black income and jobs, the demise of legal segregation, and how attitudes among whites had changed from 1940 to 1968—all of which occurred without the economic redistribution proposed by the commission. The United States was not moving toward two societies; it was moving away from two societies.

Or if it was moving toward two societies, they were not "one black, one white." Rather, one society was middle class, biracial, and multiethnic, growing more prosperous and secure economically, and the other was an underclass, mostly but not all black, in which single parenthood, welfare dependency, and crime were rising at disastrously high rates. From 1965 to 1975, crime and welfare dependency, highly concentrated in the black ghettoes of central cities, roughly tripled in America. And these problems, large as they might be, did not move American voters to consider espousing the socialism King called for or the "unprecedented levels of funding" the Kerner Report demanded. Yet there was a moment when it seemed Congress might enact a guaranteed annual income. It came when bipartisan majorities in both houses seemed ready to vote for the Family Assistance Plan drafted by Daniel Patrick Moynihan when he was chief domestic policy adviser to President Richard Nixon. But, in the end, that bill was defeated by a combination of doubters in the Senate Finance Committee and by left Democrats, including black congressmen, who denounced its guaranteed income levels as too low.[108]

Another problem, fatherless families, nurtured by generous welfare programs, produced an urban underclass which no one in 1968 expected, and for which the medicine prescribed by the Kerner Report turned out to be iatrogenic. For fatherlessness is not an inevitable consequence of poverty; as Orlando Patterson points out, "In nearly all the other ethnic groups in America, including Mexican-Americans with higher levels of poverty than Afro-Americans, and in nearly all other known human societies, including India with its vast hordes of people in grinding urban poverty and unemployment, poverty does not lead to the large-scale paternal abandonment of children."[109]

Racial quotas and preferences, also products of this period, though not foreshadowed in the Kerner Report, proved more enduring—but not necessarily more helpful to their intended beneficiaries. The idea that racial discrimination should be gauged by the percentage of blacks in a preferred position—that is, not by evidence of acts of discrimination or segregation but by racial percentages—was first endorsed in a 1968 Supreme Court unanimous decision in a southern school desegregation case. The justices, understandably frustrated by southern officials' evasions of the *Brown* v. *Board of Education* decision of 1954, struck down a freedom-of-choice plan that put no whites in black schools. This was the first time the federal government used race-counting to determine whether segregation existed. Then came the 1971 Supreme Court case authorizing school busing for Charlotte and Mecklenburg County, North Carolina, as the only way to provide similar percentages of blacks in schools throughout the district.[110] The Equal Employment Opportunity Commission surreptitiously imposed quotas for jobs in the late 1960s, despite specific language in the Civil Rights Act of 1964 forbidding them, and in 1969 and 1970 the Nixon administration required racial quotas in hiring, first in the building trades (the Philadelphia Plan) and then in all federal contracting.

Thus the federal government turned a ban on discrimination by race into a requirement that decisions be made according to race. Failure to fill a quota could result in litigation, heavy fines, and bad publicity; a contractor who filled his quota would be left alone.[111] The Supreme Court approved this rewriting of the Civil Rights Act of 1964, although in 1989 and 1995 the court threw out race-based quota schemes. State and city governments passed racial quotas, preferences, and set-asides as well, especially, but by no means in every case, when blacks held majority control.

This subversion of the Civil Rights Act created opportunities for black officials to engage in the kind of patronage politics that the Irish political machines once practiced. Public jobs and government contracts went to those who backed politicians in elections. By the late 1970s "affirmative action" programs—the label given to racial quotas, preferences, and set-asides—were firmly entrenched in the civic life of most of America's large cities.

These policies encouraged the creation of "minority-owned" businesses that were often shells, effectively owned and operated by larger contractors with a straw man who was not required to put up significant capital or to have a knowledge of the business.

But, of course, racial quotas, preferences, and set-asides have their costs. They are hugely profitable for a small number of well-connected businessmen and provide jobs for some blacks who otherwise might not get them. But the rise of the black middle class has been no faster since quotas came into existence in the early 1970s than it was in the pre-quota years from 1940 to 1970.[112] Quotas increase the cost of doing business for the public and teach the cynical lesson that race matters more than performance. They also cast doubt on the legitimate achievements of the people they are intended to benefit. Most important, the continued existence of quotas strengthens the sense of aggrievement of many blacks. The very existence of quotas is based on the assumption that in a fair society all groups will be equally represented in all jobs and schools—an assumption refuted by common experience and common sense. Quotas therefore strengthen the habit of mind that the larger society is fundamentally unfair even when it is not—a habit of mind that strengthens the dysfunctional idea that the aggrieved class has no obligation to obey the larger society's rules.

In the days of the Irish-controlled machines, elite opinion condemned preferences for Irish machine supporters in government hiring and contracting. Politicians who engaged in such practices tried to deny they were doing what they were doing, and in time such practices died out. But since the 1970s, those who have employed racial quotas, preferences, and set-asides have done so under a claim of right and with the enthusiastic support of articulate elite opinion. This support continued even when it became clear that in some cases set-asides had moved from garden-variety patronage to predatory politics similar to that of James Michael Curley.

The two prime examples were the mayoral reigns of Coleman Young in Detroit (1973–1993) and Marion Barry in Washington (1978–1990 and 1994–1998). Both were men of high intelligence and great charm. Both had backgrounds in leftist politics. Both were highly skilled politicians who were able to build loyal constituencies among elites and voters alike. But both left their city governments and very large parts of their cities in shambles.

Young was born in Alabama and moved to the Black Bottom neighborhood of Detroit as a child.[113] In his engaging, profane autobiography he describes how, as an articulate and light-skinned fourteen-year-old, he was barred from boarding the boat to Boblo, an amusement park on an island in the Detroit River. Young went to college, worked in factories, and got a job in the United Auto Workers (UAW) when it was controlled by pro-Communist leaders before the election of Walter Reuther as president in 1947. "If Coleman wasn't a Communist, he cheated them out of their party dues," said UAW president Douglas Fraser, one of Reuther's successors. Young worked on the assembly line, started small businesses, and was elected from the Black Bottom neighborhood to a state constitutional convention in 1961 and then to the state senate in 1964. In the late 1960s and early 1970s Detroit was immersed in controversy over police treatment of black suspects; Young supported Judge George Crockett, also a former pro-Communist, who convened court and freed several blacks arrested for shooting policemen.

In 1973, when blacks were on the verge of becoming a majority in the city, Young was elected mayor over the incumbent police commissioner. His strategy for governing was to seek large federal grants, to prevail on the Detroit area's big businessmen to make large investments in the city, and to provide set-asides for black contractors and city jobs for black supporters. His tactics worked, but failed to prevent the slide in the city's economy. Federal money turned out to be less plenteous than expected, especially after the election of Ronald Reagan in 1980.

Ford and General Motors made huge investments—the Renaissance Center on the riverfront, the Poletown auto factory in what had been a Polish neighborhood—but downtown real estate emptied out and the storefronts on the city's radial avenues were 90 percent vacant. Young's inflamed racial rhetoric (one black opponent was "the white man's candidate") and his seeming indifference to crime (except when committed by white suburbanites against blacks) helped persuade most remaining whites to move out of the city. Detroit's tax base withered, as property became essentially worthless,* and the city's finances were in disarray. Undeterred, Young used racial quotas to hire police, with the result that many unsuitable police officers were hired.[114] Then in the 1980s he announced that the police would no longer patrol the freeways; when blacks began beating white motorists who pulled over, the governor finally sent in state police to patrol.

Under Young, Detroit's population declined from 1.5 million to less than 1 million—a creative effort kept it at just over that number in the 1990 census—and crime destroyed many black neighborhoods. Young retired in 1993 and was succeeded by Dennis Archer, a well-connected black Democrat whose governing strategy was to control crime, lower taxes, cut the city payroll and improve services, and encourage small businesses as well as big projects—none of them priorities for Young. (Interestingly, the business elite was still at least outwardly supportive of Young to the end, even though his policies wreaked ruin on the city.)

---

* In 1989 I visited the brick-bungalow neighborhood in Detroit where I lived from 1948 to 1956. I counted one hundred vacant houses in a square-mile area. I was told that the house my parents had bought new in 1948 for $11,500 would now fetch $15,000 on the market, but if it became vacant for a day it would be worth $3,000—less than the salvage value of the fixtures and materials. In effect the land had negative value. When I asked neighbors how the police treated them, they said, "The police? They never come here, except maybe if there is a murder." In 1997, four years after Coleman Young had left office, house prices had risen to between $35,000 and $45,000—far less than in mostly white working-class suburbs but enough to yield some wealth to homeowners who had made payments on their mortgages for years.

Marion Barry grew up in Mississippi and Memphis and completed the non-thesis requirements for a Ph.D. in chemistry at the University of Tennessee in the 1960s. He left that career and moved to Washington.[115] There he emerged as a militant in opposition to the long-settled "black bourgeois" leadership, staged a successful bus boycott, and formed Pride, Inc., to hire ghetto youths.[116] Barry was elected to the school board—the first elective body in Washington since Reconstruction—and then to the city council. In 1978 he challenged Mayor Walter Washington, a career housing bureaucrat picked by President Lyndon Johnson as mayor and then elected in 1974; in a three-cornered race against Washington and longtime Washingtonian Sterling Tucker, he won by a narrow margin. Key to his victory were the endorsement of the *Washington Post* and his large majority among white voters.

Barry sought to govern by propitiating downtown business interests, seeking large federal payments (the federal government had long subsidized D.C. budgets to offset the fact that the city could not tax federal buildings), and providing set-asides for black contractors and jobs for black supporters. In 1989, to hire more black police officers, he lowered standards in such a way that many felons were able to join the force. The District's payroll zoomed to 53,000, in a city of fewer than 600,000. Contributing to the poor performance of city government was Barry's cocaine addiction, which resulted in his arrest in 1990; instead of running for reelection, he went to jail.

In 1994 Barry was reelected mayor with a much smaller majority, but by then the District was bankrupt, unable to float bonds or obtain even short-term loans from banks. The Republican Congress, with leadership from Republican Tom Davis of suburban Virginia and Washington's nonvoting delegate, Democrat Eleanor Holmes Norton, imposed a control board that actually ran the government while Barry presided. Barry's policies, as bad as they were, were unable to ruin Washington's downtown—with ever more law firms and lobbyists maintaining Washington offices, it boomed—

and the mostly white high-income neighborhoods west of Rock Creek Park continued to grow. But under Barry the city lost more than 100,000 residents, and many mostly black neighborhoods were destroyed by crime. Barry even lost elite support by the late 1980s as the results of his governance were becoming apparent. In 1998 he did not win reelection; the new mayor was Anthony Williams, the chief financial officer of the control board, who cut the payroll down to 32,000 and improved services. But by then most Washington area blacks lived outside the District, most in black-majority Prince George's County, Maryland, which had a much smaller and more competent government.

Detroit and Washington were extreme examples. Most black mayors and city officials in large cities did not produce the kind of predatory politics of Marion Barry, Coleman Young, and James Michael Curley. Indeed, many black politicians were successful in constituencies with non-black majorities, like Tom Bradley, who served twenty years (1973–1993) as mayor of Los Angeles when no more than 15 percent of the city's residents were black. When David Dinkins, in his single term as mayor of New York, seemed to be moving in the same direction as Young and Barry, and when he failed to provide police protection for Brooklyn Jews attacked by black rioters, he was defeated by Republican Rudolph Giuliani in 1993. As we have seen, Giuliani's policing tactics—targeting minor offenders (who often turned out to be major offenders), pouncing on any manifestation of social disorder (squeegee men at traffic lights and toll booths, turnstile jumpers), targeting policing at high-crime sites, and holding precinct commanders responsible for cutting crime—produced much lower crime rates; violent crime declined 50 percent in five years. Other mayors, black and white, copied Giuliani's tactics or came up with their own, helping national crime rates to decline sharply.

At the same time, welfare reforms pioneered in Wisconsin and other states, and the 1996 welfare reform act passed by the Republican Congress and signed by Bill Clinton, cut welfare dependency nearly in half in five years. The vicious cycle of high crime and welfare dependency that started in the 1960s was in the 1990s being replaced by a virtuous cycle. All the while, the black middle class had grown, to the point that the incomes of black married couples reached the same level as the incomes of white married couples with the same levels of educational achievement.[117] Racial discrimination in jobs, public accommodations, and housing has clearly been decreasing, to the vanishing point in some cases. With crime and welfare dependency declining, the ground has been laid for a similar decline in the number of fatherless families, which produced so much crime and welfare dependency for a long generation. There is reason to hope that, for millions of blacks, the gains already made by millions of others may now be in sight.

The political agenda of most black voters and black politicians over the last third of a century has had both successes and failures. The drive to stigmatize racial segregation and discrimination as illegitimate has been spectacularly successful. But the push for an ever larger and more generous government has been unavailing or, where it has succeeded in promoting heavy spending on welfare, has arguably proved harmful. The effort to stop abuses of authority by police has too often resulted in high crime rates, which have devastated black communities and destroyed the property values of black homeowners. Racial quotas and preferences, while helpful to some blacks, have not produced any greater gains since 1970 than were produced without them in the previous thirty years. In municipal politics, where party labels are not always important, black voters have repudiated some of these policies: the politics of Marion Barry and Coleman Young are dead even in Washington and Detroit.

But in national and state politics, where party labels tend to freeze opinions, black voters and elected officials have continued to embrace these policies almost unanimously. Some predicted that as black voters grew more affluent they would vote less solidly Democratic. But if anything, more affluent black voters are more liberal and Democratic in their views than older and less affluent blacks. In 2000, blacks voted for Al Gore by a 90 to 8 percent margin; despite George W. Bush's attempts to appeal to black voters, he won a smaller percentage among them than Bob Dole had four years before. In the days after the 2000 election, Jesse Jackson led protests in Florida where he charged that blacks had been excluded from the polls in "another Selma"—an exaggeration, to say the least—and polls showed that most black Americans regarded Bush's victory in the Florida contest as illegitimate. Politically, black Americans seem to have not only different opinions on public policy but also different perceptions of public events. It is worth remembering that the Irish, sixty years after their great migration began, were also alienated from the political process and remained almost unanimous in their support for one political party.

CONVERGENCE

On balance, progress has been made in interweaving blacks into American society sixty years after the beginning of the great northward migration. But we have much farther to go. While overt racism has diminished in America in that time, other barriers to convergence remain.

Among them are the racial quotas, preferences, and set-asides enthusiastically endorsed by corporate, media, and university elites. They continue to nurture a sense of racial grievance and strengthen the habit of mind that the system is so fundamentally unfair as to erase any obligation to obey its rules. Their very existence suggests that the leaders of major institutions want to keep blacks out—when in fact they go to great lengths to get them in. And while quotas and preferences confer on their donors a sense of generosity, they impose on their recipients a sense of inferiority. As Shelby Steele writes, "Under affirmative action the quality that earns us preferential treatment is an implied inferiority."[118] At elite universities, the presence of quotas and black-only dormitories, orientation sessions, and dining tables has encouraged racial consciousness and separation and has fostered an oppositional frame of mind. Many black students at Stanford University, though unable to cite examples of racial hostility, are convinced that it is present and tend to segregate themselves.[119] Racial quotas and preferences encourage what Stephan and Abigail Thernstrom call "civil rights pessimism—the belief that racism remained pervasive and undiminished—[that blinds civil] rights advocates to a changed America."[120] The temptation for blacks is to revel in the role of victim; Shelby Steele writes, "We have a hidden investment in victimization and poverty. These distressing conditions have been the source of our only real power, and there is an unconscious sort of gravitation toward them, a complaining celebration of them."[121]

It is hard to avoid the conclusion of John McWhorter that "black America is currently caught in certain ideological holding patterns that are today much more serious barriers to black well-being than is white racism."[122] McWhorter argues that too many blacks are caught up in a "cult of victimology," which treats "victimhood not as a problem to be solved but as an identity to be nurtured." In response, blacks are encouraged to believe that their aggrieved status makes them "an unofficial sovereign entity" within American society, and many draw the conclusion that they are "morally exempt" from "the rules other Americans are expected to follow."[123] "To conceive of ourselves today as eternal victims impedes our progress toward equality—because there comes a point when refraining from drawing a line between oppression and 'occasional inconvenience,' as a black cousin of mine perfectly phrases it, is infantilization. The person one considers incapable of coping with any hardship whatsoever, who one considers capable of achievement only under ideal conditions, is someone one pities, cares for, and perhaps even likes, but is not someone one respects, and thus is someone one does not truly consider an equal."[124] Or in Shelby Steele's words, racial preference "never raises expectations for blacks with true accountability, never requires that they develop *as Americans*, and absolutely never *blames* blacks when they don't develop. It always asks *less* of blacks and exempts them from the expectations, standards, principles, and challenges that are considered demanding but necessary for the development of competence and character in others."[125]

A century ago the Irish were held back by the callous disdain of the elite of the day; today blacks are being held back by the well-intentioned but misguided policies of the elite of the day. But there are also signs of progress, and they are largely the work of blacks themselves. Black voters have recoiled from the predatory politics that prevailed in some major cities. Young blacks are committing fewer crimes and falling into welfare dependency far less often than only a few years ago. The black middle class continues to grow and gain strength. It is possible to hope that the separatism and anti-intellectualism John McWhorter describes in black students will be transformed into attitudes more likely to produce success in American life, especially if racial quotas and preferences are ended by court decision or popular vote, as they have been in state universities in Texas and California. We can hope that the preoccupation with victimhood, which in McWhorter's words "condones weakness and failure" and "subtly makes criminality seem excusable,"[126] will give way to a more realistic vision of where blacks stand in American society, with opportunities open and genuine achievement possible. There is evidence that the dysfunctional habits of mind blacks brought from the rural South are growing weaker and are being replaced by habits of mind similar to those that have helped other racial and ethnic minorities to move upward in American life. It took 120 years from their initial inrush for the Irish to be fully interwoven into the fabric of American society. For all the mistakes Americans—ordinary people and elites of all races—have made, there is still reason to hope that it will not take as long for the American blacks whose mass migration began sixty years ago.

☆ PART 2 ☆

ITALIANS AND LATINOS

"Family solidarity was the basic code of [Italian] family life and defiance of it was something akin to a cardinal sin."
—LEONARD COVELLO

"Not unlike other immigrant groups—most notably the Italians—the Latino path to the middle class is marked more by a steady, intergenerational ascent than rapid individual progress in education, which better characterizes the Asian and Jewish immigrant experiences.... Latinos are, by and large, struggling upward and following the momentum of the great waves of European immigrants who came before them."
—GREGORY RODRIGUEZ

There is a close, almost uncanny resemblance between the Italian immigrants who arrived in the United States in great numbers from 1890 to 1924 and the Latino immigrants who began arriving in great numbers in the late 1960s.

Both the Italians and the Latinos came from an old country whose government and culture were characterized by ineffective centralism and in which trust in institutions was extraordinarily, and justifiably, low. Individual initiative was discouraged and rewards came only to those in privileged positions. They began their journey at a time when population was growing rapidly but economic growth was producing little or no perceptible improvement in living conditions and was lagging behind that in other countries, especially the United States. What began as a migration of work-seeking men, intending only to sojourn in the new country and send money home, became a migration of whole families, though there was much movement back and forth between the new and old countries. The Italians, who came at a time when many other immigrants were arriving from eastern Europe and elsewhere, never became the largest visible immigrant group in any major city. The Latinos, in contrast, became the numerically dominant ethnic group in several large metropolitan areas.

Both groups of immigrants, having little trust in institutions, relied heavily on hard work and family. They were willing to take the most menial jobs, though Italian women avoided domestic service. More often than was common in the new country, wives stayed home to take care of children. The authority of the father in the home was strong. Rates of family formation and stability were higher among both groups than among other economically struggling groups in the new country.

Both the Italian and the Latino immigrants, though nominally Catholic, showed less than total attachment to the Catholic Church in America, which under its Irish hierarchy had little resemblance to the folk Catholicism, with local saints and festivals, that they had known in the old country. But over time they responded differently: second- and third-generation Italians tended to become conventionally Catholic, while first- and second-generation Latinos were often attracted to the Protestant evangelical churches that were also drawing many converts in Latin America.

Neither the Italian nor the Latino immigrants placed much value in education: the schools were just another institution in which they had little trust. Their children tended to leave school early, usually to work, and relatively few went on to college. Italian children nonetheless mastered the English language in school, while Latino children, cordoned off in Spanish-speaking "bilingual education," sometimes failed to master English well enough to qualify for good jobs. Despite publicity about Italian organized crime and Latino gangs, neither group had crime rates far above the American average.

The Italians and the Latinos showed relatively little interest in politics. They became naturalized U.S. citizens less often than other immigrant groups, and even those that did become citizens were not likely to register and vote. Coming from societies in which government was mistrusted, and in which politics was typically rigged, they did not see government as a savior and were not much interested in getting on government payrolls. They did not gravitate in a uniform way to either of the two American political parties. Instead, their party preferences seemed to result from some combination of attitudes formed in the particular part of the old country from which they came and their responses to the political situation they found in the state and city where they lived. It never made much sense to speak of a single "Italian vote" or "Hispanic vote."

America's articulate elites seldom celebrated the strengths of the Italian and Latino immigrants. The Italians were stereotyped as revolutionary anarchists and violent criminals, though only a very few Italians were either. The Latinos were characterized as welfare seekers and criminals, though in fact they worked exceedingly hard and often did not apply for welfare benefits for which they qualified. Their move upward in American society was quiet: they maintained strong families and, despite below-average education levels, rose in income and occupation status each generation. They produced some sports heroes and entertainment figures—mainly baseball players and singers. But they suffered serious insults in the public realm—Franklin Roosevelt's "dagger in the back" comment for the Italians and California's passage of Proposition 187 and the Elian Gonzalez case for Latinos. Italians responded by proving their loyalty to America in the crucible of World War II, while Latinos, unlike many of their neighbors, quietly persevered in hard work and family stability.

By the early 1970s Italians seemed to have become interwoven into the fabric of American life. Despite the *Godfather* movies, the Mafia stereotype seemed to be fading into the past. In the Watergate crisis, two Italian-Americans, Judge John Sirica and Chairman Peter Rodino, played key roles in upholding the rule of law. Later, the highly publicized success of automaker Lee Iacocca and the unanimous confirmation of Antonin Scalia as Supreme Court justice showed that Italian-Americans were moving into the top ranks of American life on merit. As for Latinos, their convergence at this writing is obviously far from complete, as their numbers are augmented by hundreds of thousands of new immigrants every year. Their assimilation has been retarded by bilingual education and has not been much advanced by racial quotas and preferences. Nonetheless, signs of convergence are apparent in that U.S.-born Latinos have reached median income levels in the Los Angeles area; an assimilated but unapologetically Latino middle class is quietly growing even as the media and professors in Chicano studies departments look for protest movements and try to encourage Spanish-language separatism. The desire of young Latinos to learn English, to advance themselves by hard work, to take advantage of the opportunities that are so plentiful here, so much more plentiful than in their parents' old countries, are quietly interweaving Latinos into the fabric of American life.

CHAPTER 3

ITALIANS

THE OLD COUNTRY

A traveler in southern Italy today sees a landscape much like what he would have seen 110 years ago when the great migration from the *Mezzogiorno*—literally, noon, and in Italian the word for the South—to America began. It is a landscape of mountains and valleys, of occasional flat plains and a few domineering volcanoes—Vesuvius, Etna—a landscape of narrow, twisted roads headed toward the nodes of cramped, tiny villages, often with old castles and newer churches. Peasants set out to tend the fields and men huddle in conversation at small *caffés*. There are fields of wheat and groves of olives and vines, usually spread over irregularly rolling hills, but relatively few trees; the parched land receives little rain from spring to fall.

Civilization is old here: peasants were cultivating these fields before the young Roman Republic conquered them in the third and second centuries B.C. and have been cultivating them ever since. It has not been a happy history. Southern Italy was conquered and ruled by one autocratic monarch after another. Its great cities—Naples, Palermo—had grown to enormous size by the Middle Ages but have remained much the same size since; their economies depended less on free trade than on connections with a royal court, and even today there is little of the light industrial development that spreads over so much of northern Italy. The North, political scientist Robert Putnam has written, has a vibrant civil society with roots in the independent city-republics of the 1100s. But the Mezzogiorno developed no such tradition under the autocratic rule of Norman kings and their descendant, the Holy Roman Emperor Frederick II, in the 1100s and 1200s, or under the various foreign-based monarchs who followed—the French Angevins, the Aragonese and Spanish, the Austrian Habsburgs, and Napoleon's relatives and the Spanish-origin Bourbons who ruled what became the Kingdom of Naples and the Two Sicilies until 1861.[1] Southern Italy was part of the domain of Emperor Charles V and his son, King Philip II of Spain, whose government has been aptly described as ineffective centralism—a government that gave minutely detailed orders but was unable to enforce them. Effective political power was held by an indolent viceroyalty or monarchy and powerful barons.[2]

This southern kingdom came to be part of unified Italy in 1861 only by happenstance. (Even that great centralizer Napoleon had created separate kingdoms of Italy and Naples.) The architect of Italian unification, Camille Cavour, a Piemontese from the Far North who spoke better French than Italian, was interested only in uniting northern Italy, south to Rome. But his hand was forced by Giuseppe Garibaldi's lightning conquest of Sicily and defeat of the last Bourbon king, at which point he made a gift of the territory to the Piemontese king, Victor

Emanuel II.[3] Even then, the new Italian government had to send in 100,000 troops to crush local rebellions during the next five years.[4]

The Mezzogiorno did not fit easily into the new kingdom. Most people in the new unified Italy spoke not standard Tuscan Italian but dialect; one linguistic scholar has estimated that "when Italy's political unity was achieved in the 1870s, fewer than 180,000 people were able to speak and write it correctly."[5] Southern dialects—Neapolitan, Calabrian, Apulian, Sicilian— were incomprehensible from Rome northward. Nor was the Church a unifying force: Pope Pius IX, protected by French troops, held on to his temporal possessions around Rome and, when Italian troops took them over in 1870, refused to recognize the authority of the new Kingdom of Italy. This conflict between church and state continued until Mussolini negotiated the Concordat of 1929, five years after most Italian immigration to the United States was cut off by the 1924 immigration act. Italy had free elections, but the franchise was limited, and political power in the South was in the hands of indolent nobles, jaded bureaucrats, and a few rising local notables, just as in the years before 1861. As the noble protagonist of Giuseppe Tomasi di Lampedusa's great novel of Sicily, *The Leopard*, said, "Everything must change so that everything can remain the same."[6]

In the years after unification, northern Italy rapidly industrialized while southern Italy remained economically stagnant: no one wanted to invest there. In 1870 a higher proportion of northern Italians than of southern Italians still worked on the land; by 1911, the percentage of northerners working the land had decreased sharply, while the number of southerners who worked on the land had actually *increased* in forty years.[7] Criminal organizations—the Mafia in Sicily, the 'Ndrangheta in Calabria, and the Camorra in the Campagna around Naples— thrived in southern Italy, corrupting local government and choking off legal commerce.[8] As late as the mid-twentieth century,

southern Italy, with 40 percent of the nation's population, produced only 20 percent of the gross domestic product and had
incomes not much more than half those in the North.[9]

Thus, southern Italy until well into the twentieth century
was—and arguably is, even today—as Richard Alba writes,
"rigidly stratified" and "essentially rural, with most of its people
eking out an existence in agriculture" under a system "that still
bore the evident imprint of its feudal past."[10] It was not so far in
the past: feudal land tenure was abolished only in 1806.[11] There
was a rigid class system: as Jerre Mangione and Ben Morreale
write, "An individual would be born into the family of a *contadino*,
an *artigiano*, or a *galantuomo*, and this circumstance of birth
would largely settle his or her destiny."[12] Gentlemen and even
artisans were few in numbers; *contadini*—peasants—were of
course the overwhelming majority of the population. Theirs
were lives of *pane e lavoro*—bread and work.[13] This was a largely
illiterate population—84 percent in the mid-nineteenth century,[14] 70 percent in 1901[15]—with no experience of modern
urban industrial society. The idea that government could allevi-
ate their condition was foreign: government officials were
regarded as *ladroni*—thieves—and laws were simply the means
by which thieves did their work.[16] To rely on them seemed
utterly foolish.

Regard was scarcely higher for the Catholic Church and its
officials.[17] Rome was distant and alien; southern Italian religious
belief was not so much an acceptance of the official doctrines of
the Church as, in Donald Tricario's words, "a folk religion, a
fusion of Christian and pre-Christian elements, of animism,
polytheism, and sorcery with the sacraments of the Church."[18]
Nor were there the mediating institutions and voluntary associations so often found in the United States. In this society, it was
considered completely out of place for a peasant or laborer to
take the initiative in work or self-improvement, much less seek a
voice in public or political affairs.[19]

The only institution that was trusted and respected was the family—not the nuclear family, but the *casa* of close relatives and the more distantly related *parenti*.[20] As an early-twentieth-century student of southern Italy wrote, "Life in the South exalts the family. It has been said of Sicily that the family sentiment is perhaps the only deeply rooted altruistic sentiment that prevails."[21] This has been an enduring condition, going back, as Putnam shows, to the Middle Ages. In the 1950s, after spending a year in a southern Italian town, Edward Banfield described it as "amoral familism," with social ties and moral obligations limited to the family. Banfield wrote that the villagers "act as if they were following this rule: Maximize the material, short-run advantages of the nuclear family; assume that all others will do likewise."[22] In such a society, he said, "deliberately concerted action will be very difficult to achieve and maintain."[23] Leonard Covello tells the story "of the old woman who saw a village boy stealing fruit from a tree. She ignored this. But after she saw him do it a second time she severely reprimanded the boy. Why? Because the first time he was stealing from someone who was not part of his family, a 'stranger,' and this was all right."[24] Toward *forestieri*—strangers—it was only sensible to behave with *furberia*, shrewdness; only toward family, and to *paesani*, people from the same village, with whom one must live, did one have ethical obligations, the first because of morality, the second out of prudence.[25] Family imposed obligations as well, especially the obligation to contribute to the family's economic well-being: children were expected to work starting at age twelve, the boys in the field and the girls in the household.[26] Toward outsiders, the prevailing attitude was mistrust. The story goes that Mario Puzo called his mother, an immigrant living in an Italian neighborhood on Long Island, with the good news that he had sold the paperback rights to *The Godfather* for $600,000. Before he had finished talking, she blurted out, "Don't tell nobody!"

THE JOURNEY

Italians immigrating to the United States came mostly from the Mezzogiorno and moved mostly to large American cities: more than 80 percent were from southern Italy, and about 90 percent settled in big cities, mainly in the East.[27] Italian immigration came in a rush, but it seems not to have been precipitated by a cataclysmic event like the potato famine that sent so many Irish across the Atlantic or a technological development like the mechanical cotton picker that sent so many southern blacks to the big cities of the North. From 1789 to 1880 just 25,000 Italians crossed the Atlantic to the United States. Then the numbers accelerated. In the 1870s, the decade following unification, 55,000 came to America. In the 1880s, 267,000 came, followed by 603,000 in the 1890s and 3,035,000 between 1900 and 1914. Another 585,000 came, mostly after World War I, until the 1924 immigration act virtually cut off the flow. Altogether, some 5 million Italians immigrated to the United States, 4.2 million of them in the third of a century between 1890 and 1924.[28]

Why did Italians migrate to America when they did? Just as immigration declined in places that were winners in the late-nineteenth-century industrial revolution, such as England and Germany, it increased in places that were bypassed by industrialization. Crop prices fell in the late nineteenth century as new transport techniques brought the produce of the American Midwest, Argentina, and Australia into the world market; in the 1880s the availability of American wheat and citrus crops plunged many southern Italian landowners into insolvency.[29] Moreover, erosion of topsoil and deforestation, the products of centuries, made land in southern Italy less and less productive, and the large landholding system gave farmers on year-to-year leases little incentive to improve the land.[30] Then, in 1884–1887, the Mezzogiorno suffered from a cholera epidemic, and in 1890 the Phylloxera parasite destroyed most of southern Italy's grapevines. Later came the volcanic eruptions of Vesuvius and Etna and the earthquake and tidal wave that in 1908 killed 100,000 in Messina.[31]

Improvements in public health brought declining child mortality in southern Italy, but the increase in population was not matched by an increase in jobs. As industry advanced elsewhere, employment in mining, artisan work, home piecework, and small-scale industry became scarcer in southern Italy. As scholar Virginia Yans-McLaughlin writes, "The demographic and economic changes occurring after 1870, then, upset the close interdependence of peasant agriculture and household production on the one hand, and domestic, artisanal, and small-scale industry on the other. Thus the reduced opportunities for alternate work, coupled with an increasing demand for scarce land, encouraged young individuals and ultimately entire families to emigrate."[32]

A substantial majority of Italian immigrants were men looking for work who either were unmarried or left their families behind. Between 1899 and 1910, 79 percent of southern Italian immigrants were men.[33] Many sent for their families when they became established, but many others returned to Italy: according to one estimate, 3.8 million Italians came to the United States between 1899 and 1924, but 2.1 million left in the same period.[34] These emigrants tended not to be the most impoverished and downtrodden of southern Italians; they had above-average (though still low) rates of literacy and had evidently achieved enough minimal competence at dealing with the larger world to give them confidence that they could take advantage of life in America—the minimal levels of cultural and psychological capital needed to finance emigration.[35] As Humbert Nelli describes, the back-and-forth migration was continual: "Some of the returners simply stayed in Italy until they needed money again and then repeated the process; eventually many of these settled in the New World, although often not before they made the voyage back and forth several times and sometimes to both North and South

America. After the turn of the century, immigration gradually became more stable as women and children joined the men who came seeking their fortunes."[36] This pattern, completely new to America, was familiar to Italians, who often returned after migrating to other parts of Europe and to Argentina.[37] In the meantime, men sent money back to their families; remittances to Italy totaled nearly $2 million in 1902 and $15 million in 1914.[38] Italian immigrants, far from being cut off eternally from the old country, in many cases remained in close touch with family back home, regarding the passage across the ocean as an almost routine part of their lives.

Italian immigration, like Irish immigration and the black migration from the rural South, was "chain migration": first a few hardy individuals would make the journey; then others from the same family or community, hearing of those individuals' success and believing that they would be met by people they knew, came also; then others, often in very large numbers, would follow. The total number of immigrants would swell in size so long as conditions and prospects in the old country did not noticeably improve. Virginia Yans-McLaughlin gives the example of Francesco Barone, who in 1887 left the Sicilian village of Valledolmo for Buffalo, New York; fourteen of his relatives from this "not especially large place" were in Buffalo by 1905, and by the mid-twentieth century eight thousand Valledolmesi had emigrated.[39]

THE NEW COUNTRY

The vast majority of Italian immigrants landed in New York harbor—97 percent in the years of peak immigration[40]—and settled not far away. Even at the end of the twentieth century nearly half of Italian-Americans still lived within a hundred miles of Manhattan.[41] Small numbers of Italians settled in rural areas, mostly in the West—most famously in what they made the California wine country—and San Francisco had a sizeable community of mostly northern Italians, who worked in banking, small industry, fishing, and horticulture and had relatively high incomes.[42] Very few Italians immigrated to the American South. As a rule, Italian immigrants settled in large cities, a large majority of them in New York, followed distantly by Philadelphia, Chicago, and Boston.

There they settled in tenement neighborhoods that became known as "Little Italies." They might better have been known as "Little Sicilies" or "Little Calabrias"; the peoples of the various villages in the southern Italian peninsula and on the island of Sicily spoke different and often mutually incomprehensible dialects,[43] and people from the same village or province tended to cluster once in America. Thomas Kessner, an early chronicler of Italian immigration, provides a map of the settlements in New York City: "Mott Street between East Houston and Prince held the Napolitani; the opposite side of the street was reserved for Basilicati. Around the corner the Siciliani settled Prince Street, while two blocks away Calabresi lived on Mott between Broome and Grand. Mulberry Street was strictly Neapolitan, and Hester Street, running perpendicular to Mulberry, carried the local color of Apulia."[44] Similarly, the Italian First Ward of Newark was settled primarily by immigrants from towns in the Campagna provinces of Avellino, Salerno, and Potenza.[45] Given the importance of family to southern Italians, it is not surprising that one-quarter of 765 families surveyed on New York's Elizabeth Street in 1905 had relatives living nearby—and that was probably an underestimate.[46] The North End of Boston, once the home of Paul Revere, became a Little Italy starting in the 1870s; in the 1930s it had 42,000 people, 95 percent of them Italian.[47] Chicago's Little Italy was around Taylor Street on the Near West Side; when the University of Illinois built a new campus there, a new Little Italy formed at the western edge of the city.[48]

Outside of these Little Italies, neighborhoods seldom became exclusively Italian; there were too many immigrants from other countries to permit that. But Italians still tended to cluster with others from the same village, province, or region, and created something like southern Italian village life in the brick-and-brownstone streets of America's big cities. Vincenza Scarpaci paints the picture: "Butchers kept goats for Easter; grocers imported olive oil from the region favored by their clientele; saloons sold beer and wine and provided tables for Italian card games; and boardinghouses often expanded into simple *casalingo* restaurants, offering Italian dishes. Spoken Italian and dialects filled the streets; familiar smells of cheese, salami, and garlic wafted on the breeze; street music was provided by the hurdy gurdy and organ grinder; women compared produce bought from a huckster's cart; and posters announced Italian theater and opera performances or proclaimed the street entertainment of the puppet shows."[49] Italians also clustered beyond the city limits, on Long Island and in Westchester County, where several towns had nuclei of Italian craftsmen, gardeners, and other workers.[50]

Clustering was also a result of the fact that so many of the early Italian immigrants were brought over by labor contractors called *padroni*. Charles Morris writes, "In the 1880s and 1890s, they arrived almost as serfs under the control of a *padrone*, who financed their passage, provided room and board, collected their wages, and paid a risible living allowance."[51] *Padroni* often abused their workers, but they found them jobs, such as on railroads and construction projects, that the immigrants could not have found on their own; *padroni* also wrote letters and sent money back home for the often illiterate workers. In 1897 *padroni* controlled two-thirds of the Italian workers in New York, but over time, as immigration increased and states passed laws to regulate labor agents, their numbers declined markedly.[52] As chain migration increased, Italian immigrants, with the help of relatives and townsmen who had come before, could find work for themselves.

WORK

Pane e lavoro was the lot of the *contadini* of southern Italy; so it was of southern Italian immigrants in the United States. Most who came in the years of heavy immigration worked unskilled jobs.[53] Of the 1.7 million Italians with previous occupational experience who arrived between 1899 and 1910, less than 1 percent were professional and only 15 percent skilled workers;[54] 32 percent had been farm laborers and 43 percent "other" laborers, and so they naturally sought laboring jobs in America.[55] Their "fluid, unstable work experiences" proved to be useful when they reached America, where they often worked in outdoor jobs and, writes Virginia Yans-McLaughlin, "compensated for the seasonal unemployment just as they had in Italy; they took any available day laborer's job in the city [Buffalo, in this case] or drifted around the Niagara Frontier region seeking work as construction, railroad, or agricultural laborers."[56] In 1910, 59 percent of Italian men worked as laborers or operatives and 23 percent as craftsmen, with only 9 percent in professional or sales work.[57] Italians made up three-quarters of the construction labor in New York City and almost the entire workforce on the new New York subways.[58] More skilled Italian immigrants worked as stonemasons, shoemakers, and tailors. Women often worked, too, especially in the garment industry, on piecework at home or in sweatshops,[59] and in the artificial flower industry; many of the workers killed in the tragic 1911 Triangle Shirtwaist fire in New York were Italian immigrant women.

Yet even among the first generation of Italian immigrants there was some occupational upward mobility; in short order a significant percentage worked their way to skilled and white-collar jobs.[60] The entrepreneurial impulse, so visibly absent among the Irish, was somewhat stronger among Italians: as early as 1910 Italians in Boston were much more likely to own businesses than the more settled and more numerous Irish.[61] To be sure, Italian entrepreneurship was concentrated in a few trades in which they had had experience in Italy. In St. Louis's Hill neighborhood, for example, almost all the Italian-owned businesses were saloons, grocery and fruit stores, and barbershops (restaurants were much more likely to be owned by Greeks), while in Buffalo they owned shoe repair and tailor shops or sold real estate.[62]

But Italian immigrants also founded several well-known businesses. Amadeo Obici, an immigrant from the Veneto, started the Planter Peanut Company in 1908 and, with the Mr. Peanut symbol he designed in 1916, made Planters Peanuts the dominant firm in the industry; operating in segregated Virginia, he insisted on paying his black workers the same wages as whites.[63] In another case, the four Paterno brothers became major forces in construction in New York, building luxury apartments on Fifth Avenue, Sutton Place, Gracie Square, and West End Avenue.[64] Italians disdained receiving welfare from the state or charities and instead founded their own mutual aid societies, usually with others from the same village or province; by 1910 there were two thousand of these mutual aid societies in New York and four hundred in Chicago.[65] They also formed banks to receive deposits and send money to relatives in the old country. Often located in grocery stores and saloons, these were small institutions with little capital and under no legal control. In time they came under regulation, both through state laws and when the Italian government designated the Bank of Naples as the sole agent for transmitting savings to Italy from all parts of the world.[66] But one, A. P. Giannini's Bank of Italy, the only bank open in San Francisco after the earthquake of 1906, ultimately became one of the largest banks in the United States, the Bank of America.[67] Italians also created their own ethnic organizations, including the Sons of Italy, many of which raised money to erect statues of Columbus, Mazzini, Verrazano, Garibaldi, and Verdi.[68]

Much has been written about Italians' role in labor unions, but it was largely a passive one: Italian immigrants were often strikebreakers and seldom union organizers.[69] Italians led the 1912 Industrial Workers of the World (IWW) strike in Lawrence, Massachusetts,[70] but this was the exception rather than the rule. Many Italian laborers were members of the Hod Carriers Union, which was headed by Italian-Americans starting in 1909, but, writes Nathan Glazer, it "became *padronismo* on a larger scale and was a scandal to the labor movement"; the Hod Carriers held no conventions from 1911 to 1941.[71] Many Americans entertained a stereotype of Italians as anarchists, but this was based on anecdote rather than data. The prime examples were the anarchists Sacco and Vanzetti, executed in 1927 for armed robbery and murder (despite much protest about the fairness of their trial, it seems clear that they were in fact guilty), but they were hardly typical of Italian immigrants.

FAMILY

Close family ties: this was a defining—perhaps the defining—characteristic of Italian immigrant communities. "Family solidarity was the basic code of such family life and defiance of it was something akin to a cardinal sin," writes Leonard Covello.[72] Studies in New York in 1905 showed that 93 percent of Italian families had "husband or father present" and less than 3 percent of households were "male-absent" and headed by women under forty.[73] Italians were also the ethnic group least likely to apply for welfare and, when they did, the least likely to give desertion or nonsupport as the reason.[74] Much has been written, sometimes with a note of disapproval, of the unchallenged authority of the father in the southern Italian family. But if those fathers took their authority for granted, they also took their responsibilities very seriously, to the point that desertion, so common among the Irish, was almost unheard of among the Italians. This carried over into employment. "Men traditionally addressed the outside world as breadwinners," writes Donald Tricario, while "women supplemented family earnings in a way that minimized the disruption of family solidarity and, more specifically, their roles of wife, mother, homemaker, daughter."[75] Young unmarried women often worked in factories, but usually quit on being married, and almost always lived at home with their parents;[76] at least in the early years of immigration there were "hardly any Italian prostitutes," notes Thomas Sowell.[77] Children were expected to work from an early age,[78] and parents regarded with scorn the recess periods of the public school. They preferred the Sicilian proverb: "a cane, hard work, and bread make for beautiful children."[79]

The family made great demands, but it also offered great support. It provided a safe harbor against the rest of the world, a basis for pride in upholding one's responsibilities, an identity, and a particular set of traditions—every family believed its tomato sauce was the best.[80] And families stayed close together. Married daughters and sons almost always lived in the same blocks, often the same buildings, as their immigrant parents.[81] This pattern persisted even as the first and second generations became better off economically. Families would buy houses they had formerly rented, renovate and modernize them, and furnish them more commodiously. As Nathan Glazer writes, "The old houses would be rebuilt on the inside (there is always a great amount of skilled building and crafts labor in an Italian community), new furniture is brought into the old apartments, new cars line the streets, and even the restaurants reflect quality and affluence, for they serve not only friends and relatives who come back to the neighborhood but also those who have never moved away, and who now have an income far greater than the cost and quality of their housing would suggest." Such neighborhoods remained persistently Italian, even as other immigrant neighborhoods were abandoned by their original residents and turned over to other ethnic or racial newcomers.[82]

The second generation of Italian-Americans hewed fairly closely to the habits their parents brought over from Italy. They tended to live with their parents until they married, and they usually married other Italians. Young couples generally chose to live in heavily Italian neighborhoods, although often in farther reaches of the city or in the suburbs. The second generation tended to leave school early and to work hard.[83]

RELIGION

Most Italian immigrants did not trust the major institutions of America any more than they had those in southern Italy. This included the Catholic Church. The Italian government was anticlerical, and many men shunned the Church except when they were baptized, married, and buried: "Italian men left it to the women to attend Mass and keep the faith," Leonard Dinnerstein and David Reimers write.[84] Most Italians, they go on, regarded the Church as "a cold and almost puritanical organization" and priests as "lazy, ignorant hangers-on who merely earned their living off the community."[85] For the Irish, the Catholic Church had been the one institution they and not the English controlled, and adherence to its rules and attendance at Mass were the most important assertion of their Irishness. For the Italians, however, the Church was an alien institution, controlled by Rome and distant bishops; the folk wisdom of their own local communities was frequently more important. As Dinnerstein and Reimers write, "They were flexible about doctrine, ignorant of many traditional aspects of Roman Catholicism, and devoted to their festivals and *festas*. The southern Italian immigrant feared 'the evil eye' and its effects, and, as one historian tells us, 'through the use of rituals, symbols, and charms, they sought to ward off evil spirits and to gain the favor of powerful deities.'"[86]

In the United States, unlike Germans and Poles, who typically built their own churches, Italians tended to inherit their
churches from the suburbanized Irish; this was the pattern in
South Philadelphia, in New York's Little Italy and Greenwich
Village, in Boston, and in Chicago.[87] Italians, accustomed to a
church that venerated local saints and celebrated local festivals,
disliked the rigorous and grim Irish priests and their astringent,
impersonal creed. Italians preferred to celebrate *feste* for their
local saints, the images of which typically weren't entrusted to
unsympathetic Irish priests but rather were kept in the loft of
an Italian saloon. Robert Orsi, the chronicler of the Madonna
of 115th Street in East Harlem, describes how in 1913 "Italians
would hold their *feste* on the steps of the local church, crowding
the streets, while inside the priest said Sunday mass before
empty pews."[88]

But as each generation in America passed, the Italians became
more conventionally Catholic. Charles Morris tells the story:
"Italian-American religious practice tended to approach the Irish
Catholic norm in the second, and even more strongly in the third,
generation. In contrast to first-generation Italians, both Irish
Catholics and second- and third-generation Italians had much
higher rates of weekly Mass attendance and were quicker to call
a priest during a dangerous illness. (First-generation Italians
were worried about frightening the patient.) Parochial-school
attendance was very low among first-generation Italian children,
but approached that of the Irish by the third generation. First-
generation Italians prayed to local saints or to the Blessed Virgin;
Irish Catholics and assimilated Italians prayed, austerely enough,
to God. Third-generation Italians showed the same deference to
the clergy as Irish Catholics did. Irish Catholics and third-
generation Italians did not cry at funerals."[89] Still, Italians were
much less likely than Irish to have five or more children, and they
produced far fewer priests than did Irish Catholics. The first
Italian-American bishop was not appointed until 1954.[90]

EDUCATION

"Fesso chi fa i figli meglio di lui," ran an old Italian proverb: stupid is he who makes his children better than himself. Italian immigrants came to America with little schooling, and, valuing family and not trusting outside institutions, they discouraged their children from staying in school and from using education to rise in economic or social status.[91] "Laws mandating school attendance up to a certain age were regarded as a particularly obnoxious intrusion on the prerogatives of the family," writes Richard Alba. "Only a few years of schooling were viewed as necessary to impart to children what they would need to survive. Additional years were destructive of their moral fiber, instilling in them ideas that were alien to their parents and the family ethos."[92] Dropout rates were high, and there were few Italian high school or college graduates.[93] Among Italian-Americans in New York City in 1908, there were only one-tenth as many children in the eighth grade as in the third grade.[94] Nationally, in 1910 only 31 percent of Italian immigrants age fourteen to eighteen were enrolled in school, far below the rate for Irish (48 percent) or Jews (56 percent).[95] Boys were encouraged to work as soon as possible, to bring money into the family; girls were kept home, rather than be exposed to unsuitable young men. Coming from a society in which the game of getting ahead was fixed by those born on top, they assumed that upward social mobility was impossible and that sensible people simply concentrated on working hard enough to earn a decent living for their families.

These attitudes changed only slowly. Nathan Glazer writes, "Nor, despite a strong desire for material improvement, did the Italian family see a role for education in America. One improved one's circumstances by hard work, perhaps by a lucky strike, but not by spending time in a school, taught by women, who didn't even beat the children. Parents felt that the children should contribute to the family budget as soon as possible, and that was

years before the time fixed by the state for the end of their education. Truancy and dropouts were a constant problem, and were
often abetted by the parents, who wanted the children to help
out in the shop or store." He concludes, "For the children of
south Italian peasants in New York to get college educations in
the 1920s and 1930s was a heroic struggle."[96] In the early 1930s
only 11 percent of Italian-American high school students graduated, far below the average of 42 percent. In those same years
Italians were the least educated ethnic group in St. Louis, below
even blacks, and 35 percent of Italian immigrants were illiterate.[97] Yet the public schools did give Italian children a solid command of English and knowledge of math, even if they did not
acknowledge the students' Italian heritage in any way.[98]

There were exceptions, of course, individuals who worked
hard in school to become doctors and lawyers and who often
practiced their profession in Italian-American communities.[99]
These men pursued their educations and practiced their professions with a fierceness, acquiring an unshakable authority in their
families and communities. One wonders how they would have
fared in Italy, where they would have been far less likely to
become professionals.

CRIME

In the years when heavy Italian immigration began, the stereotype of the Italian as criminal was common in America. This was
partly because of the fame of the Mafia and other criminal societies and because Italians, as Richard Alba writes, were believed
to be "prone to crimes of passion and vengeance, a tendency
symbolized for Americans by the stiletto." As the writer of an
1890 article entitled "What shall we do with the 'Dago'?" put it,
"The knife with which he cuts his bread he also uses to lop off
another 'dago's' finger or ear."[100] But in fact Italian immigrants

had lower crime rates than immigrants generally (although there was more crime among Italians than among urban blacks).[101] In close-knit Italian communities, with their strong families, robbery and burglary were proscribed. A Buffalo doctor in 1898 noted that when Italians got control of Canal Street, "once famous as America's toughest thoroughfare," crime plummeted. "A woman can now walk through this section of town with impunity."[102] As Thomas Sowell writes, "The casual Irish approach to brawling was foreign to southern Italians, to whom fighting was a very serious matter. The Italian immigrant was often armed with a knife or a gun, and an attack on him was a deadly risk."[103] Crime rates among Italians fell as they became integrated into the industrial workforce.[104]

In the nineteenth century, as noted, criminal organizations existed in much of southern Italy, though they were not as tightly structured or centralized as their image in American popular culture suggests.[105] Vestiges of these organizations did make their way to the United States. In the first decade of the century, the "Black Hand" became notorious; these were organizations of extortionists who set off bombs if their targets did not pay up.[106] By the 1920s some Italian-Americans had formed more elaborate local syndicates. In Greenwich Village, for instance, a syndicate created an underground economy, furnishing locally valued goods and services and becoming a kind of invisible government whose main objective was to guarantee a marketplace for illicit ventures.[107] As it happened, Italians became leaders of large criminal organizations just as Prohibition produced opportunities for enormous profits; the thriving speakeasies in big cities drove demand for illegal alcohol. After Prohibition's repeal in 1933, Italian gangsters concentrated on gambling, drugs, and (with the collusion of unions) the waterfront, and by the early 1950s, when Senator Estes Kefauver conducted his highly publicized investigation of organized crime, gambling and other rackets seemed to be largely under the control of Italians.[108]

Keep in mind, however, that the Irish, the Jews, and other ethnic groups also produced criminal organizations practicing extortion in a more or less organized manner. Dinnerstein and Reimers observe, for example, that "one study of the top underworld figures in Chicago in 1930"—the heyday of the notorious Al Capone—"estimated that 30 percent were of Italian background, 29 percent of Irish background, and 20 percent of Jewish background."[109] Nevertheless, the image of the *mafioso* has become a familiar stereotype, thanks largely to vivid (and by no means entirely accurate) portrayals in popular culture—from the gangster films of the 1930s and 1940s, to the television program *The Untouchables* and its imitators in the 1950s and 1960s, to the 1960s book *The Godfather* and the 1970s and 1980s movies based on it, to the successful cable television series *The Sopranos* of today. The prominence of this image is disproportionate to its actual magnitude. It bears repeating that the very large majority of Italian-Americans were in no way associated with these criminal organizations. The code of *omerta*—silence—which many adhered to when questioned about organized crime, was observed partly out of fear and partly out of the southern Italian reticence to get involved in any but one's own family—a reticence that also accounted for their tolerance for the very un-Italian behavior of Bohemians in heavily Italian Greenwich Village. "Oddities that did not affect the group could easily be ignored," Glazer writes. "Concern for odd or immoral behavior is limited to one's own family; the rest of the world, as long as it poses no threat, can be ignored."[110]

POLITICS

Nothing in the background of immigrants from southern Italy encouraged them to participate in American politics. Few had ever voted—only 2 percent of the Italian population qualified to vote during the early decades of the Kingdom of Italy—and Italian elections were in any case manipulated by local notables. Allegiance to the Kingdom of Italy, which had ruled the Mezzogiorno only since 1861, was not strong. Nor did the villagers of southern Italy place any reliance on what they called *lo stato ladro*—literally, the state-thief.[111] The early sojourner immigrants, who expected to return to Italy and often did, had no interest in American politics,[112] and up through the 1920s only a minority of Italian immigrants in many cities chose to become U.S. citizens; the rate of naturalization from 1899 to 1910 was only 16 percent.[113]

When Italians did enter the electorate, they did not do so as a unified bloc. Neither the Yankee-dominated Republicans nor the Irish-dominated Democrats had any intrinsic appeal to the Italians, whose background was so different and whose inclination to trust institutions was so weak. Partisan preference instead seems to have been a result of different origins in Italy and of different local situations in American cities. In some cities, like New Haven, Italian voters, shut out by the Democrats, became Republicans;[114] in others they became strong Democrats, as in Cleveland, whose mayor Anthony Celebrezze became the first Italian-American cabinet member in 1962.[115] In New York, where they were most numerous, Italians voted in large numbers for Democrats and Republicans, with different preferences in different neighborhoods—Republican in Staten Island and Bay Ridge, Brooklyn; Democratic in Manhattan's Little Italy; and for left-wing candidates of various stripes in East Harlem, where Fiorello LaGuardia was elected to Congress on the Republican and Socialist lines, James Lanzetta and Alfred Santangelo[116] on the Democratic line, and the pro-Communist Vito Marcantonio on the American Labor Party line. Italians in Philadelphia up through the early 1930s were, like just about everyone else in the city, Republicans. Thomas Foglietta, a liberal Democratic congressman in the 1980s and 1990s and Bill Clinton's second ambassador to Italy, was the son of a Republican politician and began his career in that party.

The first successful Italian politicians had atypical backgrounds. Anthony Caminetti, elected as a Democrat to the House in 1890 and 1892 and later Woodrow Wilson's commissioner of immigration, was of northern Italian descent and grew up in San Francisco and the Gold Rush country of California.[117] Fiorello LaGuardia, whose father was of Genoese and mother of Trieste Jewish stock, grew up in Arizona, where his father was an army musician. He was an Episcopalian and a Republican. He was elected to the House six times and mayor of New York three times with support from left-wing parties; in 1941 he received much lower percentages from Italians than from Jews.[118] The first Italian-American governor, Charles Poletti of New York, who served one month in December 1942 after Herbert Lehman resigned, was Protestant.[119] It is a measure of the lateness of Italian success in American politics that the first Italian-American elected governor and senator, John Pastore, died as recently as July 2000. Pastore, a Catholic of southern Italian origin, was slated by the Rhode Island Democratic machine for lieutenant governor in 1944, an obvious ticket-balancing move in the state with the highest percentage of Italian-Americans. He became governor in October 1945 when incumbent J. Howard McGrath resigned to become U.S. solicitor general, and he was elected in his own right in 1946 and 1948. In 1950 he was elected to a short term in the Senate seat vacated by the same McGrath when he became U.S. attorney general, and he was elected to full terms by wide margins in 1952, 1958, 1964, and 1970.[120] Pastore, an able man with a distinguished record, would probably have risen even without McGrath's propensity to switch jobs,* but not so fast.

---

* McGrath resigned as attorney general in 1951 amid charges of scandal and had no further political career.

DISTINCTIVENESS

Italian immigrants were a visually distinctive group whom many in the articulate elite regarded as another "race." "Swarthy" was a term often used to describe them, and, as Richard Alba notes, "to the eyes of Americans they bore other physical signs of degradation, such as low foreheads."[121] Dinnerstein and Reimers write that, in addition to using the epithets "wop," "dago" and "guinea," "old-stock Americans" referred to Italians as "the Chinese of Europe" and "just as bad as the Negroes."[122] Many Americans doubted that Italians were "white"; a witness in a congressional hearing in the early twentieth century, asked if he considered an Italian a white man, replied, "No, sir, an Italian is a Dago." In the American South, Italians were often segregated like blacks or were classified as yet another race—"between." As one southern newspaper put it, "The average man will classify the population as white, dagoes, and Negroes."[123] Eleven Italians were lynched in New Orleans in 1891, which led to protests from the Italian government,[124] and five Italians were lynched in Tallulah, Louisiana, in 1899; after these incidents, very few Italian immigrants headed to the American South.[125] As Richard Alba notes, "Their problematic racial position is suggested by a common epithet for them, *guinea*, which is probably derived from a name attached to slaves from part of the western African coast."[126] The notion that all immigrants from Europe were regarded as white Europeans and accepted without prejudice is an artifact of 1990s "multiculturalism" and an anachronism with no historical basis.

SPORTS AND ENTERTAINMENT

Despite these negative stereotypes and despite habits of mind that Italians brought from the old country and that proved dysfunctional in the new, Italians over time became interwoven into the fabric of American life. As with other groups, this was facilitated by the emergence of sports and entertainment heroes. The most important were two who appeared just on the eve of World War II, Joe DiMaggio and Frank Sinatra. Their enduring qualities were not at first fully apparent: DiMaggio was patronized by some sportswriters ("Italians, bad at war, are well suited for milder competitions")[127] and Sinatra dismissed as a heartthrob of teenage "bobby-soxers." But DiMaggio demonstrated his cool excellence with his hitting streak in 1941 and his leading the Yankees to nine World Series titles; Sinatra's career, revived after a few fallow years in the late 1940s, made him the premier American singer for four decades. DiMaggio's brief marriage to Marilyn Monroe and Sinatra's dalliance with organized crime figures, which caused the Kennedys to drop him as a social companion, did not dim their luster; they were fondly remembered figures when they died in the 1990s. They seemed not just Italian but American; they showed that Italian-Americans could rise to the very top in American society.

CONVERGENCE

Other Italian-Americans rose more slowly. The first Italian immigrants were slow to learn English and clung to their dialect. But relatively few spoke standard Tuscan Italian,* and their dialect was adulterated by anglicisms like *shoppa* (shop), *fatoria* (factory), and *giobba* (job). Still, as Richard Alba writes, "Once they did learn English it rapidly replaced Italian."[128] The hold of the family over children also loosened over the decades. "Most second-generation Italian children used English to hide their

---

* My grandfather Charles J. Barone, born in Buffalo in 1894, could speak Sicilian but not Italian.

teenage secrets from their parents," writes Vincenza Scarpaci. "Many developed linguistic non-reciprocity, that is, they understood the Italian spoken by their parents but spoke only English."[129] By the late 1930s, when sociologist William Whyte observed gangs in the Italian North End of Boston, he was able to distinguish significant groups of both "corner boys" and "college boys," members of gangs who hung out together and boys who concentrated on schoolwork in search of upward social mobility.[130] Negative attitudes toward staying in school remained until World War II, as Italians continued to have much higher dropout rates than other groups.[131] Intermarriage with those from other ethnic groups, very uncommon among the first and second generations, became more common among the third, and family size dropped rapidly as infant mortality declined and the cost of raising children rose.[132] Second- and especially third-generation Italians, as we have seen, were much more likely to be conventional American Catholics and homeowners.[133]

World War II played a critical part in the rise of Italian-Americans. Many Italian-Americans expressed admiration for Mussolini's fascist regime in the 1920s and early 1930s, but there was little sympathy for it by the outbreak of the war.[134] Still, many Italian-Americans were outraged when, after Mussolini invaded France in 1940, Franklin Roosevelt said, "The hand that held the dagger has struck it into the back of its neighbor"—not because they sympathized with Mussolini but because it evoked the stereotype of Italians as criminals—and Roosevelt got fewer votes than Wendell Willkie or racket-busting Thomas Dewey in Italian districts of New York City in 1940 and 1944.[135] But the loyalty of Italian-Americans proved not to be in doubt. The 600,000 Italian citizens in the United States were required to register as "aliens of enemy nationality" in 1941,[136] but restrictions on them were lifted on Columbus Day 1942.[137] Meanwhile, hundreds of thousands of ethnic Italians served in America's famously multiethnic military, memorialized in wartime movies and in postwar novels by Norman Mailer, James Jones, Henry Brown, and John Hersey.

When Italian-Americans returned from the war, many took advantage of the G.I. Bill of Rights; college attendance among Italians rose from 15 percent in 1940 to 30 percent in 1954 and 38 percent in 1960.[138] Like other ethnics who had grown up in central city neighborhoods, Italian-Americans joined the march to the suburbs, producing very large Italian percentages in the Westchester County, Long Island, and New Jersey suburbs of New York, and in suburbs of other large cities as well. By the 1960s Italian-Americans had risen above the national average in income, even though they still had fewer years of schooling than average. That latter statistic had changed by the 1970s, as the educational level of young Italian-Americans reached the national average.[139] By the beginning of the 1980s, Thomas Sowell could write that "in income, education, IQ scores, and other indices, Italian Americans are very much like other Americans today,"[140] and Census Bureau statisticians could speak of "an overall Italian population that is similar to the rest of the population in this country."[141]

In the 1990 census, those who identified themselves as having Italian ancestry had household incomes and mean family incomes 17 percent above the national average and were nearly 50 percent more likely to have college degrees. And the rate of business ownership among Italian-Americans was 70 percent above the national average.[142] In Richard Alba's pithy summary, "Italian Americans have risen from ragpickers and ditchdiggers to virtual parity within three generations."[143]

In the process, Italians have become much more likely to marry non-Italians. As late as the early 1960s, about 60 percent of Italian-Americans chose spouses of unmixed Italian ancestry. By 1979 a majority were marrying non-Italians, and less than 20 percent of Italian-American children under age five were of entirely Italian ancestry.[144] Of Italian-Americans born since

1950, more than two-thirds of those of entirely Italian-American parentage and four-fifths of those with partial Italian parentage married non-Italian Americans.[145] By the 1970s Italian child-rearing practices and spousal relationships came to resemble the family lives of most Americans and not the practices of the first generation of immigrants.[146] To some these numbers suggest a dilution of the Italian heritage, but they also mean that a much larger number of Americans are of Italian ancestry than would be the case if the rate of intermarriage had stayed as low as in the first or second generation.

In these postwar years, Italian-Americans also made great strides in politics and business. In politics they continued to back neither party consistently: they voted more heavily than the Irish for John F. Kennedy in 1960, then just ten years later cast key votes that made Conservative Party nominee James Buckley senator from New York. In the 1950s there were few Italian-Americans in high office, and the first Italian leader of Tammany Hall, Carmine De Sapio, was regarded as a sinister figure. In the 1980s New York governor Mario Cuomo was a national figure and in 1984 Congresswoman Geraldine Ferraro was the Democratic nominee for vice president. Italian officeholders, once a rarity, became commonplace. Ella Grasso was the first woman elected a governor in her own right, in Connecticut in 1974; New York elected Alfonse D'Amato to replace Jacob Javits in the Senate in 1980; and Cuomo himself was beaten in 1994 by George Pataki, who is of Hungarian and Italian descent. Italian-Americans were elected senator in such unlikely states as New Mexico (Pete Domenici, in 1970), Vermont (Patrick Leahy, in 1974), and Wyoming (Mike Enzi, in 1996). "Where would we find an honest Italian-American?" Richard Nixon was heard to say on the White House tapes. But he was brought down in the Watergate scandal in large part because of the efforts of Judge John Sirica, who handed down harsh sentences to the Watergate burglars, and Congressman Peter Rodino, who chaired the House

Judiciary Committee hearings on impeachment. It was no accident when the conservative Antonin Scalia was confirmed unanimously in 1983. What liberal senator wanted to vote against the first Italian Supreme Court justice? In the private sector Italian-Americans were achieving spectacular success. Lee Iacocca became a national figure as president of Ford and CEO of Chrysler (and a best-selling author) in the 1970s and 1980s. A. Bartlett Giamatti became president of Yale in 1978 and commissioner of baseball in 1989.

But there were dozens of other CEOs of Italian ancestry in the 1980s and 1990s, so many that no one bothered to count. By the 1970s Italians were thoroughly interwoven into the fabric of American life. It took eighty years.

CHAPTER 4

LATINOS

THE OLD COUNTRY

On the road from Mexico City to Teotihuacán, where the messages on the giant Pyramids of the Sun and Moon remain undeciphered, a traveler can see much of today's Mexico. There is the giant city, its center in the historic Zocalo, the same place where Cortés enticed Montezuma to become a prisoner in his palace,[1] and its monumental statues on the Paseo de la Reforma commemorating the heroes of the nation's past— Cuahetmoc, the last Aztec emperor; Benito Juarez, the first *indio* president and nemesis of the Catholic Church; the *niños heroes*, the military cadets who died defending Chapultepec Castle against U.S. troops in 1847.[2] To the north, the traveler passes by the industrial residential districts and suburbs, nestled between rising mountains on fill land in what was once the lake surrounding the city, with their littered streets and small houses with open spaces in place of windows, tiny stores and ubiquitous street peddlers. Over another mountain, the houses grow scarce, and the traveler sees the farm fields, still laid out in Aztec geometric patterns, punctuated by occasional crossroads villages, packed with the green leaves of maize and other crops, spread out up to the volcanic mountains that ring this seven-thousand-foot-high Valley of Mexico. This is one of the thousands of Latin American landscapes that have produced the Latino immigrants who have come, by the hundreds of thousands and millions, to the United States in the last third of the twentieth century.

Latinos, of course, are not entirely strangers to the territory that is now the United States; they have lived there longer than any other identifiable group except American Indians. Spanish soldiers founded St. Augustine, Florida, in 1565 and Santa Fe, New Mexico, in 1609. Texas was part of Mexico until 1836, and the United States acquired California, Nevada, New Mexico, and most of Arizona in the Treaty of Guadalupe Hidalgo, which ended the Mexican-American War in 1848. But these lands were lightly populated: the lands ceded by Mexico in 1848 contained only 75,000 Spanish speakers, with only 7,500 in all of California;[3] there was no permanent Latin American community in Los Angeles for most of the nineteenth century.[4] The only demographically significant Spanish-speaking communities in this territory are in northern New Mexico and south Texas.

Immigration from Mexico and other parts of Latin America was negligible for most of this country's existence. The 1924 immigration act did not impose quotas on Western Hemisphere countries, and for years the border was unpatrolled. People would cross the river in the Lower Rio Grande Valley to work in Texas fields during the day and then return to their homes in Mexico at night, or they might live in Texas; no one outside the area much cared, for there was no mass migration any farther north.[5] The United States was so much more affluent than

Mexico or other Latin American countries and its culture so different that the possibility of migrating evidently did not occur to many Latinos, except in times of severe political instability.

Despite their proximity in the Western Hemisphere, the differences between the United States and Latin America have been profound, greater probably than the differences between Britain and Spain. Latin America is an older civilization than the United States, older because Spanish rule was established more than a century before British colonies were established in North America and because elements of the culture of pre-Conquest Mesoamericans and South Americans persisted beneath the veneer of the Spanish language and the Catholic religion. Indian languages are still spoken today in parts of Mexico, Central America, Ecuador, Peru, Bolivia, and Paraguay,[6] and Indian folkways persist in mountain-bound provinces and in great cities to which their residents have migrated. A wondrous example: tourists arriving at the astonishing Machu Picchu ruin in the mountains of Peru are told that it was discovered by an American, Hiram Bingham, in 1911, but it seems that the ruin was always known to the local Indians, who kept it a secret from Spanish speakers from the Conquest in 1535 until Bingham's discovery—376 years.

Mexico in particular has a culture of *mestizaje*—mixedness, a fusion of the European and Mesoamerican. "Although the Conquest destroyed the indigenous world and built another and different one on its remains," writes Mexico's greatest intellectual, Octavio Paz, "there is an invisible thread of continuity between the ancient society and the new Mexican order."[7] The Catholic Church, adaptive as always, took on much of the character of indigenous Latino religions. Paz again: "The bloody Christs in our village churches, the macabre humor in some of our newspaper headlines, our wakes, the custom of eating skull-shaped cakes and candies on the Day of the Dead, are habits inherited from the Indians and the Spaniards and are now an inseparable part of our being."[8] Like the peasants of southern Italy, the peasants of Mexico and other Latin American countries pray to local saints and celebrate local festivals that have their roots in pre-Christian times.

Also like southern Italy, Latin America was ruled by Emperor Charles V, in his capacity as king of Spain, by his son Philip II (who, on becoming king of Portugal in 1580, became ruler of Brazil), and by the kings of Spain for two hundred years thereafter. Philip II read carefully his dispatches from viceroys in Naples, Palermo, Mexico City, and Lima, and sent back detailed directives which, in the case of Latin America, would not be received for nearly a year but which he expected to be obeyed to the letter. Such centralism was bound to be ineffective, all the more so when employed by less hardworking kings. This "centralist mainstream of Castilian and imperial policy" continued, historian Claudio Veliz argues, even after most of Latin America became independent in the early nineteenth century (the conspicuous exceptions being Cuba and Puerto Rico, ruled by Spain until 1898). In the mid-nineteenth century, Veliz goes on, this centralism "was overwhelmed by the rising tide of European commercial and political liberalism," but the economic travails starting with the depression of the 1930s brought it back. "For the past half-century—with the expected variations from country to country—Latin America has been finding its way back to its centralist mainstream."[9]

This centralism has often been accompanied by authoritarian, arbitrary governance. On gaining independence, most Latin American countries declared themselves republics, modeled on the United States (though Mexico briefly and Brazil for six decades were empires). But most (prominent exceptions are Chile, Uruguay, and Costa Rica) also have had political systems in which insiders have manipulated power and, often, fixed elections. Dictatorships have been common, and the Mexican government under the Party of the Institutional Revolution (PRI) from 1929 to 2000 was in many respects authoritarian, if not dictatorial. Business interests were typically intertwined with government; labor unions have had little independence; voluntary associations have been few and not very influential. Nor has the Catholic Church been a real source of countervailing power. Mexico since 1929, like Italy between 1870 and 1929, has been an officially anticlerical nation; only in the 1990s were priests allowed to appear in public in clerical collars. Trust in institutions, and indeed trust in anyone outside the family, has typically been very low.

Of course, to any generalization about Latin America there must be exceptions. After his first multistop trip to Latin America, President Ronald Reagan exclaimed, just as sophisticated travelers do, even while knowing how hackneyed it sounds, "Every country is different." Here the primary focus must be on Mexico, which was the old country for almost half of America's Latino immigrants, with side glances at other countries that have produced sizeable immigrations—Cuba and the Dominican Republic, El Salvador and Nicaragua, Colombia and Peru, Argentina and Brazil—plus the American Commonwealth* of Puerto Rico.

THE JOURNEY

So let us begin with Mexico in the 1960s, just when the great Latino migration to the United States was beginning. With a stable government and a fast-growing economy, Mexico in those years seemed unlikely to produce a flood of immigrants. It had enjoyed political stability for three decades—since 1929 when Plutaro Elias Calles, one of several contending generals jousting for power, formed what became the PRI and established the six-

---

* An English term that is perhaps misleading. The Spanish term is more exact: *estado liberado asociado*, free associated state.

year presidential term and the tradition that no president should be reelected. Each president selected his successor by a process that came to be known as *dedazo*—literally, placing his finger on him; the anointed successor won every election from 1934 to 1994.[10] This system—a sort of term-limited absolute monarchy, with its calendrical regularity and its grant of all power to a single individual who after six years effectively vanished from public life—was congenial to the Aztec sensibility. "The thread of continuity between the ancient society and the new Spanish order," writes Paz, "has not been broken: the Spanish viceroys and the Mexican presidents are the successors of the Aztec rulers."[11]

PRI governments built trade barriers around Mexico, confiscated foreign oil holdings, distributed farmland in collective *ejidos* to landless peasants, and built factories and resort centers. They encouraged nationalist and anti-American feelings and, by putting leading intellectuals, artists, and writers on the public payroll, harnessed these natural rebels to the service of the regime. For many years these policies produced splendid results: the economy grew at 6 percent annually between 1946 and 1970.[12] But growth does not necessarily mean stability. In this period millions of Mexicans left the farms for cities. As Jonathan Kandell writes, "The migrants were expelled from the countryside by prolonged droughts, the inability of ejidos to sustain families, the mechanization of private farms, and the rise of population resulting from health care improvements that cut mortality rates of infants and adults." By 1960 most Mexicans lived in cities, with one in five in Mexico City and its sprawling suburbs.[13]

Increasing numbers of Mexicans also made their way to the United States. For centuries most Mexicans had lived on farms, seldom moving from their places of birth. Now, in the 1960s, they had grown up in cities or had moved from the countryside to cities. Many were ready to move again. And in fact, many Mexicans had had experience in the United States through the *bracero* program. Originally a war measure, this program temporarily imported

Mexicans to work on farms in California, Texas, and other states.[14] Between 1956 and 1959 the *bracero* program was at its peak, bringing in, and then returning to Mexico, more than 430,000 workers a year,[15] far more than the annual average of 40,000 Mexican immigrants.

Before these years of economic upheaval and urbanization, Latinos migrated to the United States in large numbers only during years of revolution and political unrest—they were more refugees than immigrants. Between 1910 and 1930, 713,000 Mexicans fled to the United States during the violent years of the Mexican revolution. When stability was established in 1929, many of these Mexicans returned home (the number of Mexicans in the United States dropped from about 600,000 to about 400,000 in the 1930s),[16] and American immigration authorities deported many others. Similarly, political upheaval spurred 495,000 Cubans to come to the United States between 1959, when Fidel Castro came to power, and 1970, with another 305,000 coming between 1970 and 1996. The exception to this rule is the special case of the Puerto Ricans, U.S. citizens since 1917. Starting in the 1940s, as its population started growing robustly and peasants headed to the cities, Puerto Rico also produced a huge movement to the mainland, almost entirely to New York City. In 1940 New York had 70,000 Puerto Rico–born residents, then 187,000 in 1950 and 613,000 in 1960.[17] The peak migration year was 1952–1953, when 58,500 arrived. But Puerto Rico's economy grew rapidly in the 1950s, and net migration from Puerto Rico to the mainland United States has since 1961 been negligible.*

---

* By 1961 Governor Luis Munoz Marin's Operation Bootstrap was rapidly creating jobs and raising incomes in Puerto Rico, and the economic incentive to migrate diminished sharply; there had never been a political motive to immigrate, since Puerto Rico was part of the United States. When Leonard Bernstein wrote *West Side Story* in 1957, he imagined a city where Puerto Ricans were by far the largest ethnic group, as they would have become if early 1950s trends had continued indefinitely.

Between 1903 and 1964, just over 800,000 Latin Americans (excluding Puerto Ricans) immigrated to the United States.[18] But since 1965 some 10 million Latin Americans have come to the United States—though the huge number of illegal immigrants in the past few decades makes this a very rough approximation. Latino immigration has increased on a steep upward curve since the late 1960s, with spikes from countries with political disturbances.*

The surge in Latino immigration was *not* a result of the Immigration Act of 1965. The immigration acts of 1924 and 1952 did not impose quotas on Western Hemisphere immigration; the 1965 act did, with a maximum quota of 20,000 for every country and a total quota of 170,000 for all of the Western Hemisphere. The hemispheric quota was repealed in 1978, however, and the family reunification provisions of the law and the amnesties for illegal immigrants granted in the 1986 and 1995 immigration laws have effectively raised the number of legal immigrants from Mexico and other Latin American countries far above the 20,000 level.[19] Few anticipated the huge volume of Latino immigration,[20] even though as long before as 1948 Carey McWilliams had written in *North from Mexico*, "It is extremely debatable whether, under any circumstances, Mexican workers can be kept from crossing the border."[21] In 1965 Attorney General Nicholas Katzenbach testified, "If you look at present immigration figures from the Western Hemisphere there is not much pressure to come to the United States from these countries. There are in a relative sense not many people who want to come."[22] Yet Mexican immigration had exceeded 20,000 in every

---

* Immigration from Latin America totaled 1.1 million from 1961 to 1970, 1.7 million from 1971 to 1980, 3 million from 1981 to 1990, and 2.7 million in the six years from 1991 to 1996. The increase from Mexico alone was quite steep—from 443,000 from 1961 to 1970, to 837,000 from 1971 to 1980, to 1.65 million from 1981 to 1990, and to 1.65 million from 1991 to 1996—a total of 8.5 million.

year since 1954, and the abolition of the *bracero* guest-worker program in 1964 created a new demand for low-wage labor that Mexicans were accustomed to filling.[23] Moreover, even as the American workforce was becoming more educated, the American economy abounded with low-wage work.

This was not conventional wisdom at the time. The Kerner Commission Report on Civil Disorders, released in March 1968, in a separate chapter explaining why the immigrant experience had no relevance to 1960s blacks, declared that "the changing nature of the American economy" meant that America would never again produce the large number of low-skill jobs needed by unskilled blacks or immigrants.[24] Therefore, the report argued, blacks in the late twentieth century, unlike immigrants in the early twentieth century, needed massive government subsidy if they were to move upward. The unspoken assumption was that mass immigration was a thing of the past. Seldom has such an authoritative report proved so utterly wrong. Government subsidy has been a poor tool for producing upward mobility, while the private sector has created millions of low-skill, entry-level jobs that have been filled by immigrants. The experience of the immigrants a century before proved far more relevant to late-twentieth-century America than the elite believed.

THE NEW COUNTRY

Latino immigration, which continues in huge numbers, has been primarily an immigration from the fading countryside and burgeoning cities of Latin America to a few fast-growing metropolitan areas in the United States—primarily Los Angeles, New York, Houston, Miami, and Chicago. In 2000, one-third of America's Latinos lived in California, and three-quarters lived in one of six states—California, Texas, New York, Florida, Illinois, and New Jersey. But it is a mistake to see Latino immigration as a single wave. Rather, it is the combination of hundreds, perhaps thousands, of chain migrations, from communities urban and rural in Latin America to particular urban neighborhoods in the United States. Proximity explains little: Los Angeles may be 140 miles from the Mexican border, but most Latino immigrants to Los Angeles had their origins in states in central and southern Mexico more than a thousand miles away, though some of these lived for a time in the fast-growing border cities of Tijuana and Mexicali. A true map of Latino immigration would show hundreds of lines—many of them thousands of miles long—overlapping, crossing, tangling with each other, but not necessarily meeting at either end.

This has been true from the beginnings of Latino immigration. Mexicans who immigrated during the revolution, from 1910 to 1930, went almost exclusively to Texas;[25] a particularly large population of educated emigrés settled in San Antonio,[26] then the largest city in Texas, which has always had a large Spanish-speaking population. Puerto Ricans, as we have seen, headed almost exclusively to New York.[27] Cubans, beginning with the outrush after Castro took power, mostly went to Miami–Dade County (the official name since 1999), with smaller but significant numbers heading to Hudson County, New Jersey, across the river from New York City—still the major concentrations of Cuban-Americans.* Among later immigrants, Dominicans headed primarily to New York, while Salvadorans went to Los Angeles, Houston, and Washington; Nicaraguans and Colombians headed to Miami.[28]

There is no single chain of Mexican immigration. Unfortunately, there are no reliable statistics revealing which part

---

* The three Cuban-American congressmen are all from these areas: Ileana Ros-Lehtinen (R–Florida), Lincoln Diaz-Balart (R–Florida), and Bob Menendez (D–New Jersey).

of Mexico immigrants originally hail from. But anecdotal evidence suggests that Mexican-Americans in Los Angeles come disproportionately from the central and southern Mexican states of Michoacán, Guerrero, and Jalisco—all more than a thousand miles from Los Angeles. Mexican-American immigrants to Houston and Dallas seem more likely to come from states in northern Mexico. A woman in the Corona neighborhood of Queens, New York, when asked which state in Mexico she was from, answered Puebla, and added, "Everyone here is from Puebla."[29]

Latino immigration often begins as sojourner migration—a father or single young man leaves to search for work in the United States. Typically, most of his earnings are sent home. In time, he might bring his wife and children or other family members to the United States. There is also much back-and-forth movement. Lives are centered on what reporter Roberto Suro calls "channels of immigration." He describes Juan Chanax, a Maya Indian from Guatemala, who made his way to Houston in 1978: "Juan was the first to move, but all it took was one man to establish a link between two worlds. Over time, his haphazard trail north has become a deep, broad channel that carries human traffic steadily in both directions. People come north to work, to visit, to stay. People go south to rest, to open businesses, to retire. After spending more than a thousand years in the Sierra de Totonicapán, fixed and immobile, the Maya of San Cristobal no longer have a permanent address. They travel the channel comfortably, because at one end they have the mountain towns and villages that sustained them for centuries, and at the other end lies a Mayan immigrant society etched into Houston's urban landscape. The link between them has changed both Houston and Totonicapán, and the travel has changed the people, as well."[30]

Over the last third of the twentieth century, more and more of these channels of immigration developed, and Latino immigration vastly increased.* But the 30 million "Hispanics"† counted in the 2000 census are not members of a single homogeneous community. In fact, Latino immigrants are more likely to feel bound to their neighborhoods in Latin America than to other Spanish-speaking newcomers or long-settled Latino Americans. To be sure, almost all Latino immigrants have the Spanish language in common—and the different accents of various countries and regions of Mexico, unlike the different local dialects of southern Italians, are readily comprehensible to those from other places. The dialects are comprehensible but not always congenial. Author Peter Skerry notes that in a child-care center serving Mexican and Central American immigrants in Los Angeles "the idiomatic differences between them are so great that composing Spanish-language materials acceptable to parents and staff usually requires heated negotiations."[31]

---

* Latino immigration from 1971 to 1980 was 153,000 annually, more than double that from 1961 to 1970; it doubled again to 311,000 from 1981 to 1990. In 1991, thanks to the amnesty provisions of the 1986 immigration law, many formerly illegal aliens regularized their status, and the number of Latino immigrants for that year was 1,236,000. For the rest of the 1990s—as this is written, figures were available only through 1996 and, for some countries, 1997—Latino immigration averaged 314,000 a year, almost exactly the same figure as that for the 1980s.

Although immigration trends vary among Latino countries, the general rule seems to be that countries produce few immigrants until they reach a certain economic level, similar to that of Mexico in the 1960s, and then immigration increases. Once the country reaches the level of economic growth and political stability that Argentina and Chile reached in the 1990s, immigration drops to the levels of advanced European countries. For example, although Mexico's economy grew during most of the 1980s and 1990s, successive devaluations of the peso in 1982, 1988, and 1994 meant that wages for the typical Mexican did not increase over that time. In short, the economic motive for immigration is stronger than ever.

† "Hispanic" is a term the Census Bureau has been using since the 1970s and is meant to include people of different races who have origins or ancestors in Spanish-speaking countries. Presumably it does not include people from Brazil or directly from Spain, but since the term is applied by self-identification, the precise definition probably makes little practical difference.

Although I use the term "Latino" in this book, I occasionally cite Census Bureau and other studies that employ the term "Hispanic"; in such cases, I am obliged to use this more imprecise term.

WORK

What America's Latinos do more than anything else is work. The Hispanic male workforce participation is 80 percent, the highest of any measured group.[32] "You go to New York," says Antonio Martinez, an immigrant from the Mexican state of Puebla, "to work, eat, and sleep."[33] On street corners on the West Side of Los Angeles at seven o'clock any weekday morning, you will see groups of Latino men waiting silently: they are looking not for welfare but for work. Go into the deserted-looking four-story buildings in the garment center just south of downtown Los Angeles, or into the 1950s factory buildings of South Central L.A., and you will see dozens of Latinos busily working. Venture into the bungalows of the entry points of Latino immigrants, in Boyle Heights or Santa Ana, and you will see bunk beds where people sleep in three shifts. "Latinos have a strong work ethic and strong loyalty to employers," says East Los Angeles real estate developer Jose Legaspi. Their attitude is, he says, "I'm asked to do this job, and I go and do it. If I need more money, I'll get an extra job."[34]

Coming from countries with no reliable welfare state safety net, in which the only economic asset of those unconnected with people in power is the willingness to work, Latino immigrants have come to the United States ready to work and work hard. Arriving typically with no specialized skills, they work in construction, as janitors, in landscaping and grass cutting, parking cars, in garment and apparel factories, in textile mills and meatpacking factories, in restaurants and hotels, in retail stores and as messengers, as maids and babysitters, driving tractors or trucks. Often they have been steered to jobs by labor contractors who in many cases are the *coyotes* who took them across the border.

Latino immigrants have excelled at what former secretary of labor Robert Reich calls "in-person servers," whose essential quality is "a pleasant demeanor."[35] In an economy with a rapidly increasing number of affluent consumers, such service jobs have proliferated, and Latinos in large numbers have been filling them. Roberto Suro cites the case of Randall's supermarket in Houston, which serves upscale customers with valet parking, neatly uniformed employees, and high levels of service. One Randall's employee explained to Suro how managers with job openings "would say to us, 'We need so many people for maintenance to be ready for such and such a date,' and when it came time, we would have everybody ready. We'd have the whole department organized, enough people for all shifts for all 24 hours, seven days. From the start, they guaranteed us those jobs, even though they were getting hundreds of applications." Current employees train the newcomers before they start working and insist on pleasant behavior. "We would tell the new men, 'If any of the Americans has a complaint or gives you an order, just listen carefully and nod your head and then come to one of us and we'll tell you what to do.'"[36] Far from discriminating against Latinos, such employers discriminate *in favor of them*—or, rather, in favor of people vouched for by their highly satisfactory employees.

Typically, Latino immigrants have sought jobs in the private sector, not the public sector, and from small employers more than large employers. In 1998 only 6.6 percent of workers in public administration and hospitals were Hispanic, the lowest Hispanic percentage in any category except computer data services. Meanwhile, Hispanics represented more than 20 percent of workers in agriculture, services to dwellings and buildings, and personal services in private households.[37] Despite Cesar Chavez's struggle to organize farm laborers in the 1960s, most farm workers today are not union members. In fact, Latinos are generally less likely than other Americans to belong to unions.[38] AFL-CIO unions, for example, have tried to organize office janitors in Los Angeles, with mixed success, and in spring 2000 the national AFL-CIO dropped its longtime support of immigration restrictions—obviously a move to make unions more attractive to low-wage Latino workers. Whether such efforts will succeed is, at this writing, far from clear.

Gregory Rodriguez of Pepperdine University writes that "millions of Mexicans have come to the United States hoping to one day finally place their families in the middle class."[39] Organized protest, in the mode of Chavez, is the exception rather than the rule. Latinos may embrace the unions, but only if they decide that they are a way up to the middle class.[40]

Are Latinos moving into the middle class? Some evidence suggests not. Hispanic household median income as a percentage of the national median income fell from 77 percent in 1980 to 72 percent in 1997.[41] But that was higher than the median household income among blacks (68 percent). The poverty rate among Hispanics, 22 percent in 1980, peaked at 31 percent in 1994 and fell to 27 percent in 1997.[42] Nevertheless, median income and poverty figures mask the progress of large numbers of individuals within a rapidly expanding group. The number of Hispanics doubled, from 15 million to 30 million, between 1980 and 2000, and the low incomes and high poverty rates of new immigrants held down the economic figures of the larger group. As Gregory Rodriguez notes, "High poverty rates for recent immigrants have the effect of pushing down overall Latino statistics—eclipsing the progress of long-established immigrants and U.S.-born Latinos. If U.S.- and foreign-born Latinos are analyzed separately, however, and the immigrant's year of entry taken into account, U.S. census data reveals that there is considerable social mobility for both immigrants and the native-born. Foreign-born Latinos make steady advances out of poverty and into homeownership and the middle class the longer they reside in the United States. And, critically, the U.S.-born children and grandchildren of Latino immigrants fare considerably better than the immigrant generation."[43]

Rodriguez's 1990s study of Latinos in the five-county Los Angeles metropolitan area (who numbered 6 million in 2000, one-fifth of all American Hispanics) reveals signs of upward mobility among Latino immigrants. The study shows that in 1990

U.S.-born Latinos had four times as many households in the middle class as in poverty and that almost precisely 50 percent of U.S.-born Latinos had household incomes above the Los Angeles area median.[44] Of these middle-class households, 59 percent had incomes over $50,000. Foreign-born Latinos had lower incomes, but one in three, 34 percent, had incomes over the Los Angeles area median. Homeownership also grew, to 52 percent of U.S.-born and 32 percent of foreign-born Latinos, and rose sharply in the 1990s.[45] Within twenty years of arrival, half of Latinos own their own homes,[46] and the percentage of Latino immigrants in poverty declines sharply the longer they are in the United States. This progress of hundreds of thousands of Latinos into the middle class is not confined to the Los Angeles area or to the years before 1990; throughout the 1990s heavily Latino areas across the country showed signs of economic progress.

There has also been a surge in Latino-owned businesses. From 1987 to 1992, the number of Hispanic-owned businesses increased 76 percent, from 489,000 to 862,000. (Figures through 1997 were not available at this writing, but they will undoubtedly show a similar surge of Latino entrepreneurship.) Latino-owned businesses amounted to 16 percent of all firms in Los Angeles County, 48 percent in Miami–Dade County, and 25 percent in San Antonio and Bexar County, Texas. These are typically small businesses; despite the spectacular success of the Cuban-American Roberto Goizueta, CEO of Coca-Cola, Latinos have not risen much in large corporations. Frank Moran, president of the Latin Business Association, explains that "a lot of the corporate people have mostly an academic understanding of Latinos. They don't understand that our values are different. We're skeptical of government and large banks. We want personal and familial relationships. Our first call is an introduction call. We do business with handshakes. We don't sue each other. We tend to back away from paperwork."[47] Undoubtedly some Latino-owned businesses have benefited from government quotas and set-asides, but it seems unlikely that many

Latinos, with their mistrust of government, would care to let their businesses rely heavily on these legally shaky programs.

Latino success in the private sector should not be surprising. Back in Latin America even landless peasants were not entirely barred from the market economy, as southern black sharecroppers and Irish tenant farmers were, and they trusted market transactions they could personally monitor far more than governments, which were typically corrupt and inclined to favoritism.[48] Hence the Latino immigrants' avoidance of public-sector jobs and their aversion to government welfare. Only 17 percent of immigrant Latinos in poverty collect welfare, compared with 50 percent of poor Anglos and 65 percent of poor blacks.[49] This seems to reflect the general Latino mistrust in institutions: to many Mexicans the idea that the government will give you money just because you meet the bureaucratic qualifications seems absurd. Latinos' success has come from working hard at private-sector jobs and in starting new businesses.

There are exceptions to this pattern. Puerto Ricans have remained stubbornly downscale, with high rates of poverty and welfare dependency and low income levels and percentages of homeownership. In New York in 1996 mainland-born Puerto Ricans had median household incomes of $21,000 and island-born Puerto Ricans $13,800, among the lowest of any measured group.[50] One reason seems to be that the Puerto Rican migration tends to be downscale; Puerto Ricans with professional and entrepreneurial talents can make an affluent and secure living in Puerto Rico. Unlike many other Latin American countries, Puerto Rico since the 1960s has had a stable government and a First World economy, with income levels similar to those in some European countries. In contrast, the first and largest waves of immigration from Castro's Cuba came disproportionately from the island's economic elite and upper middle classes. These people may have come to Miami with no economic assets, but they had the abilities and habits of mind to advance rapidly, and by and large they have done so. Cuban incomes since at least the 1970s have been well above those of other Latinos in the United States, and they have had great success as entrepreneurs.

FAMILY

Latinos work, most of all, for their families. As with the Italians, many Latino men come to the United States without their families, to establish a beachhead. Often they intend to return sooner or later to their home villages, but in the meantime they send much of their earnings to their families back home. In fact, remittances are a major component of the gross domestic products of Mexico and several other Latin American countries. Many family members ultimately follow, as the family unit remains the focus of life.

Indeed, Latino immigrants and their descendants are arguably the most family-oriented group in a society where an increasing number of people do not live in two-spouse families. In 1998, 81 percent of Hispanic households were families, and 56 percent were married-couple families—both figures being higher than those for blacks (67 percent and 31 percent) and for whites (58 percent and 47 percent).[51] Of children under eighteen, 67 percent of Hispanics live with both parents, a figure just below the national average of 71 percent and far above the 40 percent among blacks. Some 28 percent of Hispanic children live in mother-only families, compared with 56 percent of black children,[52] and 48 percent of Hispanic children had stay-at-home moms, compared to 37 percent among both blacks and whites.[53] "We did a composite of the typical Los Angeles Latino: They're a married couple in their 30s, with kids, who arrived in 1976, with a household income of $28,000," says researcher Gregory Rodriguez. "South Central L.A. has the highest rate of family formation of anywhere in Los Angeles County. Immigrants can't afford not to have families."[54]

Certainly this is not the precise equivalence of the rigid, unyielding family solidarity of the Italian immigrants. But then it does not appear that family ties in late-twentieth-century Latin America were as strong as they were in late-nineteenth-century southern Italy. And family ties among Latinos appear to be at least as strong as among Americans generally, and far stronger than among blacks. Divorce is about as common among Latinos in the United States as it is among whites, as is single parenthood. Again, however, Latinos are not a single, homogeneous community; in rates of single parenthood and divorce, Cubans are closer to whites than other Latinos, and Puerto Ricans are closer to blacks. Given the high rate of single parenthood among Puerto Ricans, writes Francis Fukuyama, the low overall rate of single parenthood among Latinos "suggests that the rate of single-parent families for Cuban- and Mexican-origin Latinos is actually lower than for whites at a comparable income level."[55] Fukuyama goes on to note, "Another study indicates that Mexican-Americans have better family demographics than do whites, with higher birth-weight babies even among low-income mothers due to taboos on smoking, drinking, and drug use during pregnancy."[56]

This confutes the assumption common in some quarters that "people of color" all have similar experiences, and thus it casts great doubt on the underlying assumption that a characteristic American racism subjects all "people of color" to discrimination that produces similar responses. Latinos were not subjected in their old country to anything like the demeaning experiences that undercut the authority of black men in the segregated South. Nor, because of their low utilization of welfare, were they subjected to anything in the new country like the perverse incentives that undercut the authority of black men in the welfare-sustained underclass black ghettoes of the post-migration North.

RELIGION

It is often assumed that all Latino immigrants are Catholics; conservative analysts in particular assume that therefore Latinos
share the beliefs and attitudes of the Irish-American Catholics of
the 1950s. The first assumption is not entirely true, and the second is almost totally false. The Catholic Church did have, in
theory, a monopoly on religious practice in the Spanish colonies,
and large percentages of Latinos do identify themselves as
Catholics. But, as noted, the Catholicism of Latin America bears
closer resemblance to the folk-religion-Catholicism of southern
Italy of a century ago than to the Catholicism of American suburban parishes in the era of incense and the Latin Mass. As Peter
Skerry writes, "Hispanic cultures also emphasize *personalismo*,
which in the religious context translates into reliance more on
ties to individual clerics or patron saints than to the institutional
Church." Moreover, Latin Americans often mistrusted the
Church as they did every other institution and felt an ambivalence reflecting, in Skerry's words, "the Church's history of
alliances with European-oriented Latin American elites and its
distance from the concerns of the indigenous populations."[57]

Nor does the Catholic Church any longer enjoy a monopoly
among Latinos. In Latin America for the last several decades the
most important religious movement has been not toward the
often celebrated Catholic "liberation theology" but to Protestant
fundamentalist and Pentecostal sects.[58] That movement has
taken place in the United States as well, and the Protestant sects
have offered a stricter code of morality and a more vibrant form
of worship that have attracted many Latinos. As a result, only
about 70 percent of American Hispanics are even nominally
Catholics; according to the U.S. Catholic Conference, the percentage of Hispanics belonging to Catholic churches fell from
77 percent in 1994 to 71 percent in 1998.[59] (Still, Latinos now
make up the large majority of Catholics in Los Angeles, and

many Latinos, unhappy with public education, are eager to enroll their children in Catholic schools.)

Protestant evangelicals are making many converts. Some are attracted by television and radio evangelists like Yiye Avila, a Puerto Rican who, in the words of one observer, "preaches the value of hard work, success and prosperity in a message that is Christ-centered and miracle-oriented."[60] Hundreds of small evangelical and Pentecostal churches are springing up in Latino neighborhoods all over the country. Just as second- and third-generation Italians conformed more than their immigrant parents to the Catholicism that was the fastest-growing and most vital faith at the time, so do many immigrant and second-generation Latinos seem to be moving to the evangelical Protestantism that is one of the fastest-growing and most vital faiths in their new country at the turn of the twenty-first century.

EDUCATION

Where Latinos have lagged behind is in education. The Latino school dropout rate in the 1990s, like the Italian dropout rate in the 1910s, is well above average. Performance on standardized tests tends to be low. In 1998, among Hispanics twenty-five and older, only 55 percent had completed four years of high school— far lower than the 76 percent among blacks and 84 percent of whites. High school enrollment is much higher in the United States than in Latin America, however, and the percentage of high school graduates was higher for those Latino groups who have been in America longer—68 percent among Cubans and 64 percent among Puerto Ricans. Even the rate among Mexicans, just 48 percent in 1998—up only slightly from the figures in 1990 (44 percent) and 1980 (38 percent)[61]—is encouraging, given the flood of relatively uneducated Mexican immigrants to America in recent years. On the whole, it appears that Latinos being educated in the United States mostly finish high school. In 1998 Hispanic school enrollment among children aged five to seventeen was nearly 100 percent, dropping to 91 percent at ages sixteen and seventeen. College is another matter. In 1998 only 49 percent of Hispanics age eighteen and nineteen were in school, and just 29 percent at ages twenty and twenty-one were enrolled.[62] Among Hispanics age twenty-five and older, only 11 percent had a college degree, lower than the 25 percent among whites and 15 percent among blacks. Of the Hispanics, Cubans and Puerto Ricans approximated the white and black experiences, respectively: 22 percent of Cubans and 12 percent of Puerto Ricans had college degrees. But the figure for Mexicans was only 7 percent.[63] The figures for Central Americans and for immigrants from the Andean countries of South America are probably similar to those for Mexicans, if not lower.

Evidently Latinos are much less likely than other immigrant groups, and significantly less likely than blacks, to see education as an avenue upward. The reason has to be more than economic— after all, the United States offers many opportunities for free or inexpensive higher education. At work here seems to be the habit of mind, brought from Latin America, of a mistrust in institutions and trust in work—not to mention the desire to send money home. In Latin America students who go to university tend to get ahead only if they are well connected, especially within government bureaucracies. There is surely some fear among parents, as there was very strongly with Italians, that higher education status will take a child away from his family. It is better to work, to bring money into the household, while you look for someone to marry.

There is also the question of how well public schools have served Latino children. American public schools in the 1910s and 1920s generally provided a rigorous education in reading and mathematics, and classes were conducted in the English language.[64] Although children of Italian immigrants often dropped out of school early, and relatively few excelled, those who stayed in school and stayed up with the curriculum acquired basic skills that enabled them to make better livings than most of their parents. In contrast, American public schools in the 1980s and 1990s generally provided unrigorous instruction, avoiding rote learning, leaving children free to learn or not learn basic reading and math skills, and promoting students without requiring mastery of course work. The children of Latino immigrants remained in school longer than the children of Italian immigrants had, but the high school diplomas they received did not guarantee that they had acquired the skills needed, in a more advanced and complex economy, to make better livings than their parents had. No wonder that the National Council of La Raza declared in 1997, "On the whole, public education has not been effective for Hispanics— especially for low-income Latinos."[65]

A major reason public schools have not been effective for Latinos is bilingual education programs, which in many cases have been neither bilingual nor education. Bilingual education was established by a 1967 federal law and encouraged by a 1974 Supreme Court decision that required schools to make some kind of special provision for students unable to speak English well. In the civil rights era of the 1960s, many activists felt that instruction in English demeaned Latino students' Spanish-language heritage, and some hoped to encourage Spanish-language separatism.[66] In time these motives were replaced by institutional interests: unions representing Spanish-language teachers wanted to perpetuate the programs and maximize the number of students in Spanish-language classes to keep money coursing through their organizations.[67] A cadre of academics issued studies purporting to show that Latino children would learn better in Spanish (there were few bilingual classes in other languages because of the relatively small numbers of children speaking each of them).[68] By the 1980s, California, with one-third of the nation's Latino children, was typically keeping children in Spanish-language classrooms for five years and discouraging exit to English-language instruction. Similar bilingual programs existed in Texas, Illinois, and New York; there were fewer in Florida, where Cuban-Americans were eager for their children to learn English and had the civic skills to make the school system do what they wanted.

The predictable result—documented by studies as early as 1977 and 1978[69]—was that many Latino teenagers emerged with a weak command of English, which held down test scores and prevented them from learning the skills required for better jobs than their parents held. And in fact, a 1996 survey showed that 63 percent of Latino parents preferred that their children be taught English as soon as possible, and only 17 percent wanted them to be taught to read and write Spanish before they aretaught English.[70] But Latino elected officials, especially in California, who were closely allied with teachers' unions, defended bilingual programs; any effort to reduce funding or channel students more quickly into English was attacked as racism.

Then in 1998 Silicon Valley entrepreneur Ron Unz, whose mother had learned English through immersion in public school, put on the California ballot Proposition 227, which would require students to be removed from Spanish-language instruction after one year unless parents requested a waiver. Although most politicians—including both major party candidates for governor—opposed the proposition and Latino politicians and activist organizations denounced it, in June the referendum passed by a 61 to 39 percent margin. About 40 percent of Latinos voted for 227; majorities had supported it in polls through April, until a series of television ads sponsored by Jerry Perenchio, owner of the Spanish-language Univision television network, moved opinion in the other direction. Arizona passed a similar proposition, 63 to 37 percent, in November 2000.

The initial evidence is that Proposition 227 has been a success. The California governor, Democrat Gray Davis, vetoed bills that would have undermined it. And despite the efforts of teachers' unions and school administrators, few parents sought exemptions to keep their children in Spanish-language classes. In 1999 and 2000, test scores rose dramatically in districts that fully implemented it, while lagging behind in one major district, San Jose, that refused to enforce it.[71] These results got publicity nationwide and seemed likely to lead to changes in bilingual education in other states. For nearly three decades many Latino children were held back because American educators and politicians failed to understand what was obvious to New York and Chicago public school leaders in 1910—that children need to be taught English as soon as possible if they are to rise in America. If that lesson is now learned and acted on, the children of Latino immigrants will likely move up more rapidly in the next two decades than they did in the 1980s and 1990s.

College and university quotas and preferences have played a relatively minor role for America's Latinos. Despite the quotas, the number of Latinos at selective colleges and universities has lagged far behind their percentage of the population. One in six eighteen-year-olds in America is Hispanic, but there are not nearly so many Latino students at selective universities.

In 1996 California passed Proposition 209, abolishing quotas and preferences in state higher education. The result was a reduction in the number of students classified as Hispanic at the elite campuses of Berkeley and UCLA but an increase in the number of Hispanics at less prestigious campuses.[72] In response, UC Riverside started programs to help students in the local area—the eastern end of the Los Angeles Basin—to improve basic skills and meet the campus's standards for admission, producing a sharp increase in the school's Latino enrollment.[73] The quota system gave many Latinos places at campuses where they ended up far behind most other students and often dropped out. An end to quotas directed attention back to secondary schools, which had been doing a poor job, and helped Latino students improve their skills and perform successfully in college.

In Texas, in the 1996 case of *Hopwood* v. *Texas*, the Fifth U.S. Circuit Court of Appeals struck down the use of quotas in public universities' admissions policies. In response to the decision, Governor George W. Bush pushed through a program guaranteeing the top 10 percent of every high school graduating class a place at a state university campus. Removing quotas did not greatly affect Latino enrollment in the system as a whole; within a few years, state universities were, overall, admitting about the same number of Latinos as before the *Hopwood* decision. But there were problems, given the wide disparity in Texas high schools—the top 10 percent are very differently prepared in Highland Park High School in Dallas as compared to a high school in the Lower Rio Grande Valley—and care had to be taken to keep students from matriculating at schools where they just would not be able to keep up.[74]

CRIME

The popular image of the Latino immigrant criminal dates from the zoot-suited teenagers of the 1943 wartime riot in Los Angeles and from *West Side Story*, first produced in 1957, at the height of the Puerto Rican migration to New York City. But the Latin American heritage of mistrust of institutions suggests that Latinos would not have a proclivity toward crime: the sensible thing is to keep your head down and work, avoiding any activity that might bring you to the attention of the often corrupt police. In point of fact, Latino immigrants and their descendants have not been much more likely than native-born Americans to commit crimes or be imprisoned. Though statistical data are unfortunately sparse, it appears that crime rates among Latinos are somewhat above the national average but well below those of blacks. The percentage of Latino immigrants among state prisoners in 1992 was lower than their share of the population in California, Texas, Florida, and

Illinois, though higher in New York.[75] The murder rates in border cities with large Latino populations and relatively few blacks have been below the national average.[76] "There are nine times more Latinos in California's colleges than there are in its prisons and jails," write Gregory Rodriguez and David Hayes-Bautista. "An estimated 11 percent of Latino males aged 20 to 29 were in the state's criminal justice system—prison, jail, probation, or parole— in 1995, compared with 39 percent of African Americans and 5 percent of whites in the same age group…. When controlling for youth and income, the estimated rate of incarceration for the state's Latinos is roughly equal to the state norm…. Latinas have lower rates of incarceration than either white or black females."[77]

It is true that Latino gangs exist in Los Angeles and other cities, and many Latino parents worry that their sons will take on the criminal lifestyle that is so prevalent among blacks in certain ghetto neighborhoods. In the Los Angeles riots of 1992, there was rioting in neighborhoods in Hollywood settled by recently arrived immigrants from violence-torn Central America, but there was no rioting at all in more well-established Latino areas like East Los Angeles, South Central, the San Fernando Valley, or Santa Ana.

POLITICS

In the late 1960s, a politics of protest seemed to be emerging among Latinos in the United States. It came at a time when the inevitable paradigm was the civil rights movement, which had done so much to change America in the previous decade. Blacks had shown how poor second-class citizens, deprived of their rights by custom and by agents of the state, could organize and use the power of nonviolent protest to expose the unfairness of the larger society and force massive change. Cesar Chavez famously organized the farm laborers of the Central Valley into the United Farm Workers. Just as Martin Luther King Jr. and so many others had preached liberation in black churches, Chavez attended well-publicized Masses, notably in the 1968 California primary campaign with Robert Kennedy. As David Hayes-Bautista and Gregory Rodriguez write, "Young Mexican-Americans, newly self-anointed as *Chicanos*, then a politically charged term defining their position against 'Anglo society,' flocked to the picket lines in support of their communities and became connected—emotionally, intellectually, and spiritually—to a world that had never been theirs. Their largely Mexican-born grandparents and U.S.-born parents, who had survived the mass deportations of Latinos in the early '30s, had been understandably reluctant to teach them Spanish or publicly express any element of their ethnicity. Periodic waves of anti-Mexican sentiment and the indiscriminate sweep that netted tens of thousands of Latinos—one-third of whom are now thought to have been U.S. citizens—put Latinness in dormancy."[78]

In this environment, new Latino activist organizations—legal clinics, social service agencies, training programs—were set up, often with support from major U.S. foundations. Many universities created Chicano studies departments, hiring activists and granting them tenure. Some Latino organizers, remembering that Texas, California, and the Southwest once were part of Mexico, proclaimed that they wanted to retake their land and talked of creating a Republic of Aztlan. National publicity followed when a group of young Latino activists formed the La Raza Unida Party in the small town of Crystal City, Texas, and took over the county government in 1970.[79] There were mass protests in Los Angeles that year following the murder of Mexican-American journalist Ruben Salazar.[80] "Chicano activists," Hayes-Bautista and Rodriguez write, "sought to bring their people together as one single proletarian voice resisting what they considered their greatest enemy—white oppression."[81] The experience of Latinos in America was, in short, seen through the prism of the civil rights movement.

But the experience of Latinos in America in the years since 1970 bears very little resemblance to this picture. The huge Latino migration that started swelling in the late 1960s and then roughly doubled in size around 1980 meant that the Latinos living in the United States in the late 1960s were vastly outnumbered by those who came later. These new immigrants had no memory of the 1954 repatriation project "Operation Wetback" or the mass deportations of the 1930s. Despite the many Spanish place names in California, Texas, and the Southwest, the immigrants understood that this was another country, one in which the language of successful people would inevitably be English. Mexican-Americans had no desire to recreate Mexican institutions or political mores in the United States—far from it! They wanted to get away from Mexican institutions, which had not provided them enough room to move upward. Political scientist Walker Conner notes that polls show "a remarkable lack of identification among the Mexican people with the Mexican state and its political institutions. One such study disclosed that more than one-third of the population was not at all affected by the Mexican state apparatus and only a tenth considered themselves as participants in the system."[82]

By the late 1960s, overt racial discrimination against Mexicans had largely disappeared in Texas and California. Latino immigrants seldom suffered from discrimination when looking for work, and in fact, as we saw in the case of Houston's Randall's supermarket, employers in many cases discriminated *in favor of* them because of their strong work habits. And whereas blacks typically saw strong-arm behavior by local police as police brutality designed to keep them down, many Latinos understood this as efforts to preserve order in everyday life—which had often been lacking in their home country. The intelligent thing to do was to stay quietly out of the policeman's—and the INS agent's—way. While many Latino politicians and activist group leaders persisted in applying the civil rights model and raising grievances, others took a different approach. Alderman Danny Solis of Chicago, for example, told a reporter, "When an immigrant comes to America, he doesn't say, 'Hey, I'm a victim of racism, I'm a victim of discrimination, and I am entitled to something because I am a victim.' But here in this country, they are bombarded by our culture, especially our leaders, that they are victims, that they are a minority, that they are Hispanic. And I believe that, in the long run, that's not the route to go."[83]

For the most part that is not the route Latinos have chosen. Their experience in Mexico and other parts of Latin America did not at all incline them to believe that protest could be effective. Consider the results of the peaceful student demonstrations in Tlatelolco in Mexico City in 1968: in suppressing the demonstrations, the Mexican government massacred a never-revealed number of students.[84] The idea that a politics of protest could change the policy of the government of the United States surely struck most Latino immigrants as counterintuitive, if not *loco*. As the 1970s went on, the Chicano movement evaporated, leaving behind only little stagnant pools in university Chicano studies departments. The word "Chicano" itself fell out of use, replaced with "Hispanic" by the Census Bureau, with "Latino" in California and Texas, and with "Mexican" or "Puerto Rican" or "Cuban" or "Dominican" elsewhere. Peter Skerry tells of the Mexican-American student who grew up in a predominantly Anglo community in San Luis Obispo, California, who said that she had never heard the word "Chicano" until she went to Berkeley.[85] As Hayes-Bautista and Rodriguez write, "The death throes of the Chicano movement signal a new consciousness among Latinos. As politically and economically marginal as many of us are today, we are more defined by hope than anger. And at more than one-third of California's population, we are now more concerned with renewing a society in decline than in preserving a minority movement."[86]

Despite the protest politics that seemed to be emerging during the time of Cesar Chavez, American politics has mostly been a low priority for Latino immigrants. Significantly, Latinos have been far less likely than other late-twentieth-century immigrants to become citizens. One reason is that many come to America intending to return to their old country, and indeed many often do. Another is that many Latinos are illegally in the United States. Of course, in the mid-1990s a surge of immigrants went through the naturalization process and became U.S. citizens; some 6.4 million immigrants applied for citizenship between 1993 and 1999, more than in the preceding twenty-seven years combined.[87] Several factors contributed to this sudden jump. For one, the amnesty provisions of the 1986 immigration law made many formerly illegal immigrants eligible for citizenship. Also, in 1994 California passed Proposition 187, which barred illegal immigrants from state services, and in 1996 the welfare reform act prohibited aid to illegal immigrants—though a federal judge prevented the former provision from going into effect and the next Congress modified the latter. Moreover, Colombia, the Dominican Republic, Ecuador, Costa Rica, Brazil, and Mexico passed laws allowing some or all who took U.S. citizenship to remain citizens of those countries.[88] Some immigrants simply acted before the naturalization fee was raised, from $60 to $90 in 1991 and then to $250 in 1999. Also playing a role was the Clinton administration's Citizenship USA program, in which the White House insisted that the Immigration and Naturalization Service speed up the naturalization process so that thousands of immigrants would be eligible to vote for Clinton in November 1996; as a result, 180,000 immigrants were naturalized without proper criminal background checks and at least 5,000 became citizens who should have been disqualified.[89]

Yet even after the surge of naturalization, the Census Bureau found that only 22 percent of Hispanic immigrants were naturalized citizens, much lower than the 35 percent among foreign-born blacks, 44 percent among Asians, and 50 percent among non-Hispanic whites.[90] The fact that only 20 percent of unnaturalized

Hispanic immigrants said they had not applied because they intended to return home hints at perhaps the most fundamental reason why Latinos have generally failed to become involved in the American political scene. That reason, of course, is that ordinary people usually avoid politics in Latin America—where dictatorships or authoritarian ruling parties have been the norm, and where many elections have been rigged—and this habit of mind has followed Latinos to the United States. Thus, like Italians in the early twentieth century, Latinos in the late twentieth century showed varying degrees of political involvement and voted differently in different places, depending partly on the local political lineup they encountered and partly on the political traditions or interests they brought with them from Latin America.

For years the Cuban-Americans of Miami were among the most politically engaged. Drawn in large part from the upper and middle ranks of Cuban society, these immigrants possessed a stinging grievance against the totalitarian dictatorship of Fidel Castro. Strong Cuban organizations have dominated the politics of Miami–Dade County. These groups were heavily conservative—Miami Latinos voted 80 to 88 percent Republican in the presidential elections of the 1980s—although it was not until 1989 that the first Cuban-American Republican was elected to the House of Representatives. Bill Clinton made inroads among Cubans in 1996, but in 2000 they voted about 80 percent for George W. Bush, as they had voted for his brother Jeb Bush, whose wife was born in Mexico and whose Spanish is flawless, for governor in 1994 and 1998.

In New York the Puerto Ricans, long the largest Latino group, showed little political engagement for years after the great migration of the 1950s, even though Puerto Ricans, unlike other Latinos, started off as U.S. citizens. New York's Puerto Ricans for years had among the lowest voter turnout levels of any demographic group. This is partly because they have tended to remain downscale economically, plagued by high rates of welfare dependency and crime, but also because they have retained their interest in the politics of Puerto Rico, where passions run high, particularly on the issue of statehood. Voter turnout levels in Puerto Rico are the highest of anywhere under the American flag. When they do vote in normal U.S. elections, Puerto Ricans have gone heavily Democratic; more than any other Latino group, their voting habits resemble those of blacks.

It has taken many years for Puerto Ricans to rise to the top levels of New York politics. The one exception was Herman Badillo, elected borough president of the Bronx in 1965, congressman from the Bronx from 1971 to 1977, and defeated (very narrowly the first time) in the Democratic primaries for mayor in 1969, 1973, and 1977. In the 1990s Badillo supported Mayor Rudolph Giuliani and became a Republican (as chairman of the board of the City University system, he opposed granting degrees to students who took courses only in Spanish), whereas New York's most prominent current Puerto Rican officeholders, Bronx borough president Fernando Ferrer and Representatives Jose Serrano and Nydia Velasquez, are aligned with New York's left-liberal orthodoxy. And although New York City's Latinos gave Giuliani 43 percent of their votes in 1997, up from 37 percent in 1993,[91] in the 2000 presidential elections, New York State Hispanics, reflecting the strong Democratic leanings of Puerto Ricans, voted 80 to 18 percent for Al Gore, according to the Voter News Service (VNS) exit poll.[92]

In California, Latino voters were for years a small target group, up for grabs between the parties. Turnout in heavily Latino districts was strikingly low: the Thirty-third Congressional District, which includes downtown Los Angeles, cast only 53,000 votes in 1992—just 9 percent of its population—while the nearby West Side Twenty-ninth District was casting 276,000.[93] By the late 1990s, however, California Latinos had become a larger and fast-growing group, voting heavily Democratic. A key factor was an oft-repeated 1994 campaign commercial for Republican governor Pete Wilson. Wilson based much of his campaign on his support of Proposition 187, to deny state benefits to illegal immigrants, and the television ads showing Mexicans running across the border while an announcer proclaimed ominously, "They just keep coming," antagonized many Latinos hitherto open to Republican appeals. As Republican businessman Jose Legaspi put it, "He was saying we don't work hard."[94] Or as Gregory Rodriguez said, "It was a big civics lesson. People felt they were being maligned as a group. We were being called lazy and loafers. There is no one more anti-welfare than a Mexican immigrant."[95]

Just as Italians were outraged in 1940 by Roosevelt's "hand that held the dagger" comment, so were California Latinos outraged by the suggestion that they were migrating only to get welfare—in each case, responding with prickly pride to an unfair negative stereotype. In 1996 Bill Clinton carried Latino voters in California 71 to 20 percent, as Latino turnout rose to 12 percent of the total. That year, conservative Orange County Republican congressman Robert Dornan alienated more Latinos when, after losing narrowly to Democrat Loretta Sanchez, he demanded an investigation of illegal immigrant voting. In 1998 the Latino vote in California increased to 14 percent of the total, with 78 percent of that vote going to Democrat Gray Davis for governor. In 2000, California Hispanics formed 14 percent of the total and voted 68 to 29 percent for Al Gore over George W. Bush, according to the VNS exit poll.[96]

Of course, although Latinos' Democratic percentages in California are nearly as high as those of blacks, one cannot assume a solid "people of color" left-wing voting bloc in that state. California Latinos differ widely from blacks on ballot issues and in nonpartisan contests. For instance, in the 1997 Los Angeles mayoral election, blacks voted 75 to 19 percent for the left-wing Tom Hayden over incumbent Richard Riordan, a liberal Republican, while Latinos cast more votes and went 60 to 33 percent for Riordan.

In California, as elsewhere, the politics of the old country seems to have influenced some Latinos' political affiliations. California's Mexicans may be more inclined to vote Democratic because of where they come from in Mexico. One Mexican state that has sent many immigrants to California is Michoacán, the political stronghold of the left-wing Cardenas family; it was the only state that Cuahtemoc Cardenas of the leftist Democratic Revolutionary Party (PRD) carried in the 2000 presidential election. Cardenas ran a close second in Guerrero, another state from which many of California's Mexicans come. In contrast, most Texas Mexicans appear to have come from northern states of Mexico, historically the heartland of the conservative National Action Party (PAN) and carried by PAN candidate Vicente Fox in 2000. Meanwhile, recent Nicaraguan and Honduran immigrants to Miami appear to give Republicans fairly high percentages, perhaps a reflection of the fact that most Nicaraguans and Hondurans have voted against leftist movements like the Sandinista Party. (These votes, together with the support of Miami's Cuban-Americans, helped George W. Bush offset the heavily Democratic votes of Puerto Ricans, who have become more numerous in Orlando, and thus carry Florida's Hispanic vote, only 49 to 48 percent. That slim victory was Bush's best showing among Hispanics in any of the nine states where there were enough to be statistically significant in the poll, and it provided him with a vote margin greater than his overall margin in the state that turned out to determine the election.)[97]

In Texas in the 1960s, Latinos were Democratic voters in a state where almost all elected officials were Democrats. There were only a few prominent Latino politicians, like Henry B. Gonzalez, a liberal elected in a hotly contested House special election in San Antonio in 1961, and Eligio de la Garza, a conservative elected to replace conservative white landowners in a House district in the Lower Rio Grande Valley in 1964. The current Latino congressmen from Texas are similarly split. Charlie Gonzalez (Henry B. Gonzalez's son) and Ciro Rodriguez are liberal Democrats based in San Antonio; Ruben Hinojosa, Solomon Ortiz, and Silvestre Reyes are moderate Democrats from the Lower Rio Grande Valley, Corpus Christi, and El Paso; Henry Bonilla is a Republican from San Antonio. Texas Latinos voted overwhelmingly for Bill Clinton in 1996, but they gave a sizeable percentage of their votes to George W. Bush for governor in 1998—49 percent according to one exit poll, 39 percent according to another. Bush carried the heavily Latino Lower Rio Grande Valley and El Paso, plus Bexar County, which includes San Antonio. In 2000, Texas Latinos voted 43 percent for George W. Bush and 54 percent for Al Gore.[98] Bush carried Bexar County and Nueces County (Corpus Christi) but trailed in the Lower Rio Grande Valley and lost El Paso County.

In Chicago, where all fifty wards elect Democratic aldermen, Latino politics has been played out in the Democratic Party. Mexicans make up about 65 percent and Puerto Ricans 22 percent of Chicago's Latinos, but the city's Latino congressman, Luis Gutierrez, is Puerto Rican. Puerto Ricans were more likely to support Harold Washington, the black mayor from 1983 to 1989; Mexicans have voted mostly for Richard M. Daley, the white mayor since 1991. Daley, understanding that Latinos provide the balance wheel between about equal-sized black and white voting blocs, has been very attentive to Latino neighborhoods and got overwhelming support from them in 1995 and 1999. Peter Skerry detects "some signs of an Hispanic coalition" in Chicago. "Through efforts like the Latino Institute, a nonprofit advocacy and research institute founded in 1974, and the *Latino Studies Journal* at DePaul University, local Hispanic leaders have tried to forge a unified Latino political agenda. But such efforts seem to reflect the long-term goals of activists and intellectuals more than on-the-ground realities."[99]

In short, as the nation's Latino population grows, Latinos are becoming an ever more important target group for America's politicians. They certainly were in the 2000 presidential race.

George W. Bush hoped to use his popularity among Latinos in Texas to make inroads in the heavily Democratic Latino vote in California, and also perhaps in Illinois and New Jersey. He failed to run much better than other recent Republicans in California, but, as noted, he carried Latinos in critical Florida; he also ran fairly well among them in New Jersey and came close to carrying them in Texas. Al Gore, meanwhile, hoped to make a Democratic Latino bloc in California a firewall preventing Bush from carrying the state, and indeed, Latinos gave him about one-third of his statewide margin. Concentrated as they are in big electoral vote states—the six states with three-quarters of the nation's Latinos cast 181 electoral votes, two-thirds of the 270 needed for election—and still forming political allegiances, Latinos seem sure to be target voters in presidential elections for many years to come.

SPORTS AND ENTERTAINMENT

In sports and entertainment, Latinos have produced stars with crossover appeal to the entire population. Yet at the same time, there seems to be no single Latino national entertainment market. Latinos have long excelled at baseball, which is played in Cuba, Puerto Rico, the Dominican Republic, Venezuela, and some parts of Mexico, and by the 1990s a very large percentage of major league baseball players were Latino. The great home run duel of 1998 was between Mark McGwire, an Anglo from California, and Sammy Sosa, who came from the community that has probably produced more major leaguers per capita than any in history, San Pedro de Macoris in the Dominican Republic. Of course, Latinos generally come to the United States with little knowledge of other American sports, and few have the physical size needed to excel in football or basketball; Danny Villanueva, the first Latino in the National Football League, was a kicker. Probably the most popular sport in Latin America, soccer, has occasionally been a moneymaking proposition in this country, thanks largely to Latinos, who have provided large crowds, not to mention many of the players.

Before the great Latino migration, there were Latino movie stars and entertainers, though many were not so identified: Carmen Miranda, Cesar Romero, Anthony Quinn, Raquel Welch, Martin Sheen. More recently, Latino singers Ricky Martin and Gloria Estefan have had crossover appeal, though both have a definite Latino style and have become spokesmen for their communities—Martin in ads promoting tourism in Puerto Rico, Estefan as a spokesperson for Miami's Cuban-American community. The *Economist* reports that "popular music performers who used to be concerned with breaking out of the Latino market now get rich from it."[100]

Spanish-language television has been financially successful in the United States. The cable station Univision has thrived running *telenovelas* (soap operas), game shows, and Mexican league sports programs produced by Mexico's leading network, Televisa. It has about 80 percent of the national Spanish-language audience[101]—large enough that in 2000 both presidential candidates made a point of being interviewed by its news anchor Jorge Ramos.[102] In 2000, Televisa's major competitor in Mexico, TV Azteca, announced a joint venture creating a new U.S. network, Azteca America, which would run TV Azteca *telenovelas* and tabloid-type infotainment shows.[103] Telemundo, a TV network based in Miami, has about 20 percent of the Spanish-language market.

But while these networks have had some success, they do not have anything like a monopoly on the American Latino audience. Latino children and teenagers seldom watch Spanish-language TV,[104] and these networks have had difficulty coming up with programming that appeals to different Latino groups. *Telenovelas* that are popular in one country do not necessarily gain an audience elsewhere. Even accent is important: Jorge Ramos, a Mexican, has worked to develop a Spanish accent that does not sound jarring to Cubans, Puerto Ricans, and other Latinos.[105] Univision seems to appeal primarily to Mexicans; the same seems likely to be true of Azteca America, which has not launched stations in New York, Chicago, or San Diego. And Cuban-influenced programming coming out of Miami does not appeal to Mexicans in California or Texas. The president of Los Angeles–based Galavision did not even seek outlets in Miami and New York, saying, "You cannot satisfy all Hispanic tastes."[106]

The situation is similar in music: *Tejano* music is wildly popular in Texas but not much heard in California, Florida, and New York. In the 1990s *technobanda* music, based on Mexican town orchestras that used tubas, trumpets, and snare drums, became the top-rated radio format in the Los Angeles metropolitan area, but it was little played in Texas, Florida, and New York.[107] Cuban music is of course most popular in Florida, but Miami's Cuban-Americans try to discourage performances by musicians based in Castro's Cuba who have found an audience elsewhere.

CONVERGENCE

Latino migration has been not one but many migrations, similar but not identical, coming from different countries and starting at different times. The difficulty of coming up with a single name for these immigrants—Chicano, Hispanic, Latino, Latin—illustrates the problem. Gregory Rodriguez denounces "the absurdity of pretending that there really is some monolithic 'Latino community,' or that all Latinos snugly fit into one cultural, economic, or political mode. Quite the contrary. Latinos make up what can best be described as a vast, dispersed, heterogeneous, multilingual, and multi-class population."[108] Yet it is possible, while keeping all this variety in mind, to speak of a single Latino migration and to make some useful generalizations about it.

One is that it is large. The roughly 10 million Latinos who migrated to the United States in the last third of the twentieth century were roughly double the number of southern Italians who arrived between 1890 and 1924. Italians were never the largest ethnic group in any great city, as similar numbers of Jews immigrated in those same years and the long-established, but still distinctive, Irish outnumbered them just about everywhere. But today Latinos are by far the largest and most visible ethnic group in Los Angeles, San Diego, Phoenix, Houston, and Miami; they are on the way to outnumbering blacks in New York and are rivaling blacks' numbers in Chicago. More than 10 million Latinos live in California, with 6 million Latinos living in the Los Angeles metropolitan area alone—more people than in most American states. In Texas there are another 6 million Latinos. Whereas Little Italies were geographically tiny and relatively self-contained, neighborhoods where Spanish is spoken regularly in daily life spread out widely over the grid streets of Los Angeles, Houston, and Miami.

This has led to fears of separatism and balkanization, of Spanish-speaking meganeighborhoods where people will grow up, live, and work entirely in Spanish and never become interwoven into the fabric of American life. And it is true that Latino immigrants have been slower than other late-twentieth-century immigrants to learn English. In 1990, according to the Census Bureau, 94 percent of the total population, but only 61 percent of Hispanics and 33 percent of foreign-born Hispanics, could speak English "very well."[109] In southern California, with the nation's largest concentration of Latinos, about one-third of Latino men and about one-fourth of the women spoke English "not at all" in both 1980 and 1990; similar percentages in both years spoke it "very well," "well," and "not very well."[110] As one expert on the topic reports, "Over time the Latino adults show fairly small increases in English ability, and their gap with other immigrants widens. This pattern may reflect the lower educational achievement of Latino immigrants, as well as the continued attachment of many to Mexico."[111] Moreover, the perverse effects of bilingual education have left many children of Latino immigrants with something less than the full mastery of English that most Americans—and most Latino immigrants—believe schools should impart.

But it is necessary to keep in mind another fact about Latino migration: it is ongoing. Many Latinos who could not speak English well in 1980 could do so in 1990, and many who could not in 1990 could in 2000. The statistics showing that the average Latino has only slightly improved mastery of English, education levels, and incomes are actually evidence of substantial gains, for overall statistics that average in the huge numbers of new arrivals mask the progress that preexisting immigrants have made. It is true that many Latino immigrants go about their daily lives, working and raising their families, speaking mostly Spanish. But polling shows that overwhelming majorities of Latino parents— 81 percent—want their children to be taught English.[112] There is no substantial number of Latino immigrants who want their children to speak only Spanish.

Latino migration is ongoing and will be ongoing for some considerable length of time, certainly for decades. But it should be kept in mind that this ongoing immigration is coming from a Latin America that is itself changing. Latin American economies have grown in the 1990s as their governments have eliminated trade barriers, privatized uneconomic state-owned enterprises, and stabilized their currencies. Democracy, too, has made substantial advances.

No country has witnessed more change than Mexico. The election of Vicente Fox in July 2000, the first time in seventy-one years the PRI was defeated, was made possible by electoral reforms and the steadiness of President Ernesto Zedillo, but most of all it signaled changes in the Mexican electorate. From 1929 up through 1982, at least 66 percent of Mexicans voted for the PRI candidate for president. In 2000, Mexican voters under forty, almost all of them too young to have voted in 1982, gave only 30 percent of their votes to the PRI candidate. These young Mexicans, representing 60 percent of the electorate, are a new Mexican people, no longer loyal to the autarkic, anti-*norteamericano* ideology of the PRI. They want free markets, an open politics, transparent government—values that are part of the American civic culture. Mexican commentator Sergio Sarmiento argues that if Mexico can achieve the South Korea–style economic growth that seems possible over the next twenty years, it will vastly reduce its economic disparity with the United States and substantially reduce incentives to immigration.[113] Fox calls for completely free trade and open borders with the United States. If Mexico leaps forward economically and continues to improve its governance, it is possible to imagine such policies in place, together with a reduced level of immigration.

It is possible also to imagine that in time Latinos will become interwoven into the American fabric. Of course, there are trends working in the wrong direction. California Latinos were angered by the passage of Proposition 187 and the imputation that they are not hardworking; Cuban-Americans were angered by the larger American public's willingness—in the case of some liberals, eagerness—to send six-year-old Elian Gonzalez back to totalitarian Cuba and its indifference to the Cubans' devotion to political freedom. These insults may be long remembered. Moreover, university departments of Chicano studies and foundation-supported advocacy organizations, still operating under the civil rights paradigm, nurture a sense of grievance that tends to retard rather than promote assimilation.[114] And some young Latinos seem to be imitating the gangs and violent behavior of the black underclass, which damages those individuals as well as the victims of their acts.

Fortunately, relatively few Latinos seem to be affected by these trends. The great majority go about their work and rise in the world. And increasingly, they are marrying non-Latinos. The Census Bureau found in 1990 that intermarriage was already common: 28 percent of Mexicans, 35 percent of Puerto Ricans, 26 percent of Cubans, and 44 percent of other Hispanic marriages were to non-Hispanics. The evidence is that intermarriage is even more common among second-generation Latinos. A study of 1991 New York City marriage records showed that 66 percent of Cuban brides, 53 percent of Mexican brides, 56 percent of Central American brides, 41 percent of South American brides, and 24 percent of Dominican brides married non-Hispanics.[115] Intermarriage increases the percentage of people who can be classified as Hispanic but at the same time reduces the distinctiveness of Hispanicness and makes the category, which government classifiers use to distinguish and fence off some Americans, less useful. As John Miller writes, "At some point, intermarriage ceases to be intermarriage."[116] It becomes instead another way of weaving the children of immigrants into the fabric of American life.

Many writers on Latino immigrants focus on isolated examples of protest, incidents that are real but are not the common experience of the very large majority of Latino immigrants and their children. The common experience is one of hard work, strong family life, progress from decade to decade and generation to generation. It is an undramatic story if one is looking for social upheaval and the overthrow of the American economic or political order, as many of these writers are. But it is an incredibly dramatic story as one examines, in person or with the help of fine writers like Sanford Ungar, Joel Millman, and Roberto Suro, the challenges and changes, the hard work and the hard-won successes, in the lives of Latino immigrants and their children. "*We are assimilating ourselves.* Now there are plenty of middle-class Latinos to model ourselves after," says Gregory Rodriguez. "Not unlike other immigrant groups—most notably the Italians—the Latino path to the middle class is marked more by a steady, intergenerational ascent than rapid individual progress in education, which better characterizes the Asian and Jewish immigrant

experiences. Rather than balkanization, the long-term prospec-
tus points to a full-scale integration of Latinos—racially, socially,
and economically—into the broader regional society. Far from
mirroring the static, stuck image of a permanently disadvantaged
minority, Latinos are, by and large, struggling upward and
following the momentum of the great waves of European immigrants who came before them."[117]

Will Latinos become interwoven into American life as the
Italians were by the 1970s? We can see on the horizon no anneal-
ing event like World War II, which accelerated the interweaving
of Italians into American life, or any political moment that certi-
fies a group's Americanness, as the election of John F. Kennedy
did for the Irish or the work of John Sirica and Peter Rodino in
the Watergate crisis did for the Italians. But the process of interweaving is already going on, even as immigrants cross the border
in great numbers. Forces active in American life and in the lives
of Latinos are working mostly in the right direction. It seems
overwhelmingly likely that Latinos will become thoroughly
interwoven into the fabric of American life. With luck, it will
take less than eighty years.

☆ PART 3 ☆

JEWS AND ASIANS

"The Broadway musical, radio, and TV were all examples
of a fundamental principle in Jewish diaspora history:
Jews opening up a completely new field in business and culture,
a *tabula rasa* on which to set their mark,
before other interests had a chance to take possession,
erect guild or professional fortification, and deny them entry."
—PAUL JOHNSON

"The Chinese, Japanese, and Koreans brought with them
from their native cultures a dense network of community
organizations, one of which was the rotating credit association …
by which coethnics pooled their savings and used them
to establish one or another of their members in business….
For such an informal system to work, there had to be a
high level of trust among the association's members."
—FRANCIS FUKUYAMA

There is a close but far from complete resemblance between the Jews who began migrating in a rush from eastern Europe in the 1880s and the Asians who began migrating in a rush from East Asia after 1965. They were both persecuted peoples, under constant threat of destruction. Indeed, the overseas Chinese in Southeast Asia have often been called Asian Jews, for they like the Jews lived as distinct minorities, often hated for their commercial success, in countries ruled by autocrats and dictators. Both groups lived in polities with a certain oppressive order but also given to bouts of internal warfare and slaughter, polities with low levels of trust. The out-rush of Jews from eastern Europe to America was sparked by the persecution of Russia's tsarist government beginning in 1881. The outrush of Asians was sparked by the passage of the Immigration Reform Act of 1965.

In the United States both Jews and Asians headed to the largest and most economically dynamic cities of their times—Jews in overwhelming numbers to New York, Asians to the metropolitan areas of New York, Los Angeles, San Francisco, Washington, and Houston. Most Jewish and Asian immigrants started off working in low-skill jobs, often in garment factories. But many had an entrepreneurial spark and started small businesses. It was not unusual for immigrants of both groups to start out working in garment factories and eventually to open garment factories of their own. Few eastern European Jews arrived in America with much money, but a fairly high proportion of Asian immigrants arrived with significant amounts of capital, and others came with (or acquired in American universities) professional degrees that enabled them to become affluent.

Both Jews and Asians were people of the book, whose religion in the case of Jews was based on the Torah and whose culture in the case of Asians was based on Confucius's Analects. Both had strong traditions of literacy and came from societies in which literacy was an economic asset. In the United States many members of both groups took immediate advantage of the opportunity offered by American schools, excelling at their studies and graduating from colleges and professional schools. Jews, barred from many universities by anti-Jewish quotas and from jobs in large corporations and traditional law firms, achieved great success in the law and medicine. Asians, for whom spaces in universities were limited by racial quotas and preferences, have achieved great success in the sciences, engineering, and medicine.

Both Jews and Asians had traditions of strong family ties. Fathers almost always remained with their families; responsibilities to elderly parents were taken seriously. Intermarriage was rare among the first generation of immigrants, though the third generation of Jews and the second generation of Asians saw large numbers—perhaps a majority—marrying outside their ethnic group. Family ties were also important in business. Both Jewish and Asian entrepreneurs typically established family businesses and raised money from relatives or from kinship groups like the Chinese *hui* or Korean *keh*.

One area in which Jews and Asians differ is religion. The Jews are a people defined by their religion, a faith they have held to even though it has made them the object of persecution for many centuries. Jewish immigrants to the United States found a country where their faith carried no civic disabilities—but where it did make them the object of prejudice and discrimination. The eastern European Jewish immigrants tended to found Orthodox congregations, but over the years more have identified with the Reform tradition. Today many Jews have eschewed religion altogether or have become secular in their beliefs, usually cherishing a tradition of social justice that has deep roots in Judaism. For most Asians, the guiding tradition has been Confucianism, which is less a religion in the Western sense than a code of ethics and conduct. There is no church or religious ritual, nor any clergy. However, most Filipinos, a near majority of Korean immigrants, and a significant percentage of Chinese and Vietnamese immigrants have been Christians, while some Asian immigrants are practicing Buddhists.

Perhaps because of their strong ethical traditions, crime rates among both Jewish and Asian immigrants have been low (this despite some involvement in organized crime).

Because of their unusual dress and identifying physical characteristics, eastern European Jewish immigrants were quite distinctive in the America of a hundred years ago. Continued discrimination against Jews, especially at the upper levels of society, emphasized their distinctiveness, and networks of Jewish firms and the establishment of Jewish clubs and resorts also tended to set them apart until the 1960s. Before then it was possible for many to live in a mostly Jewish America. After the 1960s, as discrimination lessened and in many cases disappeared, Jewish distinctiveness diminished. Many Asian immigrants, for their part, have started off in heavily Asian communities like the

Chinatowns of New York. But they have encountered relatively few obstacles to buying houses in areas that are not heavily Asian or getting jobs in firms with few Asian employees. Many of those who work and shop in Los Angeles's Koreatown, for example, live scattered across the Los Angeles Basin.

Both the Jews and the Asians approached American politics gingerly, unwilling at first to give their allegiance to either major political party. Jews, with their strong sense of social justice and their desire to prevent discrimination, have tended to favor a strong secular state. In eastern Europe at the time of the great Jewish immigration, many Jews were embracing socialism and forming labor unions—movements that would let them assert a common interest with other workers rather than face discrimination and persecution as a non-Christian minority. In the United States eastern European Jewish immigrants joined unions and in New York voted for left-leaning third political parties (though only in very small numbers for Communists). In the 1940s and 1950s the importance of the Jewish vote in pivotal New York led politicians of both major parties to move to the left on economic issues and civil rights. By the 1960s most American Jews had become strong Democrats and have remained so ever since. The emergence of the Christian right as a strong force in the Republican Party has evidently been seen as a threat by Jewish voters, who cast percentages for Bill Clinton and Al Gore almost as high as those cast by their grandparents for Franklin Roosevelt fifty years before.

The direction of Asians in American politics, however, is not yet clear. The descendants of pre-1965 Asian immigrants vote heavily Democratic, particularly in Hawaii. But in the 1990s Asians in California were fairly evenly divided between the parties. These people, some of them refugees from Communism and others living in countries where Communist China is seen as an ever present threat, evidently are much less likely than Jews to see a large state as a friend and more likely to vote in line with their economic interest as entrepreneurs or high-income professionals.

Their experience as a persecuted people has made Jews exquisitely sensitive to the changing tastes and preferences of those unlike themselves. This helps to explain the spectacular success of Jews in businesses that put a premium on understanding fast-changing consumer tastes. These include the garment trade, retail selling, and show business. As performers, writers and composers, impresarios and producers, Jews did much to create American popular culture and in the process created an image of Americanness in 1930s and 1940s movies that still helps define how we see ourselves as a people. There is no equivalent performance by Asians, at least not yet.

The interweaving of Jews into the fabric of American life has been so complete that some thoughtful Jews are worried that an increasingly secular Jewry may lose its Jewish identity altogether. The convergence of Asians into American life has not proceeded that far. But the high degrees of intermarriage and a probably inevitable weakening of the Confucian cultural heritage may mean that Americans of Asian descent may someday face that question too.

CHAPTER 5

JEWS

THE OLD COUNTRY

I t is a landscape today filled with memories of the horrors of the twentieth century. The land of northeast Poland is, as Simon Schama writes, "a brilliantly vivid countryside; the riverland of the Bug and the Vistula; rolling, gentle land, lined by avenues of poplars and aspens,"[1] but it is also "a country where frontiers march back and forth to the abrupt command of history."[2] In the 1990s it was still a land of horse-drawn plows, grazing cattle, storks with "monstrously overbuilt" nests. Schama climbed the mound of Giby, which holds the bodies of hundreds of Poles murdered by the Soviet NKVD in 1945, and looked out on the landscape. "Beyond the cross the ground fell sharply away to reveal a landscape of unanticipated beauty. A fringe of bright young trees marked the horizon floor, but at their back, like giants holding the hands of children, stood the black-green phalanx of the primeval forest. In the mid-ground a silver ribbon of river, one of the many lakes and streams feeding into the course of the Niemen, wound through reedy marshes and fields of green corn. The windows of isolated timber cottages caught the sunset beside the edge of quiet ponds where geese stood doing not very much."[3]

These are what writer Anne Applebaum calls the borderlands of Europe, plains with no natural barriers, invaded and conquered many times from east and west and north and south, the home over the years of many peoples. "There are many layers of civilization in the borderlands," Applebaum writes, "and they do not lie neatly on top of one another. A ruined medieval church sits on the site of a pagan temple, not far from a mass grave surrounded by a modern town. There is a castle on the hill and a Catholic church at its foot and an Orthodox church beside a ruined synagogue. A traveler can meet a man born in Poland, brought up in the Soviet Union, who now lives in Belarus—and he has never left his village. To sift through the layers, one needs to practice a kind of visual and aural archeology, to imagine what the town looked like before the Lenin statue was placed in the square, before the church was converted into a factory and the main street renamed. In a conversation, one must listen to the overtones, guess what the speaker might have said fifty years ago on the same subject, understand that his nationality might then have been different—know, even, that he might have used another language."[4]

To a visitor the most haunting thing about this landscape is the people who are no longer there. For this was the heartland of the Jews of eastern Europe, the largest Jewish population in the world a hundred years ago, almost vanished today. Jews first came here in the fourteenth century, when Jagiello, king of a newly enlarged Lithuania and just converted to Christianity, invited Jews to come and help settle this empty and backward land. Jews were expelled from many cities in Germany and Italy in the 1400s and from Spain in 1492; many moved to less developed territories to the east, where opportunities were greater and repression less thorough. So, as historian Paul Johnson writes, "By 1500 Poland was regarded as the safest country in Europe for Jews, and it soon became the Ashkenazi heartland."[5] Jews played a key role in creating the grain-growing estates of Polish nobles and selling their produce. Their numbers rose from 30,000 to 150,000 in the sixteenth century.[6] In the seventeenth century, "the Polish nobility leased not only land but all fixed assets such as mills, breweries, distilleries, inns, and tolls to Jews, in return for fixed payments, [and] the Jews flourished and their populations [grew] rapidly."[7] But in 1648, Ukrainian peasants, pressed by these Jewish agents of Polish nobles, revolted and massacred thousands of Jews.

This was the first of many great disasters for the eastern European Jews. The next was the partition of Poland among its neighbors between 1772 and 1795; this placed most of the Jews in resolutely tsarist Russia, which, writes Johnson, "from the very start viewed the Jews with implacable hostility."[8] The Russians responded in 1812 by confining the Jews to the Pale of Settlement, essentially the areas they seized from Poland, and which included most of present-day Lithuania, Belarus, Ukraine, and Moldova and almost none of present-day Russia. In 1827 they subjected Jewish boys and men from ages twelve to twenty-seven to service in the military, where they were often pressured to convert to Christianity.[9] There was, as Arthur Hertzberg writes, much bitterness in Jewish communities when rabbis and other leaders filled their quota of draftees by hiring "*chappers* ('grabbers'), people who roamed the streets and grabbed any teenage boy they could find to give him to the Russian military."[10]

Jews were barred from living or working in villages. Instead they lived mostly in separate *shtetlakh* or, starting in the late nineteenth century, cities. They were barred from buying land, from voting for local councils, from becoming lawyers or other professionals; higher education was mostly closed to them. In practice these restrictions were often evaded by bribery, but exemptions might easily be revoked. Many Jews came to live in Moscow and St. Petersburg, only to be expelled.[11] "The *shtetl* was a town, usually a small one; it sometimes had cobbled streets; it occasionally had imposing structures; and it rarely was picturesque," writes Irving Howe. "Because the *shtetl* lived in constant expectation of external attack, all the inner tendencies making for disintegration were kept in check. The outer world, the world of the gentiles and the worldlings, meant hostility, sacrilege, brute force: the threat of the Fist against the defenseless Word. This condition of permanent precariousness gave the east European Jews a conscious sense of being at a distance from history, from history as such and from history as a conception of the Western world."[12]

Europe's Jewish population rose from 2 million in 1800 to 7 million in 1880 and 13 million in 1914, some 5.5 million of them in Russia and another 2.5 million in the Austro-Hungarian Empire.[13] During the second half of the nineteenth century, about half of these Jews moved from the *shtetlakh* to cities,[14] where they worked as traders, craftsmen, and workers in the new clothing factories. Their native language was in most cases Yiddish, developed in the Middle Ages from Middle High German dialects with admixtures of Hebrew, Polish, and Russian. In the nineteenth century Yiddish became a literary language; it was, writes Paul Johnson, "the language of street wisdom, of the clever underdog; of pathos, resignation, suffering, which it palliated by humor, intense irony, and superstition. Isaac Bashevis Singer, its greatest practitioner, pointed out that it is the only language never spoken by men in power."[15] Yiddish, writes Irving Howe, "was a language intimately reflecting the travail of wandering, exile, dispersion; it came, in the long history of the Jews, like a late and beloved, if not fully honored, son."[16] A Yiddish thesaurus has nineteen columns of synonyms for misfortune and only five for good fortune.[17] The eastern European Jews were little affected by the Enlightenment of the eighteenth century or the intellectual currents of the nineteenth. As Thomas Sowell observes, "Eastern European Jews remained not only alienated from Christians but also, to an increasing extent, from their changing co-religionists in western Europe as well.... Followers of eastern Europe's own Jewish modernizing 'enlightenment' or *Haskalah* movement were referred to sarcastically by their more traditional compatriots as 'Berlinchiks'—imitators of German Jews."[18] But the eastern European Jews maintained a tradition of scholarship. Each *shtetl* had a school to teach boys to read the Torah and other sacred books, and men were obliged to study and analyze them throughout their lives.[19]

After the assassination of Tsar Alexander II in 1881, by terrorists whose group had many Jewish members, the Russian Interior Ministry was granted total power to operate a police state and immediately began organizing pogroms—violent mass attacks—against Jews.[20] As Russian historian Richard Pipes writes, "The Jews who were considered particularly prone to subversion were subjected in the reign of Alexander III to the full force of disabling laws which, though long on the statute books, had not been strictly applied."[21] In the 1890s the tsarist police fabricated *The Protocols of the Elders of Zion*, a purported Jewish plan to take control of the world; it was published in 1905 and propagated by Lenin's Soviet and Hitler's Nazi regimes, though the *Times* of London proved it a forgery in 1921.[22] "The object of the [tsarist] government," writes Johnson, "was to reduce the Jewish population as quickly and as drastically as possible."[23] The Orthodox Church joined in: after a Christian boy was found murdered near Kishinev in 1903, the government and church accused the Jews of killing the child in order to use his blood for Passover matzoh.[24] In these years more and more restrictive laws were passed, and major pogroms occurred in Kishinev in 1903, Odessa, Minsk, and Lodz in 1905, and Bialystok and Gomel in 1906.[25]

Tsarist hostility to Jews was premised on the idea that they were especially likely to be socialists and revolutionaries, and in point of fact this was true. Socialism and Marxism appealed to a people who, despite their adeptness at making money, were mostly barred from economic success by a hostile regime and who were attracted to a system of thought that identified them with the great mass of oppressed people. Russian Jews created a socialist party called the Bund in 1897, and many of the leaders of Lenin's Communist Party were Jews, most notably Leon Trotsky (born Lev Bronstein), whose leadership of the Red Army was indispensable to the Communists' success. Other Communist Jews included Kurt Eisner, who led a revolutionary uprising in Bavaria in 1918–1919, Bela Kun, who was dictator of Hungary for five months in 1919, and Rosa Luxemburg, the leader of the Spartacist uprising in Berlin in 1919.[26] Internationally, the Bolshevik revolution was often seen as a Jewish enterprise, yet Lenin himself quickly turned to anti-Semitic appeals against Jewish traders and Zionists, and in the 1920s and 1930s Stalin liquidated almost all of the Communist leaders with Jewish origins.[27]

The Jews who lived in the Habsburgs' Austro-Hungarian Empire were not as badly treated. In the partition of Poland in 1772 the Habsburgs annexed the province of Galicia, which covered much of present-day southern Poland and western Ukraine and a bit of Romania. It contained about 215,000 Jews, far more than the 70,000 who lived in the Habsburgs' Bohemian lands and the 80,000 in their kingdom of Hungary. Now their empire was 9 percent Jewish, with the largest Jewish population in Europe outside Russia.[28] In the 1780s the reforming Emperor Joseph II abolished the "body tax" on Jews, gave them the right to attend schools, enter professions, and start factories, and even gave them, in historian William McCagg's words, "a certain equality with other subjects before the law," although he did not abolish residence restrictions.[29]

In the nineteenth century the Jews, spread out over the Habsburgs' empire, did not share a common experience. There were the privileged professionals allowed to live in Vienna (who included the likes of Sigmund Freud, Gustav Mahler, and Theodor Herzl, the founder of Zionism),[30] the long-established traders and manufacturers of industrial Prague and Bohemia, the Magyarized Jews of Hungary, all outnumbered by the poor rural Jews of Galicia. The situation of the Jews was affected by their relations with the different ethnic groups in this multiethnic empire—Germans, Czechs, Magyars, Italians, Poles, Romanians, Croats.[31] Anti-Semitism (the word was invented in 1879) flared after a stock market crash in Vienna in 1873 and when a Jew was charged with ritual murder in Hungary in 1882. In 1897 the explicitly anti-Semitic Karl Lueger was elected mayor of Vienna, installed over the objection of the long-reigning (1848–1916) Emperor Franz Josef.[32]

THE JOURNEY

In the summer of 1881, in the wake of the pogroms that followed the assassination of Tsar Alexander II, thousands of Jews from the Russian Empire streamed into the small Austro-Hungarian border town of Brody.[33] This was one of the great funnel points of the Jewish migration that lasted until the outbreak of World War I in 1914. Jews from Ukraine and southern Russia usually crossed the border here illegally, then traveled by train to Vienna or Berlin, and on to the ports of Hamburg, Bremen, Amsterdam, Rotterdam, or Antwerp for passage to New York. It was easier for the Jews of Austria-Hungary, who could leave their country legally and make their way to these ports; some of these Jews, and also Jews from Romania, left through the Austrian port of Trieste. The thousands of refugees that often accumulated at Brody received help from philanthropic organizations established by German Jews.[34]

The numbers of migrants increased in the 1890s and then again in the decade and a half after 1900. At the same time, more and more Jews were making their way from the *shtetl* to the large cities of eastern Europe—Budapest, Berlin, Vienna, and Warsaw. Russian immigration to the United States, mostly Jewish, accelerated from 21,000 annually in the period from 1881 to 1890 to 50,000 annually from 1891 to 1900, to 160,000 annually from 1901 to 1910, and to 216,000 from 1911 to 1914—a measure of increasing anti-Semitic pressure in the Russian Empire and a prime example of chain migration. World War I interrupted this flow, but in the years from 1920 until 1924 another 653,000 immigrants arrived from central and eastern Europe, and probably well over half of them were Jews. (The total numbers are not certain because U.S. authorities did not always keep track of the religion of immigrants.) At that rate, if the 1924 immigration act had not shut off immigration (the total quota for immigrants from Russia, Poland, and Romania was 8,879),[35] more than 500,000 Jews would have immigrated in the years before World War II—and thus avoided the Holocaust. Overall, more than 2 million Jewish immigrants,[36] almost all from Russia, the Galicia province of Austria-Hungary, and Romania, made their way to the United States between 1880 and 1924.*

It was a rough passage. Emigrants from Russia or Romania had to smuggle themselves—or be smuggled—into Austria-Hungary. German authorities conducted searches of emigrants passing through. Emigrants were herded into compounds in the port cities. They then had to survive inspection from steamship agents because the steamship lines had to ship back immigrants rejected in New York. From there they had to undergo a crossing in overcrowded steerage. Once arrived, they again had to pass

---

* Of the 1,051,000 foreign-born reporting Yiddish or Hebrew as a mother tongue in the 1910 census, 80 percent were born in Russia and 14 percent in Austria-Hungary. Total immigration from Russia during this period was 3,183,000, and total immigration from other countries classified as central and eastern Europe (not including Germany) was 4,392,000. Of course, these numbers included many Poles, Czechs, Hungarians, Germans, and Slavs who were not Jewish. It appears that about one-fourth of these central and eastern European immigrants were Jews.

inspection, this time at Ellis Island in New York Harbor (or, before 1891, Castle Garden, on an island nearer Manhattan).[37]

Unlike the great Italian migration that was occurring in the same years, the Jewish migration was a migration of families.[38] The statistics that exist show that 57 percent of Jewish immigrants were males, and between 1899 and 1910 some 25 percent were children under fourteen.[39] The Jewish immigration was not at all a sojourner immigration: 95 percent of the Jews who immigrated between 1908 and 1924 stayed in the United States. There was an overwhelming desire to leave Europe, and especially Russia, behind; at Brody, Jews unable to move farther refused to return to Russia.[40] The Jewish migration from Russia was so great—21 percent of Russian Jews came to the United States between 1899 and 1914—that, as Howe puts it, "it can almost be said that a whole people was in flight."[41] In 1880 about 6 million of the world's 7 million Jews—78 percent—lived in eastern Europe and 3 percent in the United States, where they made up only 0.5 percent of the total population. By 1920 Jews made up 3.4 percent of America's population, and 23 percent of the world's Jews lived in the United States.[42]

THE NEW COUNTRY

In 1881, when the great eastern European Jewish migration began, there were approximately 250,000 Jews in the United States. Some were descended from the Jews who settled in coastal ports long before America's independence. In 1654, twenty-three Jews from Brazil arrived in Nieuw Amsterdam, before it became New York.[43] Synagogues were established in New York in 1656, Newport, Rhode Island, in 1677, Savannah, Georgia, in 1733, Philadelphia in 1745, and Charleston, South Carolina, in 1750. Both Sephardic and Ashkenazim Jews arrived in the colonial period, and together they formed united Jewish congregations and communities. Colonial Jews often became merchants, having ties with Jewish merchants in London and the Caribbean. Jews were prominent supporters of the American Revolution, and three Hebrew congregations sent congratulatory letters to George Washington on his election as president.[44] It was in response to the Touro Synagogue of Newport that Washington wrote, "It is now that tolerance is no more spoken of, as if it was by the indulgence of one class of people, that another enjoyed the exercise of their inherent natural rights. For happily the government of the United States, which gives to bigotry no sanction, to persecution no assistance, requires only that they who live under its protection should demean themselves as good citizens, in giving it on all occasions their effectual support."[45]

More than any other country, the United States granted freedom and equality to Jews, and in the mid-nineteenth century there was a considerable immigration of German Jews, mostly from Baden, Wurttemberg, Bavaria, and Posen. The nation's Jewish population increased from 2,000 in 1790 to 6,000 by 1830, 150,000 in 1860, and 250,000 by 1880.[46] As Arthur Goren writes, "The Jews were part of the German migration, and, despite religious differences and historic prejudices, were drawn into the German social and cultural milieu in the United States."[47] As they had been in Germany, in the United States they became craftsmen and traders—tailors, shoemakers, dealers in secondhand clothes and dry goods, and peddlers. Peddlers, relying on members of their families, fraternal organizations, and religious congregations for capital, in time opened dry-goods stores or became clothing manufacturers.[48] German Jews became pioneer mass clothing manufacturers—Levi Strauss in San Francisco was a prime example—and developed many of the biggest department stores in the nineteenth century: Gimbels, Filene's, Neiman Marcus, B. Altman, G. Fox, Abraham & Strauss.[49] Jews clustered in trading cities, most notably New York and Cincinnati; the latter had a large German population and in 1860 was the fourth-largest city in the United States. But there were also Jewish peddlers and merchants in smaller cities and towns in the Midwest, California, and the South.[50] There, Judah P. Benjamin, a New Orleans lawyer, was elected U.S. senator in the 1850s and was the Confederate secretary of state in the 1860s.[51]

Jewish congregations were established in 160 cities and towns before the Civil War. They often split, torn by differences between traditionalists and those opposed to rigorous adherence to Jewish traditions. Reform Judaism, first established in Germany, became very popular among American Jews; it was, in the words of the 1885 Reform platform, a "progressive religion ever striving to be in accord with the postulates of reason." In 1875 the Reform Hebrew Union College was established in Cincinnati, and by 1880 most American Jews were in Reform congregations.[52] Jews also established many philanthropic and fraternal organizations.[53]

Many American Jews achieved great economic success. In addition to department stores and clothing and shoe manufacturing companies, Jews found success in investment banking. Jews who were successful elsewhere often moved to New York: Kuhn, Loeb and Company was started by Cincinnati merchants, Lehman Brothers by southern cotton factors; the Straus family moved from Talbotton, Georgia, to New York and turned R. H. Macy and Company into a giant department store. Overall, about half of all Jews were merchants, bankers, brokers, or retail dealers, and virtually none were unskilled workers.[54]

Such was the condition of the 250,000 American Jews at the beginning of the great migration of more than 2 million mostly impoverished eastern European Jews. The older American Jews were affluent, Reform, German-oriented, conventionally dressed; the new immigrants were poor, Orthodox, Yiddish-speaking, dressed in traditional eastern European Jewish clothes. The American Jews were educated and highly cultured; although the

Jewish tradition placed great value on literacy, half the Jewish immigrants were illiterate. As Paul Johnson writes, "For the first time, American Jewry began to fear new arrivals, especially in such staggering numbers. They rightly judged that an antisemitic reaction was inevitable."[55] Similarly, Thomas Sowell observes, "The conspicuously foreign demeanor, dress, and attitudes of the 'downtown' Jews were a painful embarrassment to the 'uptown' Jews, who sought to get them to speak English, practice cleanliness, and avoid loud and demonstrative behavior."[56] Despite, or perhaps because of, their apprehensions and distaste, successful American Jews—more than members of any other ethnic group— after 1890 made massive, even heroic efforts to help the immigrant Jews adjust to American life.[57] Foremost among them was the Hebrew Immigrant Aid Society, which helped Jewish immigrants pass through Castle Garden and Ellis Island to find jobs and housing in New York and learn English.

The eastern European Jews came primarily to New York. Some 1.5 million Jews landed at New York between 1881 and 1911, and about 70 percent of them stayed there—roughly half of all Jewish immigrants. Indeed, by 1920 about half of American Jews lived in greater New York.[58] At first they clustered on a few blocks in the Lower East Side. Then, as more Jews arrived, they came to occupy almost all of the Lower East Side east of the Bowery and Chatham Square and south of Houston Street. By 1910, when Manhattan had 2.3 million residents (far more than the 1.5 million today), half of them south of 14th Street, there were some 540,000 Jews living in 1.5 square miles on the Lower East Side. In other words, there were 730 per acre—quite possibly the highest population density on earth.[59] Jews lived in five- or six-story tenement houses, sleeping three or more to a room, with most rooms opening only to narrow airshafts.[60] Conditions in the tenements were often grim—a fact publicized by Jacob Riis's *How the Other Half Lives*, published in 1890.[61] The streets were filled with pushcarts and peddlers' stalls (there were 2,500 peddlers on the Lower East Side),[62] horse-drawn carts and workers carrying piles of cloth and clothing. Some tenements were converted to garment factories. Others housed synagogues, religious schools, ritual baths; one map shows 182 synagogues in the Lower East Side.[63] There were Yiddish theaters and the *Yiddish Daily Forward* at 175 East Broadway. Philanthropic groups founded by German Jews opened more than two dozen settlement houses where social workers sought to improve housing, provided public health services, taught English, and conducted citizenship classes. Reunions of old neighbors, *landslayt*, turned into *landmanshaft* organizations, which offered social services, including life insurance, sickness and death benefits, aid in finding jobs or housing, and, since there were no cemeteries in Manhattan, burial plots.[64] Other new groups included the Hebrew Free Loan Society, several hospitals, the Workmen's Circle, and the Jewish National Workers' Alliance. No other immigrant group produced so many voluntary associations as the Jews.[65]

Jews from different places tended to cluster in certain parts of the Lower East Side. As historian Moses Ridschin tells it, "Hungarians were settled in the northern portion above Houston Street, along the numbered streets between Avenue B and the East River, once the indisputably *Kleindeutschland*. Galicians lived to the south, between Houston and Broome, east of Attorney, Ridge, Pitt, Willett, and the cross streets. To the west lay the more congested Romanian quarter ... on Chrystie, Forsyth, Eldridge, and Allen Streets, flanked by Houston Street to the north and Grand Street to the south, with the Bowery gridironed by the overhead elevated to the west.... From Grand Street reaching south to Monroe was the preserve of the Russians—those from Russia, Poland, Lithuania, Byelorussia, and the Ukraine—the most numerous Jewries of eastern Europe. To add a particularly exotic note, after 1907 a community of Levantine Jews settled among the Romanians between Allen and Chrystie Streets."[66]

The Lower East Side was not a permanent home for most of its residents: the average Jew remained there only fifteen years.[67] By 1920 part of the East Side had become heavily Jewish at midtown, near the current site of the United Nations, as had much of Harlem between Third and Eighth Avenues up to 125th Street.[68] As the subways were built—the first line opened in 1906—they moved in huge numbers to New York's outer boroughs, especially Brooklyn and the Bronx. The new neighborhoods of Brownsville and Flatbush in Brooklyn and the area along the Grand Concourse in the Bronx became heavily Jewish between 1910 and 1930; Brownsville, which had 4,000 Jews in 1890, had 230,000 in 1915.[69] By 1920 New York had 1.6 million Jews, by far the largest Jewish population of any city in the world.

Similar patterns were seen in other cities. Eastern European Jewish immigrants thronged into small ghetto-like neighborhoods, on Chicago's West Side or in South Philadelphia, usually far from the neighborhoods where affluent German Jews lived. Other cities with large Jewish immigrant populations included Boston, Cleveland, Baltimore, Pittsburgh, St. Louis, and Detroit. Chicago and Philadelphia accounted for 13 percent of the nation's Jews, and seven other eastern and midwestern cities accounted for another 14 percent.[70] Few Jewish immigrants of this era went to the South, to join the small merchant Jewish families found in almost every fair-sized town, or to the West. Relatively few went to Cincinnati, where the Jewish community remained largely German in origin and Reform in religion, or to San Francisco, where the German Jewish community had been well established since the Gold Rush created the city overnight in 1849.

The distinction between German and Ashkenazim Jews may have remained strong in San Francisco, but not elsewhere in the country, especially not in New York. Instead, in Nathan Glazer's words, "Out of a multitude of institutions and organizations, a consciously single Jewish community was formed by the time of the First World War."[71] The major Jewish organizations set up by that time—the American Jewish Committee, B'nai B'rith, the Federation of Jewish Charities—had been founded mostly by German Jews, but they set out to serve the interests of all American Jewry and proved ready to enroll Ashkenazim Jews in their ranks. In New York, uptown and downtown Jews formed the Kehillah in 1908 to deal with problems of religious morality, "social morals" (i.e., crime), and Jewish education.[72] Despite experiences of discrimination and anti-Semitism, the eastern European Jewish immigrants, like the German Jews before them, came to America determined to stay. They had the lowest rate of return of any immigrant group. Even as they cherished their identity as Jews, they embraced their new identity as Americans.

WORK

The eastern European Jews reached America not entirely unprepared to cope with urban life. The *shtetl*, after all, was a kind of small city, and many Jews came with commercial habits developed from years of lending and peddling.[73] They also had a tradition of learning, from reading the Torah and arguing about the Talmud, and a habit of forming voluntary associations, often in opposition to existing associations. Moreover, many had moved from *shtetl* to city and had experience working in Russia's growing clothing industry. As Joel Kotkin writes, "In the United States, the Jews arrived with skills more ideally suited for a rapidly industrializing economy than did other immigrants; around the turn of the century, 75 percent of the newcomers from Poland and southern Italy were either farmers or manual laborers while two-thirds of the Jews came as skilled workers."[74] Many had skills as furriers, tailors, seamstresses, watchmakers, milliners, tobacco workers, and cigar makers.[75] But most frequently they had experience and skills as garment workers.[76]

Fifty years before there had been no large clothing industry. Luxury clothes were handmade by tailors, and ordinary people bought fabric and made clothes for themselves. But the development of the sewing machine made possible the mass production of inexpensive, standard-sized clothes, and by the 1880s the garment industry was growing rapidly in both the United States and Europe.[77] In New York it was an industry dominated by German Jews, who by 1900 owned 97 percent of garment factories, 90 percent of clothing wholesalers, and 80 percent of clothing retailers.[78] "We knew how to do everything—I made my own cuts and patterns," recalled one Jewish garment manufacturer. "Everybody you sold to—at J. C. Penney's, Macy's, Gimbels, the whole ready-to-wear business was Jewish."[79] Some have argued that the Jews were lucky to have arrived in New York just as the garment industry was taking off. To such arguments Thomas Sowell replies, "I could not help thinking that Hank Aaron was similarly fortunate—that he often came to bat when a home run was due to be hit."[80] As a result of Jewish immigration, New York, which had 10 percent of the nation's clothing factories in 1880, had 47 percent by 1910.[81]

Not that working in garment factories was an easy way to make a living. The garment industry consisted mostly of small firms, in intense and never-ending competition, under pressure to extract more labor at less cost than their competitors.[82] The result was the "task system," which increased the workload faster than the paycheck. The workday was often twelve or fourteen hours long.[83] Edwin Burrows and Mike Wallace provide a vivid description of a typical garment sweatshop: "A contractor ... set up a workspace in a rented loft or his own tenement apartment. He rented or bought sewing machines—$50 to $100 would buy a few used Singers—or required employees to bring their own. Finally he supervised, and usually worked alongside, teams of eight to 28 semiskilled workers, ideally just off the boat. Labor in these 'sweatshops' was broken down into 30 or more tasks, with machine work done by operators and needlework, basting, finishing, felling, and pressing reserved for the less skilled. By 1895 there were roughly 6,000 sweatshops in New York City and 900 in Brooklyn, employing perhaps 80,000 workers. Given such fierce competition, few contractors did well."[84]

As a result, wages were low. Jews, drawing on their heritage in the Bund, the Jewish labor movement in Russia, became leaders of the labor unions that formed in the garment industry. Between 1909 and 1914 there were massive strikes, and in 1910 Jewish manufacturers and labor leaders reached a "protocol of peace," with the mediation of Boston lawyer and later Supreme Court justice Louis Brandeis.[85] The settlement prohibited contracting, lowered the average workweek to fifty hours, and provided permanent industry-labor mediation machinery. After the 1911 fire at the Triangle Shirtwaist factory that killed 168 people, mostly women, union organizing accelerated.[86] The International Ladies' Garment Workers Union, founded in 1900, and the Amalgamated Clothing Workers Union, founded in 1914, plus other heavily Jewish unions in the hat and fur industries, had 217,000 members by 1917 and set up medical plans, housing programs, and retirement benefits for their members.[87]

But this hectic and chaotic business environment also left open many roads to success. As early as 1910, only 28 percent of first-generation Jewish immigrant men worked as laborers or operatives, while 31 percent were craftsmen, 29 percent had technical or sales jobs, and 9 percent were professionals or managers—an upscale profile rivaled only by Germans among other immigrants of the time.[88] Thousands of immigrant Jews became independent businessmen, small traders, and storekeepers. The Jewish heritage of trading surely played a part here, as did a desire to be independent; entrepreneurship was deeply rooted in Jewish culture. As Irving Howe writes, "To shake loose from the domination of a boss, to be free from the stares and sneers of gentiles, to take the risk of using one's wits and gaining the rewards of one's own work—this became a commanding desire among the immigrant Jews."[89] About one-quarter of Jewish immigrants moved into self-employment in small businesses as soon as possible. "In the virtually all-Jewish Eighth Assembly District [of New York]," historian Gerald Sorin writes, "there were 144 groceries, 131 butcher shops, 62 candy stores, 36 bakeries, and 2,440 peddlers and pushcart vendors."[90] These included many shops devoted to Jewish products—kosher meat, seltzer water, bagels, bialys, knishes, blintzes, challah bread, matzoh and gefilte fish for Passover.[91] Many Jewish entrepreneurs achieved only modest success; stores required around-the-clock work and yet furnished incomes not all that much greater than those of garment workers. But a significant number of others moved spectacularly ahead; Howe cites cases of eastern European Jewish immigrants who became millionaires by purchasing tenement houses, through construction and real estate, by selling plate glass, and by manufacturing shirts, children's dresses, overalls, lingerie, sportswear, and men's clothing.[92] Great Jewish fortunes were also made in the scrap metal business, which Jews dominate even today.

A common element in these success stories is an exquisite sensitivity to the changing tastes and desires of others who are often of entirely different backgrounds—customers, consumers, wholesalers. From their experience of persecution, Jews acquired an ability to understand the often shifting attitudes and preferences of gentiles; in Russia and eastern Europe it was literally a matter of life and death to understand the whims of the *goyim*. Jewish business success came most spectacularly in fields where others were not already dominant, and where the ability to foresee what others would want offered enormous rewards.[93] The garment industry was one such business. Others included retail and advertising—Julius Rosenwald, for many years the head of Sears, and Albert Lasker, the pioneer advertising man, amassed great fortunes and were among the greatest philanthropists of their times[94]—as well as communications and entertainment and show business (this last, perhaps the most spectacular, is a story to be taken up later). It was a Jew who built the first transcontinental trucking firm, and a Jew who pioneered in the banana business and took over the United Fruit Company.[95]

Jews also had great success in the professions. This was the result of two factors: their excellence at education and their near-total exclusion from high-level jobs in large corporations. Large corporations and law firms from early on refused to hire even highly acculturated German Jews, much less the sons of eastern European immigrants.[96] Such policies continued in place for years. Even if corporate leaders had been willing to hire Jews, few Jews had any confidence that they would be promoted or treated fairly in the corporate environment. Jews were barred almost totally from jobs in banks and the large insurance companies, though many became independent insurance agents. They were also barred from white-collar jobs in the steel, coal, railroad, and automobile companies.[97] As a result, by the early 1960s less than one-half of 1 percent of executive personnel in leading industrial companies were Jews, and non-Jewish graduates of the Harvard Business School outnumbered Jewish graduates in executive positions in leading corporations by thirty to one.[98] Only by the 1970s were there a few visible CEOs, notably Irving Shapiro of DuPont; still, Joel Kotkin observes that "as late as the early 1980s more than 75 percent of surveyed business executives told the Harvard Business School that being Jewish represented a 'handicap' to achieving upper-level positions in the corporate hierarchy."[99]

So Jews sought to move forward in the professions, where they could work for themselves and not for unwelcoming gentiles. A 1935 study by the Welfare Council of New York found that of Jewish fathers born in Russia, 4 percent were professionals and 32 percent proprietors, managers, and officials—presumably mostly small businessmen. But Jewish youth, 33 percent of the total survey, were 56 percent of those in proprietary and managerial work, 43 percent of those in clerical and sales positions, and 37 percent of those in the professions.[100] Indeed, Jews came to dominate their professions in New York: by 1937 Jews were 25 percent of the city's population but 65 percent of its lawyers, 64 percent of its dentists, and 55 percent of its physicians. In Cleveland, a city perhaps typical of those where Jews were less numerous, in 1938 Jews were 8 percent of the population but 23 percent of the lawyers, 18 percent of dentists, and 21 percent of physicians.[101] Jews also achieved success in teaching, starting in the Depression of the 1930s when Jewish college graduates could get few other secure jobs; thirty years later half the city's teachers and a majority of its school principals were Jews.[102] Moreover, Jews changed the professions. Many Jewish lawyers, barred from white-shoe law firms and shunned by large corporations, became personal injury lawyers living off fees contingent on winning their cases. Such trial lawyers succeeded in persuading courts, particularly the Supreme Courts of California and New Jersey, to change the rules of tort law to allow easier recovery and to authorize class action suits. Trial lawyers operating under such rules, many but by no means all of them Jewish, have now become in effect makers of major public policies and redistributors of corporate wealth, as in the asbestos and tobacco litigation of the 1980s and 1990s.

Jewish organizations did not trumpet the great economic success that Jews of eastern European immigrant stock had achieved by the 1920s. But that success is evident in the near doubling of contributions to Jewish charities from 1918 to 1926, in the building of hundreds of new synagogues, and in the ability of Jews to finance education at elite colleges for their children.[103] By the 1940s, just a half century after the eastern European mass migration began and the first decade in which most American Jews were born in the United States,[104] Jews were as a group substantially more affluent than most Americans—an astonishing achievement.[105]

EDUCATION

"A passion for education," an "enthusiasm for schooling": this was surely the predominant characteristic of the eastern European Jewish immigrants.[106] Jews have always been people of the book, who believed themselves under obligation to teach boys to read the Torah and other sacred scripture and to demonstrate that ability on their *bar mitzvah* at age thirteen. Adult men were expected to read scripture as well, and in even the humblest backgrounds, where their religious congregations often had no rabbi, they argued about the meaning of the Torah and Talmud. Literacy was central to their identification as Jews. This was a very different heritage from that of Italian immigrants who were arriving in the same years, who believed that literacy was a luxury of the well born and reading a diversion from the duty to work, which was the source of the father's authority. For Jews, the source of the father's authority was not just the fact that he worked but also the fact that he was learned.

Curiously, Jewish children at first seemed to be performing poorly in school. Studies in 1910 and 1911 showed large percentages of Jewish children in New York and other cities to be lagging behind grade level, and in World War I Jewish soldiers had some of the lowest test scores of different ethnic groups tested by the army.[107] This may have reflected the heavy overcrowding of schools in Manhattan's Lower East Side and elsewhere. Another factor could have been that these young people's parents were literate in Yiddish and Hebrew, with their different alphabet, rather than English. Still, even though immigrant Jews did not instantly achieve superiority over upper-middle-class native-born Americans, Jewish children were less likely to fail, less likely to be tardy, and more likely to stay in school longer than other immigrant children.[108] The conventional form of eastern European Jewish education—the *heder*, in which boys studied from dusk to dawn—withered in America,[109] and parents instead sent their children to public schools, with religious instruction afterwards in Talmud Torah schools.[110]

In public schools, in the settlement houses pioneered by Lillian Wald and financed by Jacob Schiff and other rich German Jews, and in organizations like the Young Men's Hebrew Association, immigrant Jews found not only welfare services but also classes in English and civics, preschool programs, and manual training classes—all intended to promote "Americanization."[111] The New York public schools under William Maxwell, superintendent from 1893 to 1918, and Julia Richman, assistant superintendent for the Lower East Side during much of that period, consciously strived for Americanization. In that period there were few Jewish teachers. Classes were all in English, and the use of Yiddish was discouraged; hygiene and "moral education" were taught; evening and summer courses were instituted; civics and the duties of citizenship were emphasized.[112] Never was it supposed that public schools were to reinforce the culture of the immigrants' old country or to preserve its language. And Jews availed themselves of this opportunity. In 1910, among first-generation Jewish immigrants age fourteen to eighteen, 56 percent were in school, a figure higher than for any other immigrant group and far ahead of the Italians (31 percent) and Poles (27 percent).[113]

Jewish parents, unlike Italian parents, saw that schooling could lead to better jobs. Even girls, who had not been educated in eastern Europe, were encouraged to stay in school, for parents hoped they could work as bookkeepers or typists rather than in garment factories.[114] In fact, enough Jews excelled that City College of New York, with its free tuition, had a majority-Jewish student body by 1900, "which was as soon as there were enough Jews of college age to fill it," as Irving Howe put it.[115] By the early 1920s Jews amounted to 9 percent of total college enrollment, three times their proportion of the population. In 1918–1919 they amounted to 39 percent of enrollment in a group of New York colleges and universities. In medical school the proportion of Jews was double that of gentiles, in dental schools, triple.[116]

No other immigrant group produced so many college and professional school graduates, and Protestant elites who ran private colleges were fearful that their institutions would become predominantly Jewish.[117] So in the 1920s many schools began instituting quotas for Jews, limiting their numbers and in effect requiring them to meet much higher standards than other applicants.* In a very few years, the percentage of Jews was reduced at Columbia College from 40 to 22 percent and at Harvard College from 21 percent to below 10 percent.[118] A dean at Yale conceded that "in terms of scholarship and intelligence, Jewish students lead the class, but their personal characteristics make them markedly inferior."[119] Quotas at medical schools were notorious,[120] and so many hospitals refused to allow Jewish doctors on their staffs that Jewish hospitals were created less to serve Jewish patients than to provide places for Jewish doctors to practice.[121] Jews responded by attending other colleges and by taking advantage of public institutions like City College that did not refuse to admit qualified students because of their religion or ethnic origin.

FAMILY

Traditional Judaism laid down detailed rules for the conduct of family life and expected as a matter of course that men and women would marry and raise families. In this it was different from Catholicism, which encouraged religious vocations that required celibacy. Family ties among Jewish immigrants were strong, and family obligations were upheld with great rigor. Jewish immigrants

---

* By the end of the 1920s, schools that had instituted quotas included Princeton, Duke, Rutgers, Barnard, Adelphi, Cornell, Johns Hopkins, Northwestern, Penn State, Ohio State, Washington and Lee, and the Universities of Illinois, Kansas, Minnesota, Texas, Virginia, and Washington.

typically saved to bring other family members over; two-thirds of eastern European Jewish immigrants had their passage to America paid for by family members.[122] In all, family stability was surely much greater than among the Irish, if not as great among the Italians. Writing from the vantage point of the early 1960s, Nathan Glazer could confidently state, "Studies have long shown that Jewish families break up less than non-Jewish ones. Rabbis rarely seem to find it necessary to warn their congregations against marital breakup, neglect of children, cocktail partying, and the like. Although the powerful maternal overprotection that was one of the chief characteristics of the first immigrant generation is perhaps somewhat abated, Jewish parents still seem to hover more over their children and give them shorter rein for exploration and independence than other middle-class American parents."[123]

Strong Jewish family ties also played a large role in Jews' success in business. Family members were the chief source of precious capital for Jews who started small businesses, and family members were critical in the operation of these businesses. They would work long hours at low wages and could be trusted absolutely. "One notices how often Jewish enterprises involve fathers and sons or groups of brothers," Glazer wrote.[124] Even some of the greatest fortunes Jewish Americans have made have come to essentially family businesses, from the German Jewish investment banks to the great real estate entrepreneurs of the past fifty years.

But to be sure, there were strains in Jewish families. Fathers' authority weakened as they struggled to make a living and as other family members had to work, with mothers taking in piecework and children shining shoes or selling newspapers. In addition, tensions formed between immigrants who remained more or less observant Jews and their sons who ostentatiously avoided the synagogue and patronized the dance hall. Parents found themselves estranged from their college-educated children.[125] Later, there was tension between the rough-hewn small businessman and the smoother, more educated heir. Glazer again: "For the Jewish businessman, who is culturally and socially bound to the Jewish community, who perhaps speaks with an accent and would not appreciate an exclusive club even if admitted, a life of associating with largely Jewish competitors, suppliers, and retailers is comfortable and cozy. To his son, who is perhaps a graduate of the Wharton School or the Harvard Business School, such a life is not satisfying, even if the income is good."[126] This situation was not uncommon as Jews seized the opportunity for higher education; a 1935 study in New York City showed that Jewish youth were more likely than non-Jewish youth to be working at a job "of a higher socioeconomic grade than that of the parent."[127] This tension between the generations, all the greater if the son went into academic life or cultural criticism, is the subject of a vast and rich literature, in which the dazzling success the parent had always hoped for, had worked so hard for, becomes a mixed blessing, a source of separation and sadness.[128]

RELIGION

With the arrival of the eastern European immigrants, Judaism in America changed from predominantly Reform to predominantly Orthodox. In 1881 only a few of the two hundred synagogues were Orthodox; by 1890 a majority of congregations were, and by 1910, 90 percent of two thousand synagogues were Orthodox.[129] But the Orthodox were not entirely successful in replicating in America the authority the religious congregation had exercised over community life and personal behavior in eastern Europe. Few rabbis immigrated, and most new congregations did not have one.[130] Usually these were, in the words of historian Gerald Sorin, "small *landslayt* congregations, without permanent rabbis or buildings [that] reflected the need for old-country regional ties and social familiarity."[131] Sanctions against violating the Sabbath were weaker than in eastern Europe and incentives to violate it stronger; observant Jews were less successful economically than those who gave up some of the religious regimen.[132] Providing kosher food became the duty of the grocer and the butcher, and responsibility for keeping a kosher household fell on the mother. Synagogues were still thronged on High Holy Days, and after-school instruction in Jewish scripture was maintained.

But as Jews moved out of the Lower East Side and similar ghettoes in other cities, they founded synagogues and temples that, in Arthur Goren's words, "were still traditional but more lenient and moderately innovative, a compromise between their American middle-class desire for social integration and their ties to traditional culture."[133] The prestige of Orthodox rabbis declined because of disputes about their training.[134] Meanwhile, the Reform movement, eschewing traditional clothing and kosher practices and emphasizing social justice, prospered, expanding from 136 congregations in 1900 to 500 in 1944.[135] The Conservative movement, a middle ground between Orthodoxy and Reform, grew rapidly in the first two decades of the century but then tapered off.[136] As Sorin writes, "In individualistic America, 'a treyfe land where even the stones are impure,' Jewish piety never fully dissipated; but it did soften, and many Jews gradually drifted into a secular mode of life."[137] By the 1950s, American Judaism was once again more Reform than Orthodox. Yet today the movement is in the other direction, as many Reform Jews have abandoned observance, married gentiles, and in some cases shed their Jewish identity, while Orthodox communities, with their large families and enthusiastic observance, have grown.[138]

CRIME

The violent crime rate among Jews was the lowest of any immigrant group and—perhaps there was a connection—so was the rate of alcoholism.[139] But there was nonviolent crime—gambling, arson, protection rackets, fencing stolen goods, pickpocketing, horse poisoning, and prostitution. Arson and insurance fraud were common enough to create a stereotype, and "clever fraud was for some a way of survival," Arthur Hertzberg writes. "The law had always been the enemy of the Jews; to circumvent it was often the only way to survive and, therefore, to outfox authority was a praiseworthy act."[140] Prostitution received the most attention; there was evidence that prostitution rings brought over Jewish girls from eastern Europe.[141] Historians Frederick Binder and David Reimers write, "In 1909 an article in the muckraking *McClure's Magazine* referred to the Lower East Side as 'the world's brothel,' and the Dillingham Commission reported that three-quarters of the more than 2,000 prostitutes brought before the New York City Magistrate's Court between November 1908 and March 1909 were Jewish."[142] Prostitution was sometimes a family business—consider the string of brothels run by "Mother Rosie" Hertz and her husband, brothers, and cousins. And its operators shared the Jewish propensity to form voluntary associations; brothel owners established the Independent Benevolent Association to provide health and death benefits and other aid.[143]

Gentiles troubled by the presence of the fast-growing eastern European Jewry in their cities seized on and exaggerated evidence of Jewish crime. In 1908 New York police commissioner Theodore Bingham charged that 50 percent of the city's criminals were Jewish, a statement he later retracted after a storm of criticism.[144] There were Jewish criminal gangs, and there were headlines when gambler Herman Rosenthal was murdered in 1912 just after giving evidence of a vice ring operating with police protection on the Lower East Side.[145] There were Jewish gangsters in the Prohibition era, but typically they were organizers and financiers of illegal business operations rather than hit men who used violence to rub out competition—less Al Capone than Arnold

Rothstein, who is alleged to have bribed Chicago White Sox players in the 1919 World Series and who was the model for Meyer
Wolfshiem in *The Great Gatsby*.[146] But there were some tough
Jewish gangsters: Dutch Shultz (Arthur Flegenheimer) in
Manhattan, the Purple Gang in Detroit, the Woodland Four
in Cleveland, the Twentieth Ward group in Chicago, and others in
Newark, Philadelphia, Kansas City, and Minneapolis. The best
known was Meyer Lansky, who set up a cartel to provide bookies
with instant results of horse races across the country.[147] There
were also violent gangs connected with the garment industry and
its unions; these were the gangsters who prompted the crime fighting of a young assistant U.S. attorney, Thomas E. Dewey.[148]

But very few in the next generation of Jews became involved
in organized crime, or indeed in crime at all. Jewish crime rates by
1940 were probably the lowest of any identifiable ethnic group.[149]

DISTINCTIVENESS

Like all immigrant groups, the Jews were distinctive. And like a
number of other groups, they inspired fears and dislike among
many Americans. Many argued that this "race" could never be
assimilated into American life. Jews' persistence in observing the
Sabbath and dietary laws underlined the fact that, unlike other
immigrant groups, they were not Christians. In the 1890s populist
figures like Ignatius Donnelly of Minnesota and Tom Watson of
Georgia—both former congressmen and the Populist Party's vice-
presidential nominees in 1892 and 1896, respectively—attacked
Jewish bankers as oppressors of beleaguered farmers.[150] But most
of the American elite did not echo such attacks. Later, as the number of eastern European Jewish immigrants approached 2 million,
voices of anti-Semitism became louder and the focus turned from
allegedly powerful Jewish capitalists to the masses of immigrant
Jews.[151] Theodore Bingham's charge that Jews were 50 percent of

New York City's criminals was one example. Another was Madison Grant's 1916 book *The Passing of the Great Race*, in which he charged that Polish Jews' "dwarf stature, peculiar mentality, and ruthless concentration on self-interest are being grafted upon the stock of the nation."[152]

The large number of ethnic Jews in the leadership of the Communists in the November 1917 Bolshevik revolution—and especially Leon Trotsky, who led the Red Army against the Communists' opponents, which included American troops[153]— fanned fears of Jewish revolutionaries.[154] Trotsky had in fact lived in the Bronx before he returned to Russia, and many Jews were socialists at a time when the distinction between democratic Socialists and totalitarian Communists was not as clear as it later became. Attorney General A. Mitchell Palmer spread these fears in the "Red Scare" of 1919–1920, denouncing "foreign-born subversives and agitators." Palmer claimed there were "60,000 of these organized agitators of the Trozky [*sic*] doctrine in the U.S." and that "Trozky" was a "disreputable alien ... the lowest of all types known to New York City."[155] These same years saw the revival of the anti-Jewish, anti-Catholic, anti-black Ku Klux Klan[156] and the widespread dissemination of *The Protocols of the Elders of Zion* in Henry Ford's *Dearborn Independent*.[157] All of this publicity increased support for immigration restriction and national quotas legislation, which passed in 1921 and 1924 and, unlike earlier immigration restriction bills, was signed by the president.[158]

This fanning of popular anti-Semitism was not vigorously opposed by most of the American elite. Indeed, elite Protestants had long practiced anti-Semitism of their own. The economic success of so many German Jews in the 1870s raised the question of whether they would be welcome to elite social organizations and to the new large corporations that were being formed. The answer was no. In 1876 the investment banker Joseph Seligman was barred from the leading hotel in the resort of Saratoga Springs, New York.[159] This turned out to be a precedent, as Jews were barred by virtually all elite social clubs, country clubs, and elite resort hotels. In response, they built a parallel set of social clubs, country clubs, and resort hotels[160]—the most spectacular examples being Catskill resorts like Grossinger's and the Concord and, later, Miami Beach hotels like the Fontainebleau and the Eden Roc. This was similar to the way in which Jews, excluded almost entirely from the executive ranks of large corporations, built their own businesses. Around the mid-1960s discrimination against Jews diminished greatly, though it is still practiced in some clubs and country clubs. The Catskill resorts have mostly closed, and the Fontainebleau and the Eden Roc now cater to convention-goers; some Jewish downtown clubs have also closed. Jews are found more often in corporate executive ranks, though in nothing like their percentages in the professions.

Until the mid-1960s, Jews were also routinely excluded from "exclusive" high-income neighborhoods, though perhaps less so in New York, where they were so numerous, than in other cities.[161] Indeed, there are still cooperative apartment buildings on the Upper East Side of New York that exclude Jews. At the same time, Jews moved out of some neighborhoods rapidly when blacks moved in, starting with Harlem in the 1920s and continuing with the West Side of Chicago, northwest Detroit, and Brownsville in Brooklyn in the 1950s. Most major metropolitan areas today have predominantly Jewish neighborhoods and suburbs, with well above-average housing values. This happens partly because many Jews wish to live near Jewish places of worship and stores that offer Jewish food and in the past may have reflected a desire to live where their children were more likely to find Jewish spouses.

POLITICS

From Russia the Yiddish-speaking Jews brought socialist and Zionist politics—both still recognizable in the political attitudes of Jewish voters today. Both socialism and Zionism were impulses toward survival, toward preserving the Jewish people from the destruction that the tsarist state seemed eager to wreak. Zionism in the early 1900s was newly born, and immigration to Palestine was not considered a practical alternative at the time; we will examine its role in Jewish politics later. But socialism, both revolutionary and democratic, seemed on the rise in the first decade of the century. Socialists were leading opponents of the tsarist regime who tried to take advantage of the failed revolution of 1905; the Social Democrats were the leading opposition party in Germany; Britain's socialist Labour Party was electing members of Parliament; and Theodore Roosevelt worried out loud that socialism might make great gains in the United States. Moreover, socialism allowed Jews to escape their status as a hated minority and identify themselves as part of a multiethnic working class, which, Marxism assured them, was the vanguard of history and would be the new ruling class. A passion for social justice, argued novelist Abraham Cahan, owed something to the Jewish ethical traditions and to the experience of battling hostile authorities and those who controlled society.[162] So it was that the Jews, persecuted by the state and excelling at making money in the free market when allowed to do so, were inclined toward a politics of expanding the state and diminishing the free market. This inclination has remained pronounced ever since in the United States, though in Britain and France since World War II Jews have tended to favor free-market parties.

Before the great eastern European migration, American Jews had not been heavily identified with either political party. Some had been attracted to the Republican Party, out of support for the Union cause and its opposition to slavery. Some had been attracted to the Democratic Party, which in the nineteenth century was a laissez faire party, for free trade and free markets, for tolerating local policies from segregation in the South to the saloon in the North. For many years August Belmont, the Rothschilds' man in

New York, was chairman of the Democratic National Committee. But there was wariness lest Jews become too identified with either party and attract attention as a "Jewish voting bloc."[163]

The eastern European Jews felt no great attraction to either party and were ready to consider socialist-type third parties. As their numbers swelled, especially in New York, they became the object of spirited competition between Democrats and Republicans. As early as 1886 they emerged as a major constituency when Henry George ran for mayor of New York on his platform of a "single tax" on land. George, who finished second to Democrat Abram Hewitt but ahead of Republican Theodore Roosevelt, got about one-quarter of his votes from heavily Jewish wards and received the support of the Jewish Workingmen's Association, established by socialists Abraham Cahan, Louis Miller, and Morris Hillquit. In Manhattan, Jewish immigrants were often put off by the crude vote-buying and bullyboy tactics of Irish-run Tammany Hall. But shrewd Tammany leaders Richard Croker and Charles F. Murphy could count. Anti-Jewish jokes disappeared from Tammany literature; Tammany stoutly opposed immigration restriction; and Tammany-supported Jews won major offices—Henry Goldfogle for Congress in 1900, Jacob Cantor as Manhattan borough president in 1901, Aaron Levy as leader of the Democrats in the New York Assembly that same year.[164]

The fact that the Jews were most numerous in New York gave them particular leverage, for New York was the fulcrum point of American politics, the largest state with the most electoral votes and, since the Civil War, equally divided between the two parties. Successful New York politicians were automatically presidential contenders, and their chances for success in New York would be greatly increased if they could carry the Jewish vote. The flamboyant publisher William Randolph Hearst, who embarked on a political career obviously aimed at the presidency when he was elected to Congress as an anti-Tammany Democrat from

Manhattan in 1902 and then ran for mayor of New York in 1905 and governor in 1906, headlined news of Russian pogroms in his papers, called for aid to Russian Jews and for social tolerance, and even put out a Yiddish paper.[165]

President Theodore Roosevelt, mindful of the increasing Jewish vote, praised Jewish immigrants, predicted there would be a Jewish president one day, denounced the Kishinev pogrom,[166] and invited the Rabbinical Council of America to the White House. In 1906 he appointed Oscar Straus to be secretary of commerce and labor, with jurisdiction over immigration; he was the first Jewish U.S. cabinet member.[167] Roosevelt carried the Jewish vote in 1904 and nearly swept in a Republican congressman from the Lower East Side. The competition continued in 1912. President Woodrow Wilson won over Jewish voters with high-level Jewish appointments—Henry Morgenthau as ambassador to Turkey (which then had a large Jewish population), Louis Brandeis to the Supreme Court in 1916, Bernard Baruch as war-industry coordinator in 1917. Wilson's support of the League of Nations and the Balfour Declaration promising a homeland for Jews in Palestine also made the Democratic Party more attractive to Jews.[168] Prominent Jews like Jacob Schiff and the Lehman family switched from Republican to Democrat in appreciation of Wilson's policies.[169]

Also a competitor for Jewish votes was America's Socialist Party. Russian immigrants, especially after the failure of the revolution of 1905, which led many leaders of the Bund and socialist parties to come to America, were often positively inclined to socialism. Many leaders of the union movement in the garment trade were also active Socialists, including Morris Hillquit, who ran for Congress unsuccessfully in 1906 and 1908.[170] The leadership of the Socialist Party founded in 1901 was disproportionately Jewish, and Jews appear to have given the Socialist presidential candidates an unusually high share of their vote in their peak election years, 1912 and 1920.[171] The first Socialist congressman,

Victor Berger, was born an Austrian Jew, but he emphasized his Teutonic origins and was elected by a heavily German district in Milwaukee in 1910 and from 1918 to 1926.[172] Meyer London, who ran as "an entirely different type of Jew from the kind that Congress is accustomed to see," ran against Henry Goldfogle in 1910 and 1914, beating him the second time, 50 to 41 percent.[173] In 1917 Socialists in New York hit their high-water mark, electing ten assemblymen, eleven aldermen, and a municipal judge. After that, the Socialist opposition to World War I cost them votes.*

The tipping point, when Jews moved away from the Socialists and Republicans and toward the Democrats, probably came in 1922. Tammany boss Charles Murphy had long been aware of the rising Jewish vote and had supported factory and welfare legislation—a break with the Democrats' historic leaning toward laissez faire policies. His protégé, Al Smith, was elected governor in 1918, lost in 1920, but came back and won in 1922. His top policy aide was Belle Moskowitz, a social worker with ties to heavily Jewish labor unions. In the 1928 presidential election Jews voted in large numbers for Smith. That same year, Franklin Roosevelt was careful to court Jewish voters in his successful bid for governor of New York, narrowly beating a Jewish Republican.

Nevertheless, while Jews may have been voting Democratic for president and governor, this did not mean that they sat foursquare in the Democrats' camp. In 1932 Governor Roosevelt had to force Mayor James Walker out of office as the result of another Tammany scandal, and New York's Jewish voters became the strongest supporters of Fiorello LaGuardia. LaGuardia was a unique figure: he had an Italian father, a Jewish mother, an Episcopalian faith. A strong backer of unions and welfare measures, he was elected to Congress from an East Side district as a

---

* The American loyalty of the Socialists was challenged in and just after World War I, but it was Samuel Dickstein, the Democrat who beat Meyer London in a landslide in 1922, who, after helping create a committee to investigate subversive activities, became a Soviet spy, apparently for money.

Republican and Democrat, against a Socialist, in 1918; from an East Harlem district as a Progressive in 1922; as a Socialist in 1924; as a Republican and Progressive in 1926; and as a Republican in 1928 and 1930. In 1932 he lost a special election for mayor, but in 1933 he was elected to a four-year term. In the Depression years LaGuardia built housing projects and parks, expressways and an airport, often with federal aid from Roosevelt. The garment workers' unions created a new American Labor Party, on whose line members could vote for Roosevelt and LaGuardia; when this was taken over by Communists in the 1940s, they established the Liberal Party for the same purpose.[174] These parties, with mainly Jewish working-class constituencies, reflected their ambivalence toward the Democratic Party.

Another current in American Jewish politics was Zionism. Initially few eastern European immigrants or prominent German Jews wanted to create a Jewish homeland in Palestine; they saw America, with all its flaws, as the best country for Jews. That started to change in 1914, when Louis Brandeis, then a nationally prominent Boston lawyer, became head of the Federation of American Zionists. Previously unobservant and uninterested in Jewish affairs, Brandeis had become a convinced Zionist, and he persuaded others that this was entirely consistent with loyalty to America. "To be good Americans, we must be better Jews, and to be better Jews, we must become Zionists," he often said.[175] Brandeis, by then a justice of the Supreme Court, conducted negotiations with President Wilson, British Foreign Minister Arthur Balfour, and Zionist leader Chaim Weizmann to get Wilson's endorsement of the November 1917 Balfour Declaration.[176] But many prominent Jews opposed Zionism, and no consensus was reached in the aftermath of World War I, after which the focus shifted to the persecution of Jews in Poland and other new nations in central and eastern Europe.[177]

Even as they wavered between the two major parties and their competitors, Jews in overwhelming numbers embraced a

common view on issues that can be summed up in the word
liberal—for civil liberties and civil rights, against immigration
restriction and for protection of the Jewish people abroad, for
labor unions and government efforts to protect workers, for
public housing and public works projects.[178] This politics was a
response to the conditions they found in Russia and elsewhere in
Europe, as well as in the early years in the United States. On
most of these issues they were well to the left of most established
politicians of all parties. In the early 1930s only a handful of
senators—Democrats Robert Wagner of New York, Edward
Costigan of Colorado, and Burton Wheeler of Montana, and
progressive Republicans Robert La Follette Jr. of Wisconsin,
George Norris of Nebraska, and Bronson Cutting of New
Mexico—shared all these views.[179]

But so did Franklin Roosevelt. Indeed, the position of
the Jews as the fulcrum point in the political balance in New
York, which was the key marginal state between 1920 and 1960
and had as many as forty-nine electoral votes during that period,
and the importance of the Jewish vote in New Jersey, Pennsylvania, and Illinois, which were also marginal in close elections,
gave politicians of both parties an incentive to support liberal
policies on a wide range of issues. Roosevelt got 82 percent of the
Jewish vote in 1932 and 86 percent in 1936, carrying all the big
states (except for Pennsylvania in 1932) handily.[180] Hope of
making gains among Jews was the political impetus behind
the liberal Republicanism of Wendell Willkie, Thomas Dewey,
Dwight Eisenhower, and Nelson Rockefeller, all New Yorkers
(Eisenhower temporarily, when he was president of Columbia
University) and all presidential candidates in those years. Jewish
voters were effective in moving both parties—and national
policy—to the left.

The rising importance of the Jewish vote and the increasing
prominence of Jews in public life led to greater anti-Semitism. In
1938 Father Charles Coughlin used his radio broadcasts to rail

against "communistic Jews," and at the same time he republished the discredited *Protocols of the Elders of Zion.*[181] Attacks on Jews were made openly in the successful Republican campaign against the ruling Farmer-Labor Party in Minnesota in 1938.[182] The 25,000-member German-American Bund between 1936 and 1941 heartily attacked Jews.[183] In 1941 Charles Lindbergh, opposing U.S. involvement in World War II, charged that "the leaders of the British and Jewish races, for reasons which are understandable from their viewpoint as they are inadvisable from ours, for reasons which are not American, wish to involve us in the war"—implying that Jews were not loyal Americans.[184] Such charges of dual loyalty, and polls showing rising anti-Semitism, help explain why Roosevelt allowed anti-Semitic State Department officials to bar Jewish refugees almost totally from the United States and why he refused to bomb the death camps or publicize the Holocaust.[185]

Anti-Semitism, on the rise in the 1930s, seemed to peak during the war years.[186] Attacks on Jewish schoolchildren were common, and Jews were treated with brutal prejudice in the military. In 1944 nearly 60 percent in one poll said Jews had too much influence in business and government and 25 percent said that Jews were less patriotic than other Americans.[187] In response, Jewish leaders were reticent about calling for action against Hitler and confined their efforts to a few behind-the-scenes imprecations. In addition, Jewish voters overwhelmingly supported Franklin Roosevelt, giving him over 80 percent of their votes in 1940 and 1944. Evidently they trusted him as the politician most likely to protect Jewish interests in a world that seemed so hostile to them.[188] But the United States welcomed few Jewish refugees and did little to impede the Holocaust, except of course to win the war.

Anti-Semitism ebbed after the war, but in the new Cold War, Jews were threatened by the stereotypes of the Jewish radical and the Jewish Communist. These stereotypes did have some basis in fact. Jews had been numerous and influential in the American Communist Party since its founding.[189] In the 1930s Jewish students at City College of New York, mostly second-generation Jews from economically humble circumstances, were attracted in large numbers to Communism and other radical causes.[190] These were also the years in which Jewish proletarian writers like Mike Gold and Clifford Odets achieved considerable notice and in which federally supported arts programs were attacked for supporting radical playwrights and artists.[191] The prominence of young Jewish lawyers and economists in the New Deal strengthened the image of the Jew as leftist.[192] This leftism in some ways seemed adversarial to traditional American values and traditions. But this was not the full picture. As historian Howard Sachar writes, "However left-of-center, the vast majority of American Jews had remained distinctly non-Communist even throughout the Depression's locust years of procommunism and fellow traveling. Among the presidents of major national Jewish organizations, not a single one accepted Soviet-style Marxism as an American panacea. American rabbis, many of whom expressed a friendly interest in socialism, remained steadfastly anti-Communist through the 1920s and 1930s."[193]

But the image was there, and when the United States broke with the Soviet Union after World War II, it was something for the Jewish community to contend with. This was one reason why many Jewish liberals worked to oust Jewish Communists from important posts in labor unions and the Democratic Party in the immediate postwar years. And when the Rosenbergs were prosecuted for espionage, it was Irving Saypol who led the prosecution and Irving Kaufman who presided over the trial and handed down the death sentences.[194] Even Joe McCarthy had as his top staffer the Jewish Roy Cohn, the son of a Democratic politician in the Bronx and one of the prosecutors of the Rosenbergs. By the 1950s Jews had proved they were loyal Americans beyond any doubt.

Also by the 1950s, Jews had achieved income levels high above the national average—so high that Jewish leaders opposed publication of a 1957 pilot census asking people's religion.[195] But, unlike the Irish and Italians, newly affluent Jews did not trend Republican. Political scientists have found that Jews are the one group who vote consistently against their economic interest. Indeed, by the middle 1960s Jews had emerged as one of the most Democratic of identifiable demographic groups and have remained so ever since. Some of this may be defensive: some Jews fear that gentiles will resent their success, and therefore they favor propitiating them by redistribution of income and wealth. Another motive was to protect the Jewish state of Israel. In the immediate postwar years Democrats were more pro-Israel; Harry Truman recognized the state of Israel immediately, against the advice of his leading aides, at the urging of his one-time haberdashery partner Eddie Jacobson.[196] Later, in 1972 and 1980, Jews trended Republican when their Democratic opponents seemed hostile to Israel. Richard Nixon had some success with Jewish voters in 1972 by arguing that the dovish George McGovern would not be as strong a supporter of Israel. And in 1980 and 1984, Ronald Reagan, who had made his way upward in a movie industry more heavily dominated by Jews than it is today, and as philosemitic a president as we have had since George Washington, made some inroads among Jewish voters—and carried New York in both elections.

In the 1990s Jewish voters reacted very negatively to the prominence of Christian conservatives in the Republican Party, and Jewish voters cast higher Democratic percentages than any ethnic group but blacks. In this we might still be seeing a reflection of the Russian experience. Habits of mind are shaped by family lore, and stories of forced conversions and persecution in pogroms by the Orthodox Church have made Jews exquisitely sensitive to the involvement of conservative Christians in politics. Leaders of Jewish organizations bristled in 1999 when

Southern Baptists announced a move to convert Jews, even though no forcible conversions are possible in America and even though the social disabilities that prompted many Jews to convert in the past have pretty well disappeared today. One could hear in their complaints an echo of the angry response of Lower East Side Jews to proselytizing Christians in the early twentieth century.[197] One could almost say that American Jews are still voting against the tsar.

SPORTS AND ENTERTAINMENT

The first sport in which Jews excelled was boxing; many wore Stars of David on their trunks.[198] The Lower East Side, writes Howard Sachar, "was the breeding ground of great Jewish fighters, such as Abe Attell, Benny Leonard, Ruby Goldstein, and Barney Ross, all of whom were the children of immigrants. At one point in the 1920s, seven of the nine boxing championships were held by Jews. The striking exception was the heavyweight championship, simply because the Jews did not produce many physical specimens in that weight range. Even so, one of the leading champions of the 1930s, Max Baer, pretended to be a Jew, because Jews were so prominent among the fight fans."[199]

Jews also played professional baseball, where they were often the target of anti-Semitic gibes on the field. Perhaps the most famous Jewish baseball player was Hank Greenberg, who in 1938 threatened Babe Ruth's record of sixty home runs in one season; Greenberg declined to play on the Sabbath or holy days. He was drafted into the army in May 1941 and released December 5. Two days later the Japanese bombed Pearl Harbor, and he immediately reenlisted. "We are in trouble and there is only one thing for me to do—return to the service," he said.[200] Another great Jewish ballplayer, pitcher Sandy Koufax, also declined to play on the Sabbath; he pitched four no-hitters, including one perfect game, and retired at the relatively young age of thirty in 1966. Few Jews have ever been notable football players, for relatively few had the size required to play the game. More Jews played basketball, a quintessential city game, particularly on college and professional teams in the 1930s and 1940s, when the sport had a relatively small following.

To a very great extent American show business during most of the twentieth century was a Jewish business. Like the retail and garment trades, this was a new and rapidly developing business, one with no established producers, and one that paid a huge premium to those able to gauge the fast-changing tastes of people different from themselves. As Paul Johnson writes, "The Broadway musical, radio, and TV were all examples of a fundamental principle in Jewish diaspora history: Jews opening up a completely new field in business and culture, a *tabula rasa* on which to set their mark, before other interests had a chance to take possession, erect guild or professional fortifications, and deny them entry."[201]

The story of Jewish success in show business begins with the theater, both the English-speaking theater that became centered on Broadway near Times Square and the Yiddish-speaking theater that thrived on the Lower East Side. The first Yiddish theater production on the Lower East Side opened in 1882, and by 1917 there were thirty such companies. Great hits included Jacob Grodin's *Siberia* and *The Jewish King Lear*.[202] Uptown, even before 1900, Jews dominated the booking circuits, which sent plays from Broadway to theaters all over the country. A group of Jews formed a syndicate in 1900 to control the Broadway theaters; it was challenged within a decade by the Shubert brothers, who by 1929 financed and controlled 75 percent of Broadway productions. Other great Jewish producers in the early 1900s included Florenz Ziegfeld, known for his eponymous follies, and legitimate theater impresarios Charles Frohman and David Belasco. Higher-tone productions were financed by the Theater Guild, headed by well-established German Jews like Otto Kahn and Maurice Wert-heim.[203] The 1920s saw the creation of the Broadway musical, the product almost entirely of a dazzling array of Jewish composers and lyricists—Jerome Kern, Irving Berlin, George and Ira Gershwin, Richard Rodgers, Lorenz Hart, Oscar Hammerstein Jr., Leonard Bernstein, Alan Lerner and Frederick Lowe, and ulti-mately Stephen Sondheim.[204]

But the greatest financial success, and the development of a quintessentially American popular culture, came with the movies. It started with nickelodeons, where viewers could watch a five-minute silent film. These became the rage in the 1890s, and in the first decade of the twentieth century there were thou-sands, mostly owned by Jews.[205] Almost no one thought that there was a mass market for longer films, and in any case a Motion Picture Patents Trust seemed to bar entry to the busi-ness. But Carl Laemmle, manager of a clothing store in Oshkosh, Wisconsin, had the idea of moving to Los Angeles to make movies, where he dodged the trust's process servers by ducking into Mexico and setting up a studio in Universal City. Other movie pioneers who found their way to Hollywood (then a Los Angeles suburb where some, but not all, of the studios were built) were Adolph Zukor, a fur distributor; Marcus Lowe, a fur trader; Jesse Lasky, a vaudeville trooper; Sam Goldfish (later Goldwyn), a glove salesman; Louis Mayer, a junk dealer; Harry Cohn; and the Warner brothers. Critical early financing came from the Bank of America, headed by Italian immigrant A. P. Giannini. As the business grew, financial control remained in the hands of theater owners, like Lowe and Joseph Schenck, who remained in New York. But the product—the silent movies of the 1910s and 1920s and the splendid talkies of the 1930s and 1940s—was the creation of immigrant Jews who spoke fractured English, who were motivated most of all by the desire to make money, and who created the most vibrant popular culture since Dickens. As Paul Johnson writes, "Like the Jews who rationalized the retail trade in the eighteenth century and created the first big stores in the nineteenth, they served the customer. 'If the audience don't like a picture,' Goldwyn said [with characteristically bad grammar], 'they have a good reason. The public is never wrong.'"206 The rewards were immense. In 1930, a Depression year when there were 130 million Americans, average *weekly* movie attendance was 90 million.207

The movie moguls were careful to avoid Jewish themes and seldom made pictures about the Jewish experience in America, though they did spotlight Jewish entertainers, like the Marx brothers, who had a broad appeal. They were also careful not to challenge American mores, and when scandal threatened them, they hired a midwestern Republican politician, Will Hays, to head up what amounted to a censorship office. Irving Howe most dramatically sums up their achievement: "Often vulgar, crude, and overbearing, they were brilliantly attuned to the needs of their business; they commanded and used to the full a profound instinct for the common denominator of taste; and they left a deep imprint on American popular culture. Trusting their own minds and hearts, shrewd enough not to pay too much attention to the talented and cultivated men they hired, the Moguls knew which appeal to sentiment, which twirl of fantasy, which touch of violence, which innuendo of sexuality, would grasp native American audiences. It was something of a miracle and something of a joke. They had come from the Ukraine and Poland and Austria-Hungary; they still spoke with Yiddish accents; but it was they, more than anyone else, who reached the fantasies of America, indeed of the entire world—a universalism of taste which shaped the century and which they could shrewdly exploit because they innocently shared it."208

Radio and television entertainment was also largely the creation of Jews. The first nationwide radio network, NBC, was the creation of Robert Sarnoff, who as a young man had reported the SOS from the *Titanic*. Its great competitor, CBS, was the creation of William Paley, who invested money from his family's cigar business. Both excelled at creating popular programming, in the 1930s and 1940s, on radio and, after 1950, on television. The third major network, ABC, originally a spin-off from NBC, was headed for many years by Leonard Goldenson, who persevered until it became a worthy competitor of the other two in the early 1960s. In the process, all three created great news organizations, which for about three decades were Americans' chief source of information.

Neither the movies nor radio or television had many characters who were explicitly Jewish, though many actors and performers were Jewish. Actors, comedians, and singers like Al Jolson, George Jessel, Eddie Cantor, Sophie Tucker, Fanny Brice, Ben Blue, Jack Benny, George Burns, Milton Berle, Ted Lewis, Bennie Fields, and the Marx brothers made their way from the theater of the Lower East Side and vaudeville into movies, radio, and television, with for the most part neither emphasis on nor denial of their Jewishness.[209] The radio and television show *The Goldbergs*, a comedy about a Jewish family and its neighbors, was a rare exception. After World War II, Jewish comedians became more explicit about their Jewishness and flaunted Yiddish terms;[210] the high point may have come in the early 1950s, when television was available only in a few large metropolitan areas, and the audience was much more Jewish than it would be later.[211]

CONVERGENCE

The convergence of Jews into the larger American society has been different from that of other ethnic groups. First-generation immigrants of all backgrounds were typically ambivalent when their children learned English and took on American cultural ways; they wanted their children to succeed but did not want to be separated from them. But the second and third generations, even if they had moved only a little up the economic ladder, had fewer qualms about assimilating into the larger culture, confident that they could retain some quantum of the heritage of their old country while placing themselves in a position to be accepted fully as Americans. But second- and third-generation Jews were ambivalent about assimilation. They wanted to maintain their identity as Jews, an identity their forebears had cherished in the face of horrifying persecution. Scorn was often expressed for Jews who converted, or for rich German and Reform Jews who eschewed religious observance and downplayed their Jewish identity. Assimilation was seen as a threat to the survival of the Jewish people, which Jews had struggled to achieve in adverse circumstances for over three thousand years.

This was reflected in a low rate of intermarriage and intermingling with non-Jews. As late as 1957, a sample census found that only 3.5 percent of Jews were married to non-Jews. There was evidently no significant rise in intermarriage between the beginning of mass immigration in the 1890s up through the 1950s. Even when they became more affluent, Jews tended to live in mostly Jewish neighborhoods, partly out of choice but also because they were barred by elite Protestants from "exclusive" neighborhoods, as they were from elite clubs and resorts.[212] In business and the professions, they tended to associate mostly with other Jews; many Jews growing up in these years still found most of their friends among other Jews. It was easier for the relatively small numbers of other immigrant groups who achieved great success to make their way in elite institutions than it was for the relatively large number of Jews who were economically successful. To a considerable extent, Jews, with incomes far above average,[213] lived in a separate-but-equal Jewish America. Protest was limited. Jews of course backed civil rights bills and resented the discrimination, but they also saw that discrimination was helping to maintain the solidarity of the Jewish community and the survival of the Jews as a separate and distinct people.

All this started to change drastically in the 1960s. Ivy League universities, suddenly more interested in cultivating academic excellence than in maintaining social manners, had begun to loosen their quotas on Jewish applicants in the 1950s.[214] City clubs, threatened with loss of their tax exemptions, began to open up membership to Jews in 1966.[215] Restrictions on selling houses to Jews in "exclusive" neighborhoods seemed to melt away in the late 1960s, perhaps as a subconscious response by the non-Jewish elite to the passage of the federal civil rights acts it strongly supported.* Around the same time, white-shoe law firms in city after city began to hire Jewish associates and, in time, select Jewish partners.† Then again, many country clubs remained closed, and many large corporations remained inhospitable to Jewish executives.

Great changes also occurred as a result of the Six Days' War between Israel and its Arab enemies in June 1967. When Israel's survival seemed threatened, American Jews responded with an enormous and immediate outpouring of aid.[216] They urged President Lyndon Johnson, who through a long career had many close Jewish advisers and supporters, to stand by Israel, though at the outset he declared neutrality and pressured Israel to accept a cease-fire.[217] Then came the exhilaration of Israel's rapid and total victory. It was a vivid contrast to the U.S. military effort then foundering in Vietnam. But support of Israel did not seem in conflict with American interests, and supporters of Israel were not asking for American troops to be sent to aid the cause. After the Six Days' War, to a greater extent than ever before, support for Israel seemed central to Jewish identity in America.[218] In these days, when, as Howard Sachar writes, "in white America, anti-Semitism was disappearing as an effective force,"[219] American Jews were no

---

* I remember telling my friend Martin Doctoroff, when he bought a house on Willow Lane in Birmingham, Michigan, in 1968, that the days of restriction were finally over.

† It was clear to me that this was a very recent phenomenon when I was at Yale Law School between 1966 and 1969.

longer afraid to assert themselves politically to aid Jews in other parts of the world. As Arthur Hertzberg writes, perhaps too giddily, "After 1967 the Jews in America were freer, bolder, and more powerful than any community of Jews had ever been in the Diaspora."[220] American Jews did not hesitate to advocate the cause of Jews in the Soviet Union and in Israel in the 1970s and 1980s.

By 1970 Jews were, to quote Paul Johnson, "a totally assimilated community which still retained its Jewish consciousness."[221] Economically, they were more successful than any other identifiable group: Jewish family incomes by 1969 were 80 percent higher than those of other Americans. By 1990 half of Jews over twenty-five had completed college, and half of those went on to graduate school—percentages far higher than for any other identifiable group of Americans. Nearly 40 percent of employed Jews were in the professions and another 17 percent in managerial positions.[222] Since 1970, at least nineteen Jews have been elected to the Senate, many from states with small Jewish populations,* and dozens elected to the House. In 2000 Senator Joseph Lieberman of Connecticut, an Orthodox Jew, was nominated for vice president by the Democratic Party; his selection was widely interpreted as a political plus for the ticket.

Indeed, the greatest threat many thoughtful Jews have come to see for Jews in America is that they have become too assimilated. With less-than-replacement birth rates, Jews were becoming a smaller percentage of Americans—down from nearly 4 percent in the 1930s to 2 percent in 2000. Intermarriage, low in the early 1960s, rose to 50 percent in the 1990s.[223] Only 28 percent of children in mixed marriages were raised as Jews, with 41 percent raised as non-Jews, and 31 percent with no religion; only 20 percent got Jewish religious education, as com-

---

* The states include California (two Jewish senators), Connecticut (two), Florida, Michigan, Minnesota (two), Nebraska, Nevada, New Hampshire, New Jersey, New York (two), Ohio, Oregon, Pennsylvania, and Wisconsin (two).

pared to 70 percent of children whose parents were both Jews.[224] Moreover, the intermarriage rate of children of mixed marriages was 90 percent.[225] Only Orthodox Jews are producing large numbers of children, leading to the possibility that the American Jewish community two generations from now will be largely Orthodox, having eclipsed the Reform and Conservative Jewish communities.[226] As Elliott Abrams notes, "Jewish life that is not centered on Judaism is already disappearing in America, while traditional Judaism—and above all, Orthodoxy—which was expected to disappear, is stubbornly holding on."[227] Religious observance is limited or absent among most American Jews, and many believe that the essence of Judaism is the pursuit of social justice, which for them usually means liberal Democratic politics and opposing any government involvement with or endorsement of religion. But some fear that a decline in Jewish faith will result in an end to the Jewish community. As Arthur Hertzberg writes, "The embers of the classic Jewish faith still smolder, but they may be dying among the mainstream of American Jews. The rational evidence is that Jews will continue, with growing unhappiness, to bet their future as Jews on what they know. Their ethnic togetherness. But Jewish experience through the centuries has often been surprising and unpredictable. The need for and possibility of a spiritual revival are clear. If it does not happen, American Jewish history will soon end, and become a part of American history as a whole."[228]

But whatever the future, Jews have a secure place in America. They are not resented but are admired for their achievements; they are not disliked for their distinctive characteristics but appreciated for their contributions to the common culture. While no one should ever forget the persecution Jews have suffered, they are more secure in the United States today than anywhere at any time in history. Since 1970 Jews have become thoroughly interwoven into the American fabric. It took eighty years.

CHAPTER 6

ASIANS

THE OLD COUNTRY

A traveler in East Asia in the mid-1960s would have seen little evidence of the miraculous economic growth that was to come in the remainder of the century. Instead he would have seen one grim landscape after another. These were war-torn lands, mostly under the sway of dictatorships, impoverished despite a long tradition of trading and technology. The great Swedish sociologist Gunnar Myrdal, in his 1968 book *Asian Drama: An Inquiry into the Poverty of Nations*, forecast that Asia would be held down for years by overpopulation and poverty. There was little outward evidence that he was wrong. In Japan the bomb damage from World War II was mostly repaired, with the exception of central Hiroshima, which was left in ruins to show the impact of the atomic bomb; office buildings and factories were

going up, but housing was still mostly flimsy and the infrastructure shabby. Korea was still recovering from the 1950–1953 war,
which had destroyed much of this long-impoverished country.
China was ruled by a dictatorial Communist regime that killed
millions during its "Great Leap Forward" from 1958 to 1960; this
nation, with its ancient civilization and sophisticated culture, had
been in a state of civil war, with no effective central government,
for most of the years from the beginning of the Taiping rebellion
in 1850 until the Communist victory in 1949. Offshore, Taiwan
lived under the dictatorship of Chiang Kai-shek, whose hopes of
returning to the mainland were by now dashed. North Vietnam
lived under a Communist dictatorship, and South Vietnam was at
war against Viet Cong guerrillas and North Vietnamese troops.
Neighboring Laos had effectively been taken over by Communists in 1961; Cambodia, for the moment, had an independent
neutral government, which would be overrun by the murderous
Khmer Rouge in the 1970s. The Philippines, granted independence by the United States in 1946, had a democratic government, but it was riddled with corruption and in 1969 would see
dictatorship imposed by Ferdinand Marcos.

Most people in these Asian countries still lived in the countryside, in villages with ramshackle houses, dependent on unreliable
farms for their sustenance. Mass movement from the countryside
to the cities was only beginning and in China was blocked by the
totalitarian regime. The economic growth that would propel so
much of Asia into advanced economic status by 2000 was already
under way in some countries, but only in Japan was it widely
noticed. Many other countries saw growth blocked by the depre-
dations of war and the tyranny of Communist regimes.

These lands of East and Southeast Asia produced some 5 million immigrants to the United States from 1965 to 1997.[1] These
immigrants are the subject of this chapter, and as such the term
"Asian" as used in this book excludes immigrants from South
Asia and the Middle East. While the Census Bureau does classify

these peoples as "Asian," I have not included such immigrants because they do not share the similar cultural heritages of East and Southeast Asia. They also do not share the experiences of war, turmoil, and Communism that, in different ways, shaped the lives of the peoples of East and Southeast Asia for much of the twentieth century. Most of the people of this region—China, Taiwan, Hong Kong, Singapore, the overseas Chinese who dominate the economies of Malaysia, Thailand, Indonesia, and the Philippines—share what Francis Fukuyama calls a "relatively homogeneous Chinese economic culture."[2]

Some would object that these countries differ among themselves as much as the countries of western Europe do, and that Asians as defined here are a less homogeneous group than the Catholic Irish, southern blacks, southern Italians, Latinos, and eastern European Jews studied in previous chapters. And indeed, the resemblance between Asians and Jews is not as close as those between blacks and Irish and between Latinos and Italians. But there are enough similarities among the various groups of East and Southeast Asians and enough similarities between the experiences of immigrant Asians and immigrant Jews to make this examination worthwhile.

The guiding culture for almost the whole of this region is Chinese. Chinese culture is ancient, with roots that go as far back as European culture, with great material accomplishments and a sense of its own centrality and intrinsic superiority.[3] The cultures of Japan, Korea,[4] and Vietnam[5] are in many ways offshoots of Chinese culture. Central to this culture is the written language of Chinese ideographs, which are the basis also of Japanese writing. Although no common language is spoken in China, the regional languages all use the same written characters. Literacy is highly valued in the Chinese culture, and the elite mandarin bureaucracy used competitive examinations to fill its positions; that tradition, in Joel Kotkin's words, "served the Chinese much as the Talmudic tradition had aided the Jews in Europe—by providing a cultural disposition toward scholarship and academic achievement."[6] Uniting the culture also is the heritage of Confucius, which emphasizes above all duty to family.[7] "The true essence of Confucianism," writes Fukuyama, is "what Tu Wei-ming called the 'Confucian personal ethic.' The central core of this ethical teaching was the apotheosis of the family—in Chinese, the *jia*—as the social relationship to which all others were subordinate. Duty to family trumped all other duties, including obligations to emperor, Heaven, or any other source of temporal or divine authority." As a result, "There is no counterpart to the Judeo-Christian concept of a divine source of authority or higher law that can sanction an individual's revolt against the dictates of his family."[8] While the Jews of eastern Europe in the late nineteenth and early twentieth century saw as their goal the preservation of the Jewish people amid persecution, the East and Southeast Asians of the middle and later twentieth century saw as their goal the survival of their families and kinship groups amid war and dictatorship.

Until very recently, the large majority of East and Southeast Asians were peasants, but they were not barred from the commercial marketplace. The mandarin governments ordinarily provided the stability for successful market transactions and for the accumulation of property. Civil war, Japanese invasion, and Communist dictatorship hindered the workings of the market, but commercial habits of mind persisted, reasserting themselves when Deng Xiaoping loosened Mao Zedong's Communist controls. The commercial ethic has been especially strong among the overseas Chinese, who come mostly from the south coastal provinces of Guangdong and Fujian,[9] which have also been the source of most immigrants to the United States. They have built small-scale businesses with family ownership and network connections, which in some cases have become very large businesses indeed. Such firms are the norm in Taiwan, Hong Kong, and Singapore, and overseas Chinese, though heavily outnumbered, account for most of the gross domestic product of Malaysia, Thailand, and Indonesia and much of it in Vietnam.[10] "Like the Jews in Poland and elsewhere in Europe," Joel Kotkin writes, the overseas Chinese have "dominated many critical commercial niches as traders, artisans, and skilled workers, often filling the 'middleman' role between the dominant elite—made up of European merchants, plantation owners, and colonial officials—and the masses of native agriculturalists. Cut off from their native land, much like the Jews, they had little alternative but to engage in such activities as trading and money lending."[11] Also like the Jews, they have been resented for their economic success[12] and persecuted for their ethnic separateness,[13] most notably when more than 1 million Chinese ethnics were massacred in Indonesia in 1965.[14]

The experience of East and Southeast Asians over the first two-thirds of the twentieth century was one of chronic insecurity. China was racked by revolution and civil wars from 1911 to 1937; it was attacked and in large part occupied by the Japanese from 1937 to 1945; after the Communist victory in 1949 came the Great Leap Forward in the 1950s and the Cultural Revolution of the 1960s and 1970s, which killed millions and uprooted millions more. Japan occupied, and ruled brutally, Taiwan from 1895 to 1945, Korea from 1910 to 1945, and Vietnam from 1942 to 1945. War divided and devastated Korea from 1950 to 1953 and Vietnam from 1965 to 1975. After 1949, overseas Chinese, while often prosperous, were cut off from their ties with China and were always at risk of persecution.[15] But despite these woes, Asian habits of mind—the centrality of family, the respect for literacy, commercial competence—persisted.[16]

Many East and Southeast Asians fled their native countries, particularly in the two decades after World War II, and many more would have done so had they been able. How many would have immigrated to the United States is something no one can know. As we will see, due to anti-Asian prejudice the United

States passed laws that almost entirely barred Asian immigrants from this country.

THE JOURNEY

The massive Asian immigration to the United States was triggered not by an event in Asia but, inadvertently, by the Immigration Act of 1965. For many years representatives of heavily ethnic big city congressional districts had sought to repeal the 1924 immigration act's restrictive quotas on southern and eastern Europeans. Thousands of their constituents' relatives applied for entry, and under the quota system almost all would have to wait years until spaces opened up. But their proposals to increase quotas were defeated by overwhelming margins. The McCarran-Walter Act, which maintained the quotas, was passed over President Harry Truman's veto in 1952; opponents of quotas could not even summon the one-third of the votes required to prevent an override.[17] John Kennedy, who authored a small book called *A Nation of Immigrants,* called for liberalizing immigration in 1960, an obvious attempt to appeal to Italian and Jewish voters (they would have voted overwhelmingly for him regardless). But Kennedy did not press the issue as president, instead submitting a bill that would phase out national quotas but retain an overall limit of 156,700 immigrants a year.[18]

The man chiefly responsible for the Immigration Act of 1965 was Kennedy's successor, Lyndon Johnson. Johnson came to office determined to pass what became the Civil Rights Act of 1964, and he saw immigration reform as another civil rights issue; national quotas to him were "alien to the American dream." In 1964 he mentioned the issue in his state of the union address, and in 1965 he made it a major priority, telling House Speaker John McCormack, "There is no piece of legislation before the Congress that in terms of decency and equity is more demanding of passage than the immigration bill." Without Johnson's active support, it probably would not have passed.[19] The bill that passed Congress and that Johnson signed before the Statue of Liberty and with Ellis Island in the background raised the limit on total immigration to 290,000, with 170,000 from the Eastern Hemisphere; raised the quota for every nation to 20,000; expanded family unification provisions (which effectively allowed many more immigrants than the quotas provided); and rescinded all provisions that discriminated against Asians.

Evidently no one expected a significant increase in Asian immigration. Attorney General Robert Kennedy, testifying in 1964, predicted that the "Asia-Pacific triangle" would produce "approximately 5,000 [immigrants], after which immigration from that source would virtually disappear."[20] As Stephan Thernstrom writes, the framers of the bill "claimed it would alter the volume and character of immigration very little, and airily dismissed critics who worried that it would bring about a huge increase in the number of Asian and African newcomers."[21] Some have speculated that Congress would not have passed the bill had it known the effects.[22] In his speech as he signed the bill, Johnson mentioned developing countries only once.[23]

Johnson and just about everyone else apparently assumed that since immigrants had always come from Europe, they must always come from Europe. But the Europe of 1965 did not resemble the Europe that had produced the waves of immigration from 1846 to 1924. In the twenty years since World War II, western Europe had grown affluent, and immigration from its poorer regions went almost entirely toward more affluent parts of Europe. But many countries in East and Southeast Asia were advancing from underdeveloped farming to industrial economies, and individuals in areas left behind were ready to move elsewhere. One country, Japan, had already developed an advanced economy, and immigration to the United States from Japan since 1965 has been of no greater magnitude than from the advanced countries of western Europe (just over 100,000 immigrants from 1965 to 1997). To be sure, Communist dictatorships prevented people from leaving China, North Korea, and North Vietnam. But others would flee to get out of the way of threatened Communist advance or persecution.

Immigration to the United States at first accelerated slowly, then increased dramatically in the 1970s and 1980s, as family unification provisions allowed most countries to send far more than their quotas, and increased again in the 1990s. From 1965 to 1997, 840,000 immigrants came from China, Taiwan, and Hong Kong. The number of immigrants from South Korea was 491,000, with the rate of immigration dropping off sharply after 1987, when the military government was replaced by an elected civilian government and the Korean economy began to grow (per capita income reached $10,000 in 1995).[24] Immigration from the Philippines was 975,000, the largest from Southeast Asia, though only a little ahead of Vietnam's 757,000. Laos produced 183,000 immigrants—mostly refugees from a backward country; Cambodia, 128,000; Thailand, 100,000. Immigration from Indonesia and Malaysia was much lower. Of the many immigrants to come from the Philippines, Vietnam, and the rest of Southeast Asia, a high percentage were ethnic Chinese, although it is not clear exactly how many.

Immigration from some countries will likely diminish as their economies grow, as it already has from Japan and South Korea, but there is a vast reservoir of Asians, in China and elsewhere, who are potential immigrants. The current high rate of Asian immigration seems likely to continue for many years.

THE NEW COUNTRY

Unlike Latinos, Asians have not lived in the United States from time immemorial, unless one counts the native Hawaiians who are part of the census classification of "Asians and Pacific Islanders."* Chinese laborers, 90 percent of them males, came to California after the Gold Rush of 1849; they were 9 percent of the state's population in 1870 and 1880, but their numbers dropped after the nativist-inspired Chinese Exclusion Act of 1882.[25] For years these bachelor immigrants were concentrated in the Chinatowns of San Francisco, New York, Boston, and Chicago. Between 1884 and 1906, some 300,000 Japanese immigrated to Hawaii and California to work as agricultural laborers, but many were sojourners who returned to Japan. California politicians demanded a Japanese exclusion act, but the Japanese government protested bitterly, and Theodore Roosevelt negotiated the so-called Gentleman's Agreement of 1907, in which Japan barred emigration of male laborers and the United States agreed to allow family reunification.[26] Then the 1924 immigration act cut off Asian immigration completely, except from the Philippines, which was U.S. territory at the time. (Still, before 1946, Filipinos could not become U.S. citizens, which limited the number of immigrants from the Philippines.)

As a result, only a little more than 1 percent of people living in the United States in 1965 were of Asian descent. Many lived in Hawaii, where Japanese-Americans formed a Democratic political machine that has controlled the state government continuously since 1962; it has prospered by proposing balanced tickets including Chinese, native Hawaiians, Filipinos, and whites, but the Japanese-Americans who make up almost one-third of the state's population are the core of its support. California was the mainland state with the largest number of Asians, mostly Chinese, Japanese, and Filipino.

Prior to 1945 anti-Asian prejudice in this country was prevalent and often vitriolic. The Chinese Exclusion Act and the

---

* Hawaii's Senator Daniel Akaka, who is of native Hawaiian descent, proposed that native Hawaiians be included in the American Indians category. Instead the Census Bureau in 2000 had a new category, Native Hawaiian and other Pacific Islander.

Gentleman's Agreement with Japan show that when Asians migrated in large numbers they encountered hatred of a depth and virulence difficult to imagine today. During World War II, the term "Japs" was used routinely and without embarrassment in headlines and by public officials. The internment of Japanese-Americans in the three West Coast states in World War II was overwhelmingly popular, and it was not the product of political troglodytes; Earl Warren won the California governorship in 1942 by calling for internment, President Franklin Roosevelt cheerfully ordered it carried out, and the Supreme Court upheld its constitutionality in a 7-2 decision. Some 80,000 Japanese-Americans were uprooted from California, many of them vegetable farmers who lost their land; only 40,000 returned to the state after internment ended in January 1945, and they were greeted with "threats, vandalism, arson, and minor outrages," in the words of John Gunther.[27]

Such attitudes became much less common in the twenty years after World War II. Racial prejudice declined generally in those years, and the well publicized record of the Japanese-American military units, among the most heavily decorated in history—and the fact that the sons of internment camp detainees petitioned for the right to serve—inspired widespread admiration. It may have helped that Japan, after its government and economy were reformed by General Douglas MacArthur, became an American ally. Americans also fought wars to preserve freedom for Koreans and Vietnamese, and, while government policy was not always popular during these conflicts, there was no public outcry against American boys dying to save Asians. Indeed, by the late 1960s Asians were being called the "model minority,"[28] a term used in a 1966 *New York Times Magazine* article in which the author argued that, through their own efforts, without government aid, Japanese-Americans had become model citizens. "By any criterion of good citizenship that we choose, Japanese Americans are better than any other group in our society, including native-born whites."[29] This characterization has come to be resented by leaders in many Asian-American organizations, who are inclined to focus on the problems and any discrimination faced by those in whose name they speak. But it is an opinion that has come to be broadly shared. When asked in 1985 whether immigrants of different nationalities generally benefit the country or create problems, respondents to a *USA Today*/CNN poll gave a favorable response to Chinese by a 69 to 13 percent margin, to Koreans by a 52 to 23 percent margin, and to Vietnamese by a 47 to 30 percent margin. The poll also found that 74 percent thought Asian immigrants "work very hard" and that 77 percent thought they "have strong family values."[30] It is hard to find in Americans' attitudes toward Asians in the years after 1965 more than a trace of the hostility that prevailed from the 1880s to the 1940s.

The 1 percent of Americans of Asian descent in 1965 were soon heavily outnumbered by the new Asian immigrants and their children. Like the Jews nearly a century before, Asians tended to head to large cities and metropolitan areas. Most Chinese immigrants went to New York, to Chinatown in Lower Manhattan. Later the "new Chinatowns" developed in Flushing, Queens, and Sunset Park, Brooklyn, and in recent years Chinese immigrants have typically started off in Manhattan and then headed quickly to Flushing or Sunset Park.[31] (The number 7 subway line in Queens, which terminates in Flushing, is known as "the Orient Express.") These new Chinatowns are crowded neighborhoods, with apartments where men sleep three to a room and overcrowded schools. Stores have signs with Chinese characters, Chinese food and other merchandise is widely available, and the local library carries Chinese-language books and periodicals. Some scholars focus on the poverty of residents, the poor working conditions and pay in garment sweatshops, and the dirt and disorder. But others emphasize the fact that immigrants with little or no English can easily find jobs and have a good opportunity to rise.[32]

California has become the second most common destination of the Chinese. As in New York, immigrants tend to start off in the Chinatowns of the central city but move to outlying neighborhoods or suburbs. In the San Francisco Bay area, Chinese immigrants have moved in large numbers to the ocean-facing neighborhoods of Richmond and Sunset, to the adjacent suburbs of Daly City and Pacific, and, among scientists and techies, to Silicon Valley. In Los Angeles County, many Chinese have headed to Monterey Park, a suburb ten miles east of downtown Los Angeles that by 1990 was 63 percent Chinese. Chinese have also moved in large numbers to nearby Alhambra, Rosemead, Diamond Bar, and Hacienda Heights, and to the nearby high-income suburbs of San Marino and South Pasadena.

Much attention has been given to the poverty of Chinese immigrants and to the smuggling of immigrants into the United States, an issue that drew notice in 1993 when the freighter *Golden Venture* ran aground off Queens, New York, and ten illegal immigrants were killed. But a large minority of Chinese immigrants are middle-class and arrive with substantial amounts of capital.[33] Some are part of what Joel Kotkin calls "Chinese global networks," connecting businessmen with family and others as far away as Hong Kong, Taiwan, Thailand, Indonesia, and Canada.[34] These "Uptown Chinese," as Peter Kwong calls them,[35] often are professionals or come over as students who already know English; between 1965 and 1985 some 150,000 Taiwanese came to the United States to study in college or graduate school, and many remained here as professionals.[36] Higher-skill Chinese are more likely to head to California,[37] whereas low-skill Chinese tend to go to New York, where low-skill jobs are plentiful in the city's Chinatowns. The Uptown Chinese generally avoid Chinatowns and low-income areas, moving instead into comfortable or affluent suburbs. There is some clustering—in Monterey Park, California, and in Fort Lee, New Jersey, which is one-fifth Asian—but Uptown Chinese and other similar Asians are, as Nancy Foner writes, "generally dispersed among many heavily white suburban communities where the Asian share of the population tends to be small."[38]

Like the Chinese, many Korean immigrants have come from a commercial background. One study showed that nearly half of Korean immigrants in the 1970s had worked in professional and technical jobs in Korea.[39] And although only about 20 percent of the Korean population is Christian, almost half of Korean immigrants are Christians.[40] The favorite destination for Korean immigrants has been Los Angeles, whose Koreatown neighborhood, centering on Western Avenue and Olympic Boulevard, became internationally known when black rioters destroyed hundreds of stores in the 1992 riot. Koreans have also immigrated in large numbers to New York and to metropolitan Washington, and in lesser numbers to other large cities. As noted, the rate of Korean immigration fell sharply in the 1990s, due in large part to growth in South Korea's economy.

Many Filipino immigrants, meanwhile, have come looking for low-wage work, but a number of nurses and other medical professionals have immigrated as well. They have gone in the largest numbers to California and Hawaii. There are particularly large Filipino communities northeast of San Francisco Bay, in the towns of Vallejo, Pittsburg, and Martinez.[41]

The first wave of Vietnamese immigrants came after the fall of Saigon in 1975; most of the 130,000 who fled to America were middle class. Another 400,000 boat people followed, as did 20,000 who arrived by land (having fled on foot to Cambodia in the 1970s and 1980s), and these immigrants were not necessarily middle class. When in 1989 the Communist government of Vietnam agreed to an orderly departure program, it permitted many more to leave; in the 1990s the United States accepted some 90,000 Amerasians (the biracial children of U.S. servicemen) and 165,000 survivors of Communist reeducation camps.[42] The number one destination for Vietnamese immigrants has been California, with a large concentration around "Little Saigon"—Westminster and Garden Grove in Orange County.⁴³ Many Vietnamese have also gone to Texas—at first fishermen plying their trade on the Gulf of Mexico, then others in larger numbers to Houston.

Most immigrants and refugees from Laos have been Hmong, an aboriginal people with little or no experience with urban life. Their biggest concentrations are in Fresno, California, and in Minneapolis.⁴⁴ The most frequent destination of Cambodian immigrants has been the old mill town and now high-tech town of Lowell, Massachusetts.⁴⁵

In 1998 the Census Bureau estimated that there were 10 million "Asian and Pacific Islanders" in the United States, ten times as many as in 1965 and 4 percent of the total population. California has 4 million Asians, 12 percent of its population; Hawaii has 756,000, nearly two-thirds of its population.

WORK

Of Asians it could be said, as Nathan Glazer said of eastern European Jews, that wherever they went, they became in large proportions businessmen and showed a fierce passion to have their children educated and become professionals. But there are considerable differences among the various nationalities. Koreans have been very entrepreneurial: surveys of Korean immigrants have shown that 45 percent in Los Angeles and Orange Counties and over 50 percent in New York City are self-employed (the national average is just 7 percent).⁴⁶ Many Chinese immigrants have started off working in garment, toy, or other factories located in Chinatowns, but, like immigrant Jews, a number have become owners of such businesses. As Kotkin reports, "Spurred by mass migration, Chinese and other Asians—including Vietnamese, Filipinos, and Koreans—by 1990 accounted for nearly three-fifths of all sewing contractors in [California], which at that juncture had surpassed

New York as the largest center of American garment production."[47] Some groups with little experience with commerce, notably the Hmong, have formed few businesses and have had high rates of unemployment.[48] Others have tended to hold relatively low-skill and low-paying jobs.

For the most part Asians have worked hard—their male workforce participation rate, 75 percent, is almost precisely the same as the national average[49]—and have very often become business owners. Examples are familiar: the Korean groceries of New York, the Chinese apparel factories of Los Angeles, the Vietnamese convenience stores of Orange County. Success is not guaranteed and is sometimes resented: Korean stores were the target of many Los Angeles rioters in 1992, as well as of a much-publicized (by the Reverend Al Sharpton) boycott in a black neighborhood in Brooklyn in 1993.[50] But success has been the story more often than failure.

One key to Asian entrepreneurial success is a practice brought over from Asia—the rotating credit association, what Richard Alba and Victor Nee call a formalized means of using "ethnic resources and solidarity in the accumulation of startup capital."[51] The Chinese *hui* and the Korean *keh* consist of a dozen or more members selected from among kin and people from the same village or lineage. Each month every member contributes a certain amount to a common pool, which is then given to one member, who typically uses it to buy a small business or a house. "As these associations turned larger and more sophisticated, they grew into quasi-credit unions, paying interests on deposits and lending out money," Francis Fukuyama writes. "For such an informal system to work, there had to be a high degree of trust among the association's members, which in turn was the result of preexisting social ties based on kinship or geographic residence in the native country."[52] The *hui* and the *keh* have provided backing for thousands of businesses that commercial banks would never have financed.

These businesses in turn have provided jobs to new immigrants, even those with limited or no English. One scholar estimated that in the 1980s 41 percent of Koreans in the New York area ran small businesses and that 80 percent of Korean immigrants in New York and 90 percent in Los Angeles worked in Korean-owned firms.[53] A high proportion of Chinese immigrants in the 1980s worked in Chinese-owned restaurants, garment factories, grocery stores, and other small businesses;[54] in New York's Chinatown, some 450 restaurants employ about 15,000 people, mostly men, and 500 garment factories employ about 20,000 women, almost all Chinese.[55] Of course, not all immigrants prosper, at least immediately, which is why the smuggling of immigrants has drawn attention. In fact, there is a lively trade in which gang members known as "snakeheads" smuggle illegal aliens, often Chinese from the Fujian province, into New York and other cities under conditions—a fee in the range of $30,000, to be repaid in three years—that result in something like indentured servitude.[56]

Chinese and other Asians also achieved great success in engineering and the sciences.[57] Many who enroll in American graduate schools stay on to work in American firms—or start their own. Indeed, without these immigrants the United States would face a severe shortage of engineers and scientists.

Despite the continual arrival of large numbers of poor immigrants, Asians' income levels are well above the national average. In 1997 the median household income among Asians was 22 percent higher than the national average. This is all the more astonishing in that about 70 percent of Asians are foreign-born. Even among Vietnamese, who are more likely than average to rely on public assistance, median household incomes had reached the national average by 1990.[58] Unemployment among Korean and Chinese immigrants seems to be very uncommon. In all, Asians appear to be rising even more rapidly economically than did the Jews and far more rapidly than any other immigrant group.

EDUCATION

The Confucian tradition placed a high value on education and literacy,[59] and the mandarin system of choosing government officials by competitive examination, used in Korea as well as China, meant that education was an economic asset in Asian society. [60] So Asians arrived in America with a high regard for education. Indeed, most early Korean immigrants had already graduated from college in Korea,[61] and many Korean and Chinese immigrated precisely because they wanted their children to get a degree at an American university. Even among first-generation immigrants, education levels have been high. In New York City in 1990, 20 percent of post-1965 Chinese immigrants were college graduates and another 16 percent had some college education. The figures were even higher among Koreans—31 percent college graduates and 21 percent with some college. And among Filipinos, 63 percent were college graduates and another 22 percent had some college.[62]

In their drive for education, Asian immigrants often avoid the troubled-plagued central city public schools and instead struggle to buy the least expensive houses in high-ranking suburban school districts.[63] Or if they do live in central cities, they work to keep their children away from what Min Zhou and Carl Bankston call "the oppositional youth culture that surrounds them."[64] Asian-Americans have avoided the perils of "bilingual" education because few school districts are prepared to offer instruction in the many Asian languages (although, interestingly, it was a Chinese-American who brought the Supreme Court case which produced the requirement that some accommodation be made to foreign-language students).

And the performance of the children of Asian immigrants in school has been spectacular. Asians have tended to score far above average on standardized tests like the SAT. Asians are only 4 percent of the nation's population, but in 1995 they made up

14 percent of those scoring 700 or better on the verbal SAT and 28 percent of those scoring over 750 on the math SAT.[65] They have won places at academically selective high schools in astonishing proportions. For example, in New York in 1995, Asian-Americans represented fully half the students at Stuyvesant High School, 40 percent at the Bronx High School of Science, and 33 percent at Brooklyn Technical High School—in a public school system in which 10 percent of students are Asian.[66] Some 15 percent of students at Stuyvesant and Bronx Science are Korean—although Koreans make up only 1 percent of total student population.[67]

This academic success seems to derive in part from the fact that Asian children are often pushed very hard by their parents. As one Korean mother told scholar Nancy Foner, "For my son's admission into Bronx High School of Science, I fasted for two years and prayed. After my son got into Bronx Science, I again fasted for a whole year for my daughter's admission to the same school."[68] The children often respond in kind. As one reporter summarized their attitude, "There's an old saying in Korea: sleep five hours, and you'll fail. Sleep four, and you'll pass. Stories of 15-hour school days with library study well into the early morning are common."[69]

The result is that Asians in the United States are very highly educated. According to the 1990 census, 37 percent of Asians (and 38 percent of foreign-born Asians) over twenty-five had a college degree, a figure far higher than the national average of 20 percent. Some 22 percent of Asians (and 25 percent of foreign-born Asians) over twenty-five had not finished high school, percentages similar to the national average of 25 percent.[70] Among those age eighteen to twenty-four, 77 percent of Chinese and 75 percent of Vietnamese were enrolled in school, as compared to 50 percent of whites and 43 percent of blacks.[71] And Asians, like Jews earlier in the twentieth century, have achieved such success despite the obstacles posed by quotas at selective colleges and universities. To be sure, the purposes of the quotas differed: the university quotas instituted in the 1920s were meant to reduce the number of Jews, while the quotas implemented in the 1970s were designed to increase the number of blacks and Latinos. But the effect has been the same as it was with the Jews—to make it more difficult for Asians with certain grade-point averages and test scores to get into selective colleges. Even so, Asians have done so well in high school that in 1998 they accounted for 19 percent of the students at Harvard, 28 percent at MIT, 22 percent at Stanford, 39 percent at the University of California at Berkeley, 38 percent at UCLA, and 10 percent at the University of Michigan, despite that school's preference for state residents in a state with relatively few Asians.[72] Some students come directly from Asian countries to attend American universities. Students of Chinese descent accounted for one-third of foreign students in American doctoral programs in science and engineering by 1990.[73] Taiwanese alone accounted for one in four candidates for doctorates in electrical engineering in the United States by 1990.[74]

One by-product of this is that Asian students in American colleges and universities tend to be dragooned into administration-approved Asian separatism. They are given "ethnic counselors," they are encouraged to sit at "Asian tables," and they are peppered with propaganda by Asian ethnic activists who are convinced that Asians suffer from terrible persecution. Evils of the past—the Japanese-American internment, the Chinese Exclusion Act—are constantly rehearsed as if they were evidence of American attitudes today, and unusual recent events—the murder of a Chinese young man by autoworkers in Detroit in 1982, the focus on Asian-Americans in the Clinton-Gore campaign finance scandals of 1996, the botched prosecution of atomic scientist Wen Ho Lee in 2000—are cited as evidence of enormous latent anti-Asian feeling.[75] All this is intended to discourage assimilation by people who, by most measures, are assimilating rapidly and excelling in the process.

But there is reason to hope that the attempts to build barriers around Asian-Americans will not succeed. Tamar Jacoby, a sensitive observer of Asian-Americans, writes, "Even the youngest and most radical do not seem to share the oppositional attitude and race-obsessed politics of today's civil rights establishment."[76]

FAMILY

Obligation to family is the strongest tenet of the Confucian heritage common to most Asians in America. In this tradition the relationship between father and son is paramount. As Francis Fukuyama writes, "Sons have the duty to defer, even as adults, to their parents' wishes, to support them economically when they are old, to worship their spirits once they are dead, and to keep alive a family line that can be traced backward to ancestors."[77] Under this tradition, property is inherited equally by sons. Daughters are less valued and become part—usually a very subordinate part—of their husbands' families when they marry. These features made sense in societies where taxation was often high and always arbitrary, where the state provided few services and no system of social security (in most Confucian societies the state still does not). Fukuyama again: "A peasant could only trust members of his own family, because those on the outside—officials, bureaucrats, local authorities, and gentry alike—felt no reciprocal sense of obligation to him and felt no constraints about treating him rapaciously."[78] Family obligation extends far beyond the nuclear family to those of the same village or who share a common lineage, which in some cases is traced back a thousand years. Although obligations to members of the immediate family are much stronger,[79] the sense of obligation is strong enough to ensure the success of the *hui* or *keh* rotating credit association.

Naturally, the tradition of family obligation has weakened somewhat among Asians in America. Most Asian children do not grow up in all-Asian neighborhoods, and they attend schools with many non-Asian children. Some come to resent or challenge the subordination of children to parents that is central to Confucian culture, to resist demands that they marry other Asians.[80] But at least for the moment, Asian families in America seem unusually strong.[81] According to the 1990 census, 78 percent of Asian households were composed of families, more than the 71 percent national average; the figure was even higher, 81 percent, among foreign-born Asians. Some 40 percent of Asian households were composed of married couples with children under eighteen, far above the national average of 26 percent; among foreign-born Asians the figure was 45 percent. Only 5 percent of Asian households were headed by women with children under eighteen, slightly below the national average of 6 percent; the corresponding figures for blacks and Hispanics were 19 percent and 12 percent, respectively.[82] In 1990, 92 percent of Chinese children and 83 percent of Southeast Asian children lived in two-parent families, as compared to 85 percent of white children and 47 percent of black children.[83] White Americans of the 1940s, whose suspicion of and hatred for Asians were so fierce, would surely be astonished to learn that Asian-Americans today are more faithfully living up to their own family values than their own descendants are.

RELIGION

Confucianism is a secular tradition, and most Asians are not religiously observant in the same ways that American Christians and Jews are. To be sure, there are Buddhist temples in the United States, the largest of which, the Hsi Lai Temple in Hacienda Heights, California, received national notice when Vice President Al Gore attended (unknowingly, he said later) a fund-raiser there in 1996. But many Asian immigrants arrived here as Christians, including about half of Korean immigrants and a not inconsiderable number of Vietnamese and Taiwanese. About 80 percent of the Vietnamese in Orange County's Little Saigon are Buddhists and 20 percent Catholics.[84] Christian missionaries, most of them Americans, in the early twentieth century produced many converts in China and Korea, and presumably these Christians are more likely than non-Christians to regard America as a congenial home. Korean and other Asian Christian churches preach a rigorous doctrine, and they probably reinforce the strong work habits and family loyalties that are also part of the Asian heritage. In many an American suburb today you can see Protestant churches, with traditional steeples or more modern architecture, sporting Korean letters on their signs announcing Sunday services.

CRIME

Asian-Americans are indeed the "model minority" when it comes to crime. Such statistics as there are suggest that a very low percentage of Asians commit crimes or are incarcerated. Some Asian teenagers and young men are members of Asian gangs, but these seem to be very much the exception rather than the rule. In addition, there are the "snakeheads," who as noted smuggle illegal Asian immigrants into the country.[85] And in New York's Chinatown there are tongs, sometimes renamed protective associations, which control youth gangs and engage in gambling, drug dealing, and extortion.[86]

DISTINCTIVENESS

Asians tend to have certain identifying physical characteristics, but such characteristics are much less noticeable among those with only one Asian parent. Golfer Tiger Woods has ancestors who were European, African, Cherokee Indian, and Thai. "Actually, I'm three-quarters Asian," he said in 1994, before he won any professional tournaments. When he won the Masters after an astonishing performance in 1997, his father, a former Green Beret, said, "We need a black in the green jacket." Woods described himself as "Cablinasian"—Caucasian, black, American Indian, and Asian—and was criticized by some black leaders for not asserting that he is black. But despite the controversy, Woods was accepted as a sports hero by a very large majority of fans, and for all his different ethnic ancestries can only be considered an American. Less frequently identified as a person of color is the movie star Keanu Reeves, famous since his role in *Speed* in 1994. Reeves's father is of Hawaiian and Chinese descent, his mother a native of England. His parents met in Lebanon, his father abandoned the mother, and his mother raised him in Canada. But he seems to be taken by most fans as just another handsome young American.

POLITICS

Like other immigrants, Asians' politics have been shaped by the countries from which they have come and the part of the United States where they live. Until recently, most Asians came from countries whose governments were dictatorial, authoritarian, or, in the cases of mainland China and Vietnam, totalitarian—governments that were at best callously indifferent to their citizens and at worst murderous. These backgrounds have left them with little experience in political and civic behavior.

Post-1965 Asian immigrants, like Jewish immigrants, have entered American politics gingerly, eager to participate but wary of prejudice. The Japanese-Americans of Hawaii, the descendants of early-twentieth-century immigrants and long inclined to group solidarity, have been at the center of the formidable Democratic machine that has run the state government for the past four decades. In trouble in 1998, the Democratic governor evoked the fifty-year-old experience of discrimination by Hawaii's big planters and the questioning of Japanese-Americans' patriotism in World War II.[87] The economically downscale Filipinos have also voted heavily Democratic.

In contrast, Korean, Vietnamese, and, to a lesser extent, Chinese immigrants, strongly anti-Communist and often entrepreneurial, have tended to vote Republican. The first Korean-American congressman, California Republican Jay Kim, was elected in 1992, 1994, and 1996 from a district including parts of Los Angeles, San Bernardino, and Orange Counties. But he was convicted of campaign finance violations for funneling money from his engineering firm into his campaign, and was defeated for renomination in 1998.[88] In California, Asian voters' Republicanism grew stronger in 1992 when Los Angeles civic leaders responded to the riot with sympathy for the rioters and indifference to the Korean and other Asian shop owners whose property was destroyed. More recently, however, California Asians have moved toward the Democrats. One reason was Proposition 187, passed in 1994, barring welfare for noncitizens; Asians, with their experience with mandarin bureaucracy, have been adept at securing Supplemental Security Income (SSI) and other aid for relatives who are not yet citizens. Also, the charges that ethnic Chinese made illegal contributions to the 1996 Clinton-Gore campaign and the targeting of Chinese-American scientists as possible spies—viewed as challenges to Asians' legitimacy and loyalty—have alienated Asian political activists and perhaps Asian voters as well.

In the 2000 election, the VNS exit poll showed Asian voters backing Al Gore over George W. Bush by a 55 to 41 percent margin. But that was due mainly to Hawaii, where Asians backed Gore, 61 to 35 percent. In California, with more than one-third of the nation's Asian voters, the vote was 48 percent for Gore and 47 percent for Bush—a reasonable facsimile of the national average. This was despite the efforts of an Asian group called the 80-20 Initiative, which sought to maximize Asian-Americans' political leverage by getting 80 percent of Asians to support one presidential candidate—in this case, the candidate was Al Gore.[89]

Asian voters, with their experience of oppressive government and their entrepreneurial drive, do not seem attracted to socialism, as so many Jewish immigrants and their children were. In fact, Asians do not seem to have the social democratic impulse toward a larger state or the sensitive regard for civil liberties so typical of Jewish Americans over the years. Their reference point is different: if Jews sometimes seem to be voting against the tsar, Asians—or at least many of them—seem to be voting against Mao. The liberal state in America—with its anti-Asian quotas and its indifference to the victims of ghetto rioting—in some ways appears to have been not the friend but the adversary of Asian immigrants. And, despite the cries of Asian-American activists on campus, the voting figures suggest that relatively few Asians see themselves as "people of color" fighting oppression and discrimination; they vote much more like whites than like blacks.

CONVERGENCE

Most Asian immigrants do not immediately blend into the larger society. Many have difficulty with the English language, especially elderly parents brought over by their sons. According to the 1990 census, only 62 percent of Asians and 49 percent of foreign-born Asians were able to speak English "very well." These numbers are roughly comparable to those for Hispanics, 61 percent of whom could speak English "very well," and somewhat ahead of foreign-born Hispanics, 33 percent of whom could do so.[90] But a considerably smaller proportion of Asians than Hispanics return to their native land, and a much higher percentage seek naturalization as citizens. Many Asian-American parents try to raise their children with respect for their Asian culture, but those efforts are not always successful. Intermarriage rates tend to be high. Among the

Japanese, long settled in the United States, the rate was over 50 percent as long ago as the 1970s,[91] and it appears to be rising among other groups. Current estimates are that 30 to 50 percent of the children of Asian immigrants marry non-Asians.[92]

Contrary to the plaints of campus activists, America seems to be more welcoming to Asians than it has been to any of the other groups studied in this book. There is no anti-Asian prejudice or discrimination comparable to the anti-Semitism that was common in America up through the 1960s—or even to the ferocious bigotry that Asians faced in the United States up through the 1940s. Tamar Jacoby is probably right in concluding that the large majority of Asians are rejecting the "oppositional" view of ethnic activists. Instead, she writes, "In cities across the country, Asians are charting [a] course, defining a vision of integration that allows for ethnic differences—sharp, flavorful, persistent differences—at home, but does not make too much of them in public life. It is an ideal that asks for tolerance, but not a public preoccupation with ethnicity. It comes with pride, but not a self-fulfilling prophecy of alienation, and it leaves to individuals to balance their ethnicity and their citizenship."[93]

Asian immigration is likely to continue at present or even higher levels; there are vast reservoirs of potential immigrants, especially from China, and one cannot rule out the possibility of a large inrush for political reasons. But the interweaving of Asians into the American fabric seems to be occurring very rapidly. It may take considerably less than eighty years.

CONCLUSION

WE'VE BEEN HERE BEFORE

S ometime in the twenty-first century, we are told in dozens of articles and books, the United States will no longer be a majority-white country. Our demographic future, it is said, will look like the California of today, where non-Latino whites make up less than 50 percent of the total population. Often these predictions are made with an air of satisfaction, even smugness, as if there is something wrong with being a mostly white nation or some virtue in being, as the phrase goes, majority-minority. Others make such predictions in anger, or in the hope of persuading Americans to stanch the flow of immigration before the racial character of the nation is inalterably changed. All seem convinced that something basic about America will be changed by the new Americans, that the country will be transformed into something it has never been before. These reactions are based on

the view of history suggested by Al Gore's mistranslation of
E pluribus unum: that we have always been a white-bread country,
and now we are on the verge of becoming a mixture of pumper-
nickel, rye, and white.

But race, as liberals have wisely insisted for years, is an arbitrary category. Americans a century ago casually referred to Irish,
Italian, Jewish, and other immigrants as separate races, just as
we refer to blacks, Latinos, and Asians as other races today.
We define race to include certain kinds of people with some
common characteristics and common backgrounds, but the cate-
gories are not airtight. Most Americans of African descent today
are also of European descent. "Hispanic" is a term invented
by government agencies to describe people who are of different
races and national origins and is determined solely by the
self-identification of the individual. Georgetown University
some years ago presumably included in its number of Hispanic
students Crown Prince Felipe of Spain, who, far from being a
member of a despised minority, is a direct descendant of King
Louis XIV and the Emperor Charles V. Asians include people
from a variety of countries with separate and often distinct ancestry. Americans today do not think of Irish, Italians, and Jews as
members of separate races; the bean counters of racial quotas and
preferences count them all as white. Americans one hundred
years from now may think of blacks, Latinos, and Asians not as
members of separate races but as Americans who share—in varying and mixed proportions—ancestry that is different from the
ancestry of other Americans.

The Americans of a hundred years ago were correct in
regarding Irish, Italian, and Jewish immigrants as different in
significant ways from native-born Americans. They were concentrated in certain city neighborhoods, bringing with them
distinctive habits of mind and patterns of behavior, unschooled in
American civic culture. The Americans of that day would have
been correct also to note, as in fact many did, that definable

groups of the native-born Americans of their day were different in significant ways from each other. The blacks of 1900 were different from the whites of 1900; southerners were different from northerners—indeed, more different than they are today, for the memory of the Civil War was still fresh; city dwellers were different from farmers; New Englanders were different from people in the western states.

Looking ahead from 1900, and using definitions of race that were common at the time, observers could have predicted that in a century a majority of Americans would be of a different race from the Americans who were here before the great waves of immigration began in the nineteenth century. That prediction has in fact come true. Most Americans today have at least one ancestor who was a post-1840 immigrant. By the definitions extant in 1900, we are already a majority-minority nation. But we are still a recognizably American nation. The descendants of the immigrants who were regarded as members of different races in 1900 have now become deeply interwoven into the fabric of American life. It is impossible to imagine what America would be like without them.

This can, should, almost certainly will happen again. There is no greater biological difference between the minority groups and other Americans of today than there was between the immigrant groups and other Americans of a hundred years ago. There is far less overt bigotry and discrimination in the early twenty-first century than in the early twentieth. And the minority groups of 2000 in important ways resemble the immigrant groups of 1900, as it has been the purpose of this book to argue.

The greatest obstacle to the interweaving of blacks, Latinos, and Asians into the fabric of American life is not so much the immigrants themselves or the great masses of the American people; it is the American elite. The American elite of a century ago may have looked on immigrants with distaste and taken care to bar Jews from elite institutions. But it also championed the cause of Americanization and promoted assimilation of immigrants into the mainstream.

Many members of the American elite today take a different view. Influenced by the civil rights movement and the Vietnam War, elites starting in the 1960s began to doubt the fundamental goodness and decency of the country they nevertheless felt entitled to lead. They became convinced that the white majority was obdurately racist and that racial quotas and preferences were needed to ensure that racism did not result in exclusion of blacks. They thoughtlessly extended that treatment to Latinos and Asians on the unexamined and erroneous assumption that their problems were similar to those of blacks. The goal of Americanization seemed suspect, and elites sanctioned policies such as bilingual education on the theory that enabling immigrants' children to master the English language was to wrongfully detach them from their native culture. When it became clear that bilingual education was retarding Latinos' chance to get ahead, elites simply ignored that fact and left in place the spoils system of the bilingual establishment. By the late 1970s, corporate, media, and university elites became dedicated to systems of racial quotas and preferences that allowed them to congratulate themselves on their open-mindedness but at the same time cast a cloud of illegitimacy over the genuine achievements of the intended beneficiaries. By holding favored minorities to lower standards than others, they practiced what George W. Bush has called "the soft bigotry of low expectations." In the process they have elicited from the favored groups a lower level of genuine achievement than was attainable.

Fortunately, there are trends in the other direction. The legal attack on racial quotas and preferences, in the courts and in referendums in California and Washington State, is leading to a moment when the elites will have to confront the fact that such programs violate the clear language of the Civil Rights Act of 1964. California's 1998 referendum abolishing the old system of

bilingual education is moving other states and localities to disman-
tle a system that has held Latinos back. Finally, after eight years of
a generally successful Democratic administration, in which the
president rhetorically paid tribute to American strengths and
virtues, liberal elites are less likely than they were in the 1980s to
take an adversarial and oppositional attitude toward the larger
society. The sense of American guilt prompted by the civil rights
movement and the Vietnam War may be waning. Confidence in
the basic goodness and decency of American institutions and the
American people may be growing, even among elites trained in
their universities to believe the worst of their country.

What is important now is to discard the notion that we are at
a totally new place in American history, that we are about to
change from a white-bread nation to a collection of peoples of
color. On the contrary, the new Americans of today, like the new
Americans of the past, can be interwoven into the fabric of
American life. In many ways, that is already happening, and rapidly. It can happen even more rapidly if all of us realize that that
interweaving is part of the basic character of the country and that
the descendants of the new Americans of today can be as much
an integral part of their country, and as capable of working their
way into its highest levels, as the descendants of the new
Americans of a hundred years ago.

NOTES

INTRODUCTION: THE NEW AMERICANS

1   Al Gore, "Address to the Institute of World Affairs," Milwaukee,
    January 6, 1994. Gore "carelessly turned the United States's most
    prized slogan into its exact opposite, a statement encouraging dissim-
    ilation." John Miller, *The Unmaking of Americans: How Multicul-
    turalism Has Undermined the Assimilation Ethic* (New York: The Free
    Press, 1998), 15.
2   Figures calculated from *Historical Statistics of the United States*
    (Washington, DC: U.S. Department of Commerce, Bureau of the
    Census, 1975), 8, 14.
3   See Robert C. Christopher, *Crashing the Gates: The De-WASPing of
    America's Power Elite* (New York: Simon & Schuster, 1989), 30; Peter D.
    Salins, *Assimilation, American Style* (New York: Basic Books, 1997), 25.
4   Howard M. Sachar, *A History of the Jews in America* (New York: Knopf,
    1992), 81–82; Douglas Southall Freeman, *Washington*, abridged (New
    York: Collier Books, 1992), 585.

5   Very similar is Peter Salins's concept of assimilation: "Immigrants
    would be welcome as full members of the American family if they
    agreed to abide by three basic precepts: First, they had to accept English
    as the national language. Second, they were expected to take pride in
    their American identity and believe in America's liberal democratic and
    egalitarian principles. Third, they were expected to live by what is
    commonly referred to as the Protestant ethic (to be self-reliant, hard-
    working, and morally upright)." Salins, *Assimilation, American Style*, 6.

6   For examples see John Miller, *The Unmaking of Americans*, 46–48.

7   Daniel Patrick Moynihan, "The Negro Family: The Case for
    National Action" (Office of Policy Planning and Research, United
    States Department of Labor, March 1965), 5.

8   Nathan Glazer and Daniel P. Moynihan, *Beyond the Melting Pot: The
    Negroes, Puerto Ricans, Jews, Italians, and Irish of New York City*
    (Cambridge, MA: MIT Press, 1963), 248.

9   Noel Ignatiev, *How the Irish Became White* (New York: Routledge, 1995).

10 John Miller, *The Unmaking of Americans*, 50.

11 Ibid., 51.

12 Ibid., 54–63.

13 Ibid., 105–113.

14 Salins, *Assimilation, American Style*, 12–18.

15 John Miller, *The Unmaking of Americans*, 120.

PART 1: IRISH AND BLACKS

1   Sir Henry Sumner Maine, *Ancient Law: Its Connection with the Early History
    of Society and Its Relation to Modern Ideas* (London: J. Murray, 1861), 170.

CHAPTER 1: IRISH

1   Colin McEvedy and Richard Jones, *Atlas of World Population History*
    (New York: Facts on File, 1978), 41–49.

2   Conor Cruise O'Brien, *The Great Melody: A Thematic Biography and
    Commented Anthology of Edmund Burke* (Chicago: University of Chi-
    cago Press, 1992).

3   Sean Duffy et al., *Atlas of Irish History* (New York: Macmillan, 1997), 84.

4   William V. Shannon, *The American Irish* (New York: Macmillan, 1966), 11.

5   Peter Quinn, "Farmers No More," in Michael Coffey and Terry Golway, eds. *The Irish in America* (New York: Hyperion, 1997), 41.

6   Shannon, *The American Irish*, 6; Andrew Greeley, *That Most Distressful Nation: The Taming of the American Irish* (Chicago: Quadrangle Books, 1972), 27–29.

7   John Bodnar, *The Transplanted: A History of Immigrants in Urban America* (Bloomington: Indiana Press, 1987), 151.

8   Ignatiev, *How the Irish Became White*, 35.

9   Patrick J. Blessing, "The Irish," in Stephan Thernstrom, ed., *Harvard Encyclopedia of American Ethnic Groups* (Cambridge, MA: Belknap Press of Harvard University, 1980), 529.

10   "Single people proliferated in the country where marriages were usually postponed due to a severe inability to inherit sufficient amounts of land on which to start a family." Bodnar, *The Transplanted*, 18.

11   Charles Morris, *American Catholic* (New York: Times Books, 1997), 30.

12   Shannon, *The American Irish*, 16-17; Greeley, *That Most Distressful Nation*, 30. The quoted phrase is Shannon's.

13   R. F. Foster, *Modern Ireland: 1600–1972* (New York: Viking Penguin, 1988), 278–285.

14   *Encyclopedia Britannica*, 11th ed., vol. 19, 991.

15   R. F. Foster, *Modern Ireland*, 298.

16   Ibid., 301.

17   Ibid., 298–302; Greeley, *That Most Distressful Nation*, 204–205.

18   R. F. Foster, *Modern Ireland*, 291, 313.

19   Kerby A. Miller, *Emigrants and Exiles: Ireland and the Irish Exodus to North America* (New York: Oxford University Press, 1985), 280–286.

20   "The potato famine only accelerated a process which would have taken place anyhow." Bodnar, *The Transplanted*, 28.

21   Kerby A. Miller, *Emigrants and Exiles*, 291.

22   Ibid., 292.

23   *Historical Statistics of the United States*, vol. 1, 105–109.

24   Shannon, *The American Irish*, 27.

25   Hasia Diner, "The Most Irish City in the Union: The Era of Great Migration, 1844–1877," in Ronald H. Bayor and Timothy J. Meagher, eds., *The New York Irish* (Baltimore: Johns Hopkins University Press, 1996), 91.

26 Blessing, "The Irish," in Thernstrom, *Harvard Encyclopedia of American Ethnic Groups*, 530.

27 Shannon, *The American Irish*, 27.

28 Frank McCourt, "Scraps and Leftovers: A Meditation," in Coffey and Golway, *The Irish in America*, 11.

29 Morris, *American Catholic*, 39.

30 Shannon, *The American Irish*, 16.

31 Kerby A. Miller, *Emigrants and Exiles*, 325–326.

32 Shannon, *The American Irish*, 16; Ignatiev, *How the Irish Became White*, 38–39.

33 Kerby A. Miller, *Emigrants and Exiles*, 325–326.

34 Thomas Sowell, *Ethnic America: A History* (New York: Basic Books, 1981), 26.

35 Diner, "The Most Irish City in the Union," in Bayor and Meagher, *The New York Irish*, 99–100.

36 Coffey and Golway, *The Irish in America*, 31.

37 Morris, *American Catholic*, 65.

38 Sowell, *Ethnic America*, 17.

39 Morris, *American Catholic*, 37.

40 Ibid., 65.

41 Frederick M. Binder and David M. Reimers, *All the Nations Under Heaven: An Ethnic and Racial History of New York City* (New York: Columbia University Press, 1995), 60.

42 Ibid., 536.

43 Ibid., 533.

44 Carl Wittke, *The Irish in America* (New York: Russell & Russell, 1970), 25.

45 Blessing, "The Irish," in Thernstrom, *Harvard Encyclopedia of American Ethnic Groups*, 531–532.

46 Binder and Reimers, *All the Nations Under Heaven*, 60.

47 Diner, "The Most Irish City in the Union," in Bayor and Meagher, *The New York Irish*, 95.

48 Binder and Reimers, *All the Nations Under Heaven*, 60.

49 Maureen Murphy, "Bridie, We Hardly Knew Ye: The Irish Domestics," in Coffey and Golway, *The Irish in America*, 141–146.

50 Wittke, *The Irish in America*, 45.

51 Diner, "The Most Irish City in the Union," in Bayor and Meagher, *The New York Irish*, 99–100.

52 Morris, *American Catholic*, 65.

53 Sowell, *Ethnic America*, 27.

54   Glazer and Moynihan, *Beyond the Melting Pot*, 219.

55   Olivier Zunz, *The Changing Face of Inequality: Urbanization, Industrial Development, and Immigrants in Detroit, 1880–1920* (Chicago: University of Chicago Press, 1982), 37.

56   Donald L. Miller, *City of the Century: The Epic of Chicago and the Making of America* (New York: Simon & Schuster, 1996), 441.

57   Sowell, *Ethnic America*, 37.

58   Joel Perlman and Roger Waldinger, "Immigrants Past and Present: A Reconsideration," in Charles Hirschman, Philip Kasinitz, and Josh DeWind, eds., *The Handbook of International Migration* (New York: Russell Sage Foundation, 1999), 225.

59   Blessing, "The Irish," in Thernstrom, *Harvard Encyclopedia of American Ethnic Groups*, 533.

60   Ibid., 536–537.

61   "Like other groups who went through generations under conditions in which they had little to gain or lose from their own actions, the Irish suffered not only the immediate losses from these [British] laws but also longer run losses from a social pattern of reduced initiative." Sowell, *Ethnic America*, 21.

62   Kerby A. Miller, *Emigrants and Exiles*, 519.

63   Ibid., 519.

64   Binder and Reimers, *All the Nations Under Heaven*, 98.

65   Ed O'Donnell, "United Front: The Irish and Organized Labor," in Coffey and Golway, *The Irish in America*, 155–158.

66   Sowell, *Ethnic America*, 37.

67   Diner, "The Most Irish City in the Union," in Bayor and Meagher, *The New York Irish*, 99.

68   Blessing, "The Irish," in Thernstrom, *Harvard Encyclopedia of American Ethnic Groups*, 533.

69   Ibid.

70   Ibid.

71   Greeley, *That Most Distressful Nation*, 100–101.

72   Sowell, *Ethnic America*, 28.

73   Zunz, *The Changing Face of Inequality*, 258.

74   Edward K. Spann, *The New Metropolis: New York City, 1840–1857* (New York: Columbia University Press, 1981), 27–28.

75   Glazer and Moynihan, *Beyond the Melting Pot*, 232.

76   Diner, "The Most Irish City in the Union," in Bayor and Meagher, *The New York Irish*, 99.

77   Ellen Skerrett, "Bricks and Mortar: Cornerstones of the Irish Presence," in Coffey and Golway, *The Irish in America*, 52; Binder and Reimers, *All the Nations Under Heaven*, 67.

78   Binder and Reimers, *All the Nations Under Heaven*, 67–68.

79   Glazer and Moynihan, *Beyond the Melting Pot*, 234–237; Daniel Patrick Moynihan, "How Catholics Feel About Federal School Aid," *The Reporter*, May 25, 1961, 36

80   Binder and Reimers, *All the Nations Under Heaven*, 69.

81   Wittke, *The Irish in America*, 91–92.

82   Coffey and Golway, *The Irish in America*, 56–57, 60–66.

83   James Carroll, "What Parish?" in Coffey and Golway, *The Irish in America*, 86–88.

84   Coffey and Golway, *The Irish in America*, 67.

85   Thomas F. O'Dea, *American Catholic Dilemma*, 152, quoted by Glazer and Moynihan, *Beyond the Melting Pot*, 231.

86   Glazer and Moynihan, *Beyond the Melting Pot*, 230.

87   Ibid., 224.

88   Shannon, *The American Irish*, 18.

89   Roger Lane, *Roots of Violence in Black Philadelphia, 1860–1900* (Cambridge, MA: Harvard University Press, 1986), 140.

90   Ibid.

91   Roger Lane, "Black Philadelphia, Then and Now," *Public Interest*, Summer 1992, 35.

92   Wittke, *The Irish in America*, 46.

93   Morris, *American Catholic*, 65.

94   Wittke, *The Irish in America*, 46.

95   Binder and Reimers, *All the Nations Under Heaven*, 62–63.

96   James McPherson, *Battle Cry of Freedom: The Civil War Era* (New York: Oxford University Press, 1988), 609–610.

97   Luc Sante, *Low Life: Lures and Snares of Old New York* (New York: Vintage Books, 1991), 201.

98   Donald L. Miller, *City of the Century*, 466.

99   Lane, "Black Philadelphia, Then and Now," 35.

100   Lane, *Roots of Violence in Black Philadelphia, 1860–1900*, 140–141.

101   T. J. English, "The Original Irish Gangsters," in Coffey and Golway, *The Irish in America*, 115–118.

102   Ibid., 115.

103   Glazer and Moynihan, *Beyond the Melting Pot*, 246.

104   Greeley, *That Most Distressful Nation*, 132.

105   Binder and Reimers, *All the Nations Under Heaven*, 61.

106   Edwin G. Burrows and Mike Wallace, *Gotham: A History of New York City to 1898* (New York: Oxford University Press, 1999), 555–556.

107   Morris, *American Catholic*, 66.

108   Greeley, *That Most Distressful Nation*, 119.

109   Sowell, *Ethnic America*, 33.

110   Ibid., 38.

111   Glazer and Moynihan, *Beyond the Melting Pot*, 246.

112   Kerby A. Miller, *Emigrants and Exiles*, 98.

113   Glazer and Moynihan, *Beyond the Melting Pot*, 225.

114   Shannon, *The American Irish*, 60.

115   See Richard Hofstadter, *The Idea of a Party System: The Rise of Legitimate Opposition in the United States, 1780–1840* (Berkeley, CA: University of California Press, 1969).

116   John Miller, *The Unmaking of Americans*, 37.

117   Binder and Reimers, *All the Nations Under Heaven*, 63.

118   Shannon, *The American Irish*, 64.

119   Bodnar, *The Transplanted*, 203.

120   Binder and Reimers, *All the Nations Under Heaven*, 64.

121   Diner, "The Most Irish City in the Union," in Bayor and Meagher, *The New York Irish*, 97.

122   Ibid., 102.

123   Irving Howe, *World of Our Fathers: The Journey of the East European Jews to America and the Life They Found and Made* (New York: Harcourt Brace Jovanovich, 1976), 367.

124   Ignatiev, *How the Irish Became White*, 175.

125   Donald L. Miller, *City of the Century*, 443.

126   Chris McNickle, "When New York Was Irish, and After," in Bayor and Meagher, *The New York Irish*, 338–339.

127   Glazer and Moynihan, *Beyond the Melting Pot*, 225–226.

128   Data calculated from *Congressional Quarterly's Guide to U.S. Elections*, 2nd ed. (Washington, DC: Congressional Quarterly Inc., 1985).

129   McNickle, "When New York Was Irish, and After," in Bayor and Meagher, *The New York Irish*, 338–339.

130   Shannon, *The American Irish*, 70.

131   Ibid., 72–73.

132   McNickle, "When New York Was Irish, and After," in Bayor and Meagher, *The New York Irish*, 338.

133   Oscar Handlin, ed., *Immigration as a Factor in American History* (Englewood Cliffs, NJ: Prentice Hall, 1959), 100.

134 McNickle, "When New York Was Irish, and After," in Bayor and Meagher, *The New York Irish*, 338.

135 Ibid., 339.

136 Henry Petroski, *Engineers of Dreams: Great Bridge Builders and the Spanning of America* (New York: Knopf, 1995), 158–170.

137 Glazer and Moynihan, *Beyond the Melting Pot*, 246.

138 Jack Beatty, *The Rascal King: The Life and Times of James Michael Curley* (Reading, MA: Addison-Wesley, 1992). See also Edwin O'Connor, *The Last Hurrah* (Boston: Little, Brown, 1956), whose chief character is modeled on Curley, and Curley's autobiographical response, James Michael Curley, *I'd Do It Again: A Record of All My Uproarious Years* (Englewood Cliffs, NJ: Prentice-Hall, 1957).

139 Coffey and Golway, *The Irish in America*, 110.

140 Shannon, *The American Irish*, 231.

141 Bob Leach, *The Frank Hague Picture Book* (Jersey City, NJ: Jersey City Historical Project, 1998), 166.

142 Donald L. Miller, *City of the Century*, 453–454.

143 Ibid., 465.

144 Michael Barone, *Our Country: The Shaping of America from Roosevelt to Reagan* (New York: The Free Press, 1990), 138–139.

145 See Adam Cohen and Elizabeth Taylor, *American Pharaoh: Mayor Richard J. Daley: His Battle for Chicago and the Nation* (Boston: Little, Brown, 2000).

146 Glazer and Moynihan, *Beyond the Melting Pot*, 229.

147 Ibid.

148 Ibid., 260.

149 Kerby A. Miller, *Emigrants and Exiles*, 325.

150 Shannon, *The American Irish*, 64.

151 Blessing, "The Irish," in Thernstrom, *Harvard Encyclopedia of American Ethnic Groups*, 541.

152 Ibid., 542.

153 Ibid., 541.

154 Samuel Lubell, *The Future of American Politics* (New York: Harper, 1952), 35–37.

155 Barone, *Our Country*, 310.

156 Sowell, *Ethnic America*, 42.

157 Blessing, "The Irish," in Thernstrom, *Harvard Encyclopedia of American Ethnic Groups*, 545.

CHAPTER 2: BLACKS

1   Barone, *Our Country*, 27.
2   Gavin Wright, *Old South, New South: Revolutions in the Southern Economy Since the Civil War* (New York: Basic Books, 1986), 74.
3   Stephan Thernstrom and Abigail Thernstrom, *America in Black and White: One Nation, Indivisible* (New York: Simon & Schuster, 1997), 40–44.
4   William Alexander Percy, *Lanterns on the Levee: Recollections of a Planter's Son* (Baton Rouge: Louisiana State University, 1984 edition), 299.
5   Thernstrom and Thernstrom, *America in Black and White*, 45.
6   John Dollard, *Caste and Class in a Southern Town* (Madison, WI: University of Wisconsin Press, 1988 edition), 62.
7   Thernstrom and Thernstrom, *America in Black and White*, 34.
8   Nicholas Lemann, *The Promised Land: The Great Black Migration and How It Changed America* (New York: Vintage Books, 1992), 17.
9   *Historical Statistics of the United States*, 320.
10   Thernstrom and Thernstrom, *America in Black and White*, 36–39.
11   Dollard, *Caste and Class in a Southern Town*, 414.
12   Lemann, *The Promised Land*, 28–29.
13   Taylor Branch, *Parting the Waters: America in the King Years 1954–1963* (New York: Simon & Schuster, 1988), 3.
14   Orlando Patterson, "Taking Culture Seriously: A Framework and an Afro-American Illustration," in Lawrence E. Harrison and Samuel P. Huntington, eds., *Culture Matters: How Values Shape Human Progress* (New York: Basic Books, 2000), 208.
15   Thernstrom and Thernstrom, *America in Black and White*, 95.
16   C. Vann Woodward, *The Strange Career of Jim Crow* (New York: Oxford University Press, 1968).
17   Thernstrom and Thernstrom, *America in Black and White*, 65.
18   Ibid., 71.
19   Ibid., 70–74; David Kennedy, *Freedom from Fear: The American People in Depression and War, 1929–1945* (New York: Oxford University Press, 1999), 763–768; James MacGregor Burns, *Roosevelt: Soldier of Freedom* (New York: Harcourt Brace Jovanovich, Inc., 1970), 123–124.
20   Thernstrom and Thernstrom, *America in Black and White*, 54; Lemann, *The Promised Land*, 6.
21   Gilbert Osofsky, *Harlem: The Making of a Ghetto: Negro New York, 1890–1930* (New York: Harper & Row, 1963), 27.

22 Lemann, *The Promised Land*, 16.

23 *Historical Statistics of the United States*, 23. Thernstrom and Thernstrom, *America in Black and White*, 80.

24 Wright, *Old South, New South*, 216–236.

25 "The invention of the cotton picker was crucial to the great migration by blacks from the southern countryside to the cities of the South, the West, and the North." Lemann, *The Promised Land*, 6.

26 Ibid., 5.

27 Ibid., 95.

28 Ibid., 65.

29 Thernstrom and Thernstrom, *America in Black and White*, 79.

30 Ibid., 56.

31 Ibid., 80.

32 Lemann, *The Promised Land*, 70.

33 Glazer and Moynihan, *Beyond the Melting Pot*, 25.

34 Thernstrom and Thernstrom, *America in Black and White*, 87.

35 Lemann, *The Promised Land*, 95.

36 Thernstrom and Thernstrom, *America in Black and White*, 515.

37 Lemann, *The Promised Land*, 81.

38 Coleman Young, *Hard Stuff: The Autobiography of Mayor Coleman Young* (New York: Viking, 1994), 16.

39 Lemann, *The Promised Land*, 81.

40 Quoted in Lemann, *The Promised Land*, 31.

41 Ibid., 52.

42 David Whitman, "The Great Sharecropper Success Story," *The Public Interest*, Summer 1991, 44–45.

43 Osofsky, *Harlem: The Making of a Ghetto*, 144.

44 Glazer and Moynihan, *Beyond the Melting Pot*, 80.

45 Alan Ehrenhalt, *The Lost City: The Forgotten Virtues of Community in America* (New York: Basic Books, 1995), 175–176.

46 Ibid., 174, 177.

47 Thernstrom and Thernstrom, *America in Black and White*, 81–82.

48 Whitman, "The Great Sharecropper Success Story," 42–43.

49 Thernstrom and Thernstrom, *America in Black and White*, 82.

50 Glazer and Moynihan, *Beyond the Melting Pot*, 38.

51 Moynihan, "The Negro Family: The Case for National Action," 21.

52 Thernstrom and Thernstrom, *America in Black and White*, 83.

53 Shelby Steele, *The Content of Our Character* (New York: St. Martin's Press, 1994), 51.

54 Glazer and Moynihan, *Beyond the Melting Pot*, 32, 33.

55 Thernstrom and Thernstrom, *America in Black and White*, 185.

56 Ibid., 186–187.

57 Ibid., 194–197.

58 Moynihan, "The Negro Family: The Case for National Action," 5–6.

59 Thernstrom and Thernstrom, *America in Black and White*, 186–187.

60 Ibid., 200.

61 Ibid., 196–197.

62 Ibid., 237–238.

63 Hortense Powdermaker, *After Freedom: A Cultural Study in the Deep South* (New York: Russell & Russell, 1968), 143, 146, quoted in Lemann, *The Promised Land*, 29.

64 Glazer and Moynihan, *Beyond the Melting Pot*, 50.

65 Moynihan, "The Negro Family: The Case for National Action," 11, 8.

66 Ibid., 12–14.

67 Lee Rainwater, *The Moynihan Report and the Politics of Controversy* (Cambridge, MA: MIT Press, 1967).

68 Thernstrom and Thernstrom, *America in Black and White*, 240.

69 Ibid., 241.

70 See, for example, Glazer and Moynihan, *Beyond the Melting Pot*, 44.

71 Thernstrom and Thernstrom, *America in Black and White*, 398–399.

72 Lane, "Black Philadelphia, Then and Now," 35.

73 Thernstrom and Thernstrom, *America in Black and White*, 381–382.

74 John H. McWhorter, *Losing the Race: Self-Sabotage in Black America* (New York: The Free Press, 2000).

75 Ibid., 100.

76 Quoted in Damon Linker, "Victimology," *Commentary*, October 2000, 77–78.

77 McWhorter, *Losing the Race*, 235.

78 Lisa Frazier and Michael D. Shear, "Despite Extra Funding, Schools Fail to Flourish; Doubts Arise About Program in Prince George's," *Washington Post*, October 26, 1997, A1.

79 McWhorter, *Losing the Race*, 123–124.

80 Ibid., 85.

81 J.Y. Smith, "Columnist Carl Rowan Dies at 75," *Washington Post*, September 24, 2000, A24.

82 Pete Hamill, *A Drinking Life: A Memoir* (Boston: Little Brown, 1994), 110, 146.

83 Thernstrom and Thernstrom, *America in Black and White*, 190–191.

84　Ibid., 192.

85　Lemann, *The Promised Land*, 31.

86　Whitman, "The Great Sharecropper Success Story," 44–45.

87　Lane, *Roots of Violence in Black Philadelphia, 1860–1900*, 170.

88　Lemann, *The Promised Land*, 65.

89　Cohen and Taylor, *American Pharaoh*, 96–97.

90　Personal recollection of Judge Wade H. McCree Jr. to author.

91　Lane, *Roots of Violence in Black Philadelphia, 1860–1900*, 170.

92　*Historical Statistics of the United States*, 413; *Statistical Abstract of the United States* (Washington, DC: U.S. Department of Commerce, Bureau of the Census, various dates).

93　See the table on page 262 in Thernstrom and Thernstrom, *America in Black and White*.

94　Ibid.

95　Michael Tonry: *Malign Neglect: Race, Crime, and Punishment in America* (New York: Oxford University Press, 1995), 49, quoted in Thernstrom and Thernstrom, *America in Black and White*, 602.

96　Thernstrom and Thernstrom, *America in Black and White*, 263.

97　Ibid., 265.

98　Lemann, *The Promised Land*, 227.

99　D. Bradford Hunt, "Anatomy of a Disaster: Designing and Managing the Second Ghetto," American Historical Association paper, 1999, 15, 19.

100　Thernstrom and Thernstrom, *America in Black and White*, 162–163.

101　Lane, "Black Philadelphia, Then and Now," 35; Lane, *Roots of Violence in Black Philadelphia, 1860–1900*, 140–41.

102　*Statistical Abstract of the United States 1999*, Table 342, p. 214.

103　Orlando Patterson, "Race Over," *New Republic*, January 10, 2000, 6.

104　Thernstrom and Thernstrom, *America in Black and White*, 56, quoting St. Clair Drake and Horace R. Clayton, *Black Metropolis: A Study of Negro Life in a Northern City* (New York: Harcourt Brace, 1945; reprint, New York: Harper Torchbook, 1962), 342.

105　See Nancy J. Weiss, *Farewell to the Party of Lincoln: Black Politics in the Age of FDR* (Princeton, NJ: Princeton University Press, 1983).

106　Thernstrom and Thernstrom, *America in Black and White*, 484.

107　Ibid., 204–209. "What the Kerner Commission saw as an inexorable demographic transformation has actually happened in only a few of the nation's largest cities." Ibid., 206.

108　See Daniel Patrick Moynihan, *The Politics of a Guaranteed Income: The Nixon Administration and the Family Assistance Plan* (New York: Random House, 1973).

109 Patterson, "Taking Culture Seriously," in Harrison and Huntington, *Culture Matters*, 215.

110 Thernstrom and Thernstrom, *America in Black and White*, 320–324.

111 Ibid., 425–429.

112 Ibid., 450.

113 For an excellent treatment of Young's mayoralty, see Tamar Jacoby, *Someone Else's House: America's Unfinished Struggle for Integration* (New York: The Free Press, 1998), 229–353, on which much of the following is based.

114 Jacoby, *Someone Else's House*, 198–199.

115 For an excellent treatment of Barry's mayoralty, see Fred Siegel, *The Future Once Happened Here: New York, D.C., L.A., and the Fate of America's Big Cities* (New York: The Free Press, 1997), 65–111, on which much of the following is based.

116 Harry S. Jaffe and Tom Sherwood, *Dream City: Race, Power, and the Decline of Washington, D.C.* (New York: Simon & Schuster, 1994), 43–44, 58–59.

117 Thernstrom and Thernstrom, *America in Black and White*.

118 Steele, *The Content of Our Character*, 116.

119 Thernstrom and Thernstrom, *America in Black and White*, 386–388. I have observed this phenomenon at Stanford myself.

120 Ibid., 482.

121 Steele, *The Content of Our Character*, 15.

122 Quoted in Linker, "Victimology," 77.

123 Ibid.

124 McWhorter, *Losing the Race*, 218.

125 Shelby Steele, *A Dream Deferred: The Second Betrayal of Black Freedom in America* (New York: HarperCollins, 1998), 125.

126 McWhorter, *Losing the Race*, 43, 44.

CHAPTER 3: ITALIANS

1 Robert Putnam, *Making Democracy Work: Civic Traditions in Modern Italy* (Princeton, NJ: Princeton University Press, 1993), 121–137.

2 See Benedetto Croce, *History of the Kingdom of Naples* (Chicago: University of Chicago Press, 1970 edition).

3 Denis Mack Smith, *The Making of Italy, 1796–1870* (New York: Walker, 1968), 323–325.

4   Jerre Mangione and Ben Morreale, *La Storia: Five Centuries of the Italian American Experience* (New York: HarperCollins, 1992), 32.

5   Masolino D'Amico, "Dante Would Have Understood It All," *Times Literary Supplement*, September 29, 2000, 10, quoting Tullio De Mauro, *Grande Dizinoario Italiano dell'Uso*.

6   Giuseppe Tomasi di Lampedusa, *The Leopard* (New York: Pantheon, 1960).

7   Francis Fukuyama, *Trust: The Social Virtues and the Creation of Prosperity* (New York: The Free Press, 1995), 104.

8   Ibid., 104, 101.

9   Sowell, *Ethnic America*, 103, citing Shepard B. Clough, *The Economic History of Modern Italy* (New York: Columbia University Press, 1964), 8–9, 371.

10   Richard Alba, *Italian Americans: Into the Twilight of Ethnicity* (Englewood Cliffs, NJ: Prentice Hall, 1985), 22–23; see Leonard Covello, *The Social Background of the Italo-American School Child: A Study of the Southern Italian Family Mores and Their Effect on the School Situation in Italy and America*, Francesco Cordasco, ed. (Leiden: E. J. Brill, 1967), 63–64.

11   Mangione and Morreale, *La Storia*, 48

12   Ibid.

13   Vincenza Scarpaci, *A Portrait of the Italians in America* (New York: Scribner, 1982), 47.

14   Sowell, *Ethnic America*, 103, citing Clough, *The Economic History of Modern Italy*, 9.

15   Alba, *Italian Americans*, 32.

16   Glazer and Moynihan, *Beyond the Melting Pot*, 197.

17   Sowell, *Ethnic America*, 105.

18   Donald Tricario, *The Italians of Greenwich Village: The Social Structure and Transformation of an Ethnic Community* (Staten Island, NY: Center for Migration Studies of New York, 1984), 10.

19   Sowell, *Ethnic America*, 106.

20   Donna R. Gabaccia, *From Sicily to Elizabeth Street: Housing and Social Change Among Italian Immigrants, 1880–1930* (Albany, NY: State University of New York Press, 1984), 3.

21   Robert F. Foerster, *The Italian Emigration of Our Times* (Cambridge, MA: Harvard University Press, 1919), 95, quoted by Alba, *Italian Americans*, 23.

22   Edward C. Banfield, *The Moral Basis of a Backward Society* (New York: The Free Press, 1967 edition), 83.

23   Ibid., 86.

24   Glazer and Moynihan, *Beyond the Melting Pot*, 195, quoting Covello, *The Social Background of the Italo-American School Child*, 166.

25   Alba, *Italian Americans*, 30.

26   Ibid., 32.

27   Humbert S. Nelli, "Italians," in Thernstrom, *Harvard Encyclopedia of American Ethnic Groups*, 547, 545.

28   *Historical Statistics of the United States*, 105–106.

29   Alba, *Italian Americans*, 39.

30   Ibid., 25, 26.

31   Mangione and Morreale, *La Storia*, 78.

32   Virginia Yans-McLaughlin, *Family and Community: Italian Immigrants in Buffalo, 1880–1930* (Ithaca, NY: Cornell University Press, 1977), 32–33.

33   Tricario, *The Italians of Greenwich Village*, 4. Yans-McLaughlin in her study of Buffalo Italians says that 81 percent "of the earliest migrants were husbands and fathers in their twenties and thirties." Yans-McLaughlin, *Family and Community*, 70.

34   Nelli, "Italians," in Thernstrom, *Harvard Encyclopedia of American Ethnic Groups*, 547. Another estimate is that 1.5 million Italians returned from the United States between 1900 and 1914. Alba, *Italian Americans*, 40.

35   John W. Briggs, *An Italian Passage: Immigrants to Three American Cities, 1890–1930* (New Haven: Yale University Press, 1978), 4–5, 10–12, 68.

36   Nelli, "Italians," in Thernstrom, *Harvard Encyclopedia of American Ethnic Groups*, 547.

37   Sowell, *Ethnic America*, 109.

38   Thomas Sowell, *Migrations and Cultures: A World View* (New York: Basic Books, 1996), 145.

39   Yans-McLaughlin, *Family and Community*, 17. The quoted phrase is from Alba, *Italian Americans*, 48. This example is of more than academic interest to me: my great-grandparents Salvatore and Sara Barone left Valledolmo for Buffalo in 1893.

40   Nelli, "Italians," in Thernstrom, *Harvard Encyclopedia of American Ethnic Groups*, 548.

41   Of those who identified themselves in the 1990 census as of Italian ancestry, 51 percent lived in the Northeast, a degree of regional concentration matched only by that of Czechs and Norwegians in the Midwest. *Statistical Abstract of the United States 1999*, Table 59, p. 56.

42   Nelli, "Italians," in Thernstrom, *Harvard Encyclopedia of American Ethnic Groups*, 549–550.

43   Glazer and Moynihan, *Beyond the Melting Pot*, 186; Sowell, *Ethnic America*, 101; Rudolph Vecoli, "The Search for an Italian American Identity: Continuity and Change," in Lydio F. Tomasi, ed., *Italian Americans: New Perspectives in Italian Immigration and Ethnicity* (Staten Island, NY: Center for Migrations Studies of New York, 1985), 91.

44   Thomas Kessner, *The Golden Door: Italian and Jewish Immigrant Mobility in New York City, 1880–1915* (New York: Oxford University Press, 1977), 20–21, quoted by Alba, *Italian Americans*, 49.

45   Michael Immerso, *Newark's Little Italy: The Vanished First Ward* (New Brunswick, NJ: Rutgers University Press, 1997), 2.

46   Gabaccia, *From Sicily to Elizabeth Street*, 59.

47   Erla Zwingle, "Boston's North Enders," *National Geographic*, October 2000, 50–67.

48   Fred Gardaphe, "Chicago's Little Pieces of Italy," *Primo*, Autumn 2000, 61–63.

49   Scarpaci, *A Portrait of the Italians in America*, xvi, xix.

50   See Salvatore LaGumina, "Italian Americans on Long Island: The Foundation Years," in Lydio F. Tomasi, *Italian Americans*, 331–340.

51   Morris, *American Catholic*, 129. See also Sowell, *Ethnic America*, 114–115.

52   Leonard Dinnerstein and David M. Reimers, *Ethnic Americans: A History of Immigration and Assimilation* (New York: Harper & Row, 1975), 60–61.

53   Sowell, *Ethnic America*, 121.

54   Glazer and Moynihan, *Beyond the Melting Pot*, 184.

55   Ibid.

56   Yans-McLaughlin, *Family and Community*, 28.

57   Perlman and Waldinger, "Immigrants Past and Present: A Reconsideration," in Hirschman, Kasinitz, and DeWind, *The Handbook of International Migration*, 225.

58   Glazer and Moynihan, *Beyond the Melting Pot*, 190.

59   Roger Daniels, *Not Like Us: Immigrants and Minorities in America, 1890–1924* (Chicago: Ivan R. Dee, 1997), 69; Gabaccia, *From Sicily to Elizabeth Street*, 64.

60   Sowell, *Ethnic America*, 121–122.

61   Ibid., 123.

62   Gary Ross Mormino, *Immigrants on the Hill: Italian-Americans in St. Louis, 1882–1982* (Urbana, IL: University of Illinois Press, 1986), 96–97; Yans-McLaughlin, *Family and Community*, 44.

63   Mike Dillon, "Working for Peanuts," *Primo*, Autumn 2000, 29–31.

64 Nelli, "Italians," in Thernstrom, *Harvard Encyclopedia of American Ethnic Groups*, 550.

65 Sowell, *Ethnic America*, 117.

66 Nelli, "Italians," in Thernstrom, *Harvard Encyclopedia of American Ethnic Groups*, 551.

67 John Gunther, *Inside U.S.A.* (New York: Harper & Brothers, 1947), 27, 28.

68 Glazer and Moynihan, *Beyond the Melting Pot*, 192–193. See the picture of the large crowd at the dedication of a statue of Columbus in St. Paul, Minnesota, in 1931, in Scarpaci, *A Portrait of the Italians in America*, 152–153.

69 Nelli, "Italians," in Thernstrom, *Harvard Encyclopedia of American Ethnic Groups*, 551.

70 John Miller, *The Unmaking of Americans*, 42–45.

71 Glazer and Moynihan, *Beyond the Melting Pot*, 191.

72 Covello, *The Social Background of the Italo-American School Child*, 150.

73 Tricario, *The Italians of Greenwich Village*, 8.

74 Yans-McLaughlin, *Family and Community*, 88–89.

75 Tricario, *The Italians of Greenwich Village*, 9.

76 Ibid.

77 Sowell, *Ethnic America*, 118.

78 Tricario, *The Italians of Greenwich Village*, 22.

79 Mormino, *Immigrants on the Hill*, 196.

80 Tricario, *The Italians of Greenwich Village*, 23.

81 Gabaccia, *From Sicily to Elizabeth Street*, 79.

82 Glazer and Moynihan, *Beyond the Melting Pot*, 187–188. See also Mormino, *Immigrants on the Hill*, 114.

83 Vecoli, "The Search for an Italian American Identity: Continuity and Change," in Lydio F. Tomasi, *Italian Americans*, 95.

84 Dinnerstein and Reimers, *Ethnic Americans*, 65.

85 Ibid.

86 Ibid.

87 Morris, *American Catholic*, 129.

88 Robert A. Orsi, *The Madonna of 115th Street: Faith and Community in Italian Harlem, 1880–1950* (New Haven: Yale University Press, 1985), 55–57.

89 Morris, *American Catholic*, 131.

90 See the good material in Morris, *American Catholic*, 131.

91 Covello, *The Social Background of the Italo-American School Child*, 286–296, 311–327.

92   Alba, *Italian Americans*, 60.

93   Glazer and Moynihan, *Beyond the Melting Pot*, 199.

94   Sowell, *Ethnic America*, 120, citing Sister Mary Fabian Matthews, "The Role of the Public School in the Assimilation of the Italian Immigrant Child in New York City, 1900–1914," in Silvano M. Tomasi and Madeline H. Engel, eds., *The Italian Experience in the United States* (Staten Island, NY: Center for Migration Studies, 1970), 131.

95   Perlman and Waldinger, "Immigrants Past and Present," in Hirschman, Kasinitz, and DeWind, *The Handbook of International Migration*, 225.

96   Glazer and Moynihan, *Beyond the Melting Pot*, 199.

97   Mormino, *Immigrants on the Hill*, 108, 103.

98   Barbara Grizzuti Harrison, "Pride and Prejudice: Growing Up Italian in Bensonhurst," *Primo*, Autumn 2000, 83–84.

99   Examples include my grandfather Charles J. Barone, who graduated from college and medical school at George Washington University and went into practice in then fast-growing Detroit. For other examples, see Claire Gaudiani, "Of Cheese and Choices," in A. Kenneth Ciongoli and Jay Parini, eds., *Beyond the Godfather: Italian American Writers on the Real American Experience* (Hanover, NH: University Press of New England, 1997), 114–125, and Betty L. Santangelo et al., *Lucky Corner: The Biography of Congressman Alfred J. Santangelo and the Rise of Italian-Americans in Politics* (Staten Island, NY: Center for Migration Studies, 1999).

100   Alba, *Italian Americans*, 67.

101   Sowell, *Ethnic America*, 118; Lane, "Black Philadelphia, Then and Now," 35.

102   Yans-McLaughlin, *Family and Community*, 78.

103   Sowell, *Ethnic America*, 118.

104   Lane, "Black Philadelphia, Then and Now," 35.

105   See Alba, *Italian Americans*, 37–38.

106   Mangione and Morreale, *La Storia*, 165–169.

107   Tricario, *The Italians of Greenwich Village*, 71.

108   Glazer and Moynihan, *Beyond the Melting Pot*, 211.

109   Dinnerstein and Reimers, *Ethnic Americans*, 169.

110   Glazer and Moynihan, *Beyond the Melting Pot*, 189.

111   Alba, *Italian Americans*, 85.

112   Mangione and Morreale, *La Storia*, 73.

113   Mormino, *Immigrants on the Hill*, 183; Nelli, "Italians," in Thernstrom, *Harvard Encyclopedia of American Ethnic Groups*, 552.

114 Robert Dahl, *Who Governs? Democracy and Power in an American City* (New Haven: Yale University Press, 1961), 39, 45–46, 216–217.

115 Author's conversation with Judge Anthony J. Celebrezze, circa 1970.

116 See Santangelo, *Lucky Corner*.

117 *Biographical Dictionary of the United States Congress, 1789–1989* (Washington, DC: Government Printing Office, 1989), 733.

118 Ibid., 1334–1335; Glazer and Moynihan, *Beyond the Melting Pot*, 213.

119 Glazer and Moynihan, *Beyond the Melting Pot*, 202.

120 *Biographical Dictionary of the United States Congress, 1789–1989*, 1615.

121 Alba, *Italian Americans*, 67.

122 Dinnerstein and Reimers, *Ethnic Americans*, 54.

123 Peter Vellon, "Black, White, or In Between?" *Ambassador*, Fall 2000, 12.

124 Mangione and Morreale, *La Storia*, 108–109.

125 Vellon, "Black, White, or In Between?" 10–13.

126 Alba, *Italian Americans*, 68.

127 Ibid., 100.

128 Ibid., 90; Mangione and Morreale, *La Storia*, 160.

129 Scarpaci, *A Portrait of the Italians in America*, xxiv.

130 Alba, *Italian Americans*, 77.

131 Sowell, *Ethnic America*, 121.

132 Morris, *American Catholic*, 131.

133 Ibid.; Mormino, *Immigrants on the Hill*, 114–117.

134 Vecoli, "The Search for an Italian American Identity: Continuity and Change," in Lydio F. Tomasi, *Italian Americans*, 96–97.

135 Author's 1986 conversation with Congressman Peter W. Rodino on the difficulty of campaigning for Roosevelt in the North Ward of Newark in 1940; Scarpaci, *A Portrait of the Italians in America*, xxix; Glazer and Moynihan, *Beyond the Melting Pot*, 214.

136 The records of this episode were for the first time required to be made public by a law signed in November 2000. "President Signs Into Law 'Storia Segreta' Bill," *National Italian American Foundation News*, December 2000, 1, 31.

137 Alba, *Italian Americans*, 79.

138 Ibid., 82.

139 Sowell, *Ethnic America*, 126–127.

140 Ibid., 126.

141 Nampeo McKenney, Michael Levin, and Alfred Tella, "A Sociodemographic Profile of Italian Americans," in Lydio F. Tomasi, *Italian Americans*, 3–31, quotation at 27.

142 Richard Gambino, "The Crisis of Italian American Identity," in Ciongoli and Parini, *Beyond the Godfather*, 282–283.

143 Alba, *Italian Americans*, 130.

144 Elliott Abrams, *Faith or Fear? How Jews Can Survive in Christian America* (New York: The Free Press, 1997), 100–101.

145 Richard Alba, "Comment on Papers by McKenney, Levin, and Tella, and by Nelli and Vecoli," in Lydio F. Tomasi, *Italian Americans*, 117–118.

146 Humbert S. Nelli, "Italian Americans in Contemporary America," in Lydio F. Tomasi, *Italian Americans*, 81–82.

CHAPTER 4: LATINOS

1 See Hugh Thomas, *Conquest: Montezuma, Cortés, and the Fall of Old Mexico* (New York: Simon & Schuster, 1993).

2 See Enrique Krauze, *Mexico: A Biography of Power: A History of Modern Mexico, 1810–1996* (New York: HarperCollins, 1997), 4–11.

3 Gregory Rodriguez, "Taking the Oath: Why We Need a Revisionist History of Latinos in the United States," *Los Angeles Times Book Review*, August 20, 2000, 1. Peter Skerry says that Spanish speakers were "at most 4 percent of the population of the Southwest." Peter Skerry, *Mexican Americans: The Ambivalent Minority* (New York: The Free Press, 1993), 23.

4 George J. Sanchez, *Becoming Mexican American: Ethnicity, Culture, and Identity in Chicano Los Angeles, 1900–1945* (New York: Oxford University Press, 1993), 69–70.

5 Author's 1986 interview with Lloyd Bentsen Sr., father of the senator and treasury secretary, who settled in the Rio Grande Valley after World War I.

6 Some 8 percent of Mexicans speak only Indian languages—a small percentage, but, given the country's population of 99 million in 2000, it represents 8 million people. *Statesman's Year-Book 1997–1998* (New York: St. Martin's Press, 1997), 900.

7 Octavio Paz, *The Labyrinth of Solitude* (New York: Grove Press, Inc., 1985), 298.

8 Ibid., 23.

9   Claudio Veliz, *The Centralist Tradition in Latin America* (Princeton, NJ: Princeton University Press, 1980), 8–9. The book was published in 1980, and it may be argued that centralism in Latin America has been in retreat since the late 1980s. On the weakness of the "Ibero-Catholic" culture, see Lawrence E. Harrison, *The Pan-American Dream: Do Latin America's Cultural Values Discourage True Partnership with the United States and Canada?* (New York: Basic Books, 1997), 26–39.

10   Jorge G. Castañeda, *La Herencia: Arqueología de la Sucesión Presidencial en México* (México: Extra Alfaguara, 1999).

11   Paz, *The Labyrinth of Solitude*, 298.

12   Jonathan Kandell, *La Capital: The Biography of Mexico City* (New York: Random House, 1988), 495.

13   Ibid., 506.

14   Carey McWilliams, *North from Mexico: The Spanish-Speaking People of the United States* (New York: Greenwood Press, 1968), 265–269.

15   Rosemarie Rogers, "Migration Theory and Practice," in Walker Conner, ed., *Mexican-Americans in Comparative Perspective* (Washington, DC: The Urban Institute Press, 1985), 183, 174.

16   Sowell, *Ethnic America*, 254.

17   Glazer and Moynihan, *Beyond the Melting Pot*, 91, 93.

18   *Historical Statistics of the United States, 1789–1971*, 107, and subsequent *Statistical Abstracts of the United States*.

19   Sanford J. Ungar, *Fresh Blood: The New American Immigrants* (New York: Simon & Schuster, 1995), 102–103.

20   Nathan Glazer, ed., *Clamor at the Gates: The New American Immigration* (San Francisco, CA: Institute for Contemporary Studies, 1985), 7; John Miller, *The Unmaking of Americans*, 105–106.

21   McWilliams, *North from Mexico*, 268

22   Glazer, *Clamor at the Gates*, 10.

23   Glazer speculates that this was one reason for increased Latino immigration after 1965. Ibid., 7.

24   "Report of the National Advisory Commission on Civil Disorders" (Washington, DC: U.S. Government Printing Office, 1968), 278–282.

25   Between 64 percent and 84 percent of Mexican immigrants arriving in the United States from 1909 to 1926 originally named Texas as their "intended future permanent residence." Only 4 percent from 1909 to 1911 and 17 percent from 1924 to 1926 named California. Sanchez, *Becoming Mexican American*, 65.

26 One such immigrant was the grandfather of Henry Cisneros, mayor
    of San Antonio from 1981 to 1989 and secretary of Housing and
    Urban Development from 1993 to 1997. Author's interview with
    Henry Cisneros, 1986.

27 Sowell, *Ethnic America*, 232–233.

28 See John J. Miller and Stephen Moore, "The Index of Leading Immi-
    gration Indicators" (Washington, DC: Center for Equal Opportunity,
    1995), 8.

29 See Joel Millman, *The Other Americans: How Immigrants Renew Our
    Country, Our Economy, and Our Values* (New York: Viking, 1997), 1, on
    "the speed with which the Mexicans had fashioned their underground
    expressway. By the summer of 1994, migrants from Mexico could
    travel from an adobe shack in Puebla to an apartment in New York
    City in less than 48 hours, at a cost of about a thousand dollars."

30 Roberto Suro, *Strangers Among Us: How Latino Immigration Is Trans-
    forming America* (New York: Knopf, 1998), 32.

31 Peter Skerry, "E Pluribus Hispanic?" in F. Chris Garcia, ed., *Pursuing
    Power: Latinos and the Political System* (Notre Dame, IN: University of
    Notre Dame Press, 1997), 19.

32 *Statistical Abstract of the United States 1999*, Table 650, p. 411. Among
    white males it is 76 percent, among black males 69 percent.

33 Millman, *The Other Americans*, 10.

34 Author's interview with Jose Legaspi, 1998.

35 Robert B. Reich, *The Work of Nations: Preparing Ourselves for 21st-
    Century Capitalism* (New York: Knopf, 1991), 176–177, quoted in
    Suro, *Strangers Among Us*, 46.

36 Suro, *Strangers Among Us*, 44–49.

37 *Statistical Abstract of the United States 1999*, Table 678, p. 428.

38 Ibid., Table 719, p. 453.

39 Rodriguez, "Taking the Oath: Why We Need a Revisionist History of
    Latinos in America," 1.

40 See Siegel, *The Future Once Happened Here*, 153–155, and Gregory
    Rodriguez, "Is L.A. the Place for a Resurgent Union Movement?" *Los
    Angeles Times*, February 16, 1997, M1.

41 *Statistical Abstract of the United States 1999*, Table 742, p. 474.

42 Ibid., Table 760, p. 483.

43 Gregory Rodriguez, "Rethinking Latino Identity," *Los Angeles Times*,
    October 13, 1996, M6.

44 Gregory Rodriguez, "The Emerging Latino Middle Class," Pepperdine University Institute for Public Policy, October 1996, 7, 9.

45 John Pitkin et al., "Immigration and Housing in the United States: Trends and Prospects," Report for the Fannie Mae Foundation Immigration Research Report, June 1997.

46 Tamar Jacoby, "Second-Generation Question Mark," *American Enterprise*, December 2000, 35.

47 Lou Cannon, "Southern California's Boom Is Latino-Led," *Washington Post*, July 12, 1997, A3.

48 See Hernando de Soto, *The Other Path: The Invisible Revolution in the Third World* (New York: Harper & Row, 1989), which shows how poor Peruvians have started and run businesses even though they must violate many laws in order to do so. The entrepreneurial impulse is strong even though the legal framework for business is lacking.

49 Gregory Rodriguez, "A Tale of Two Migrations, One White, One Brown," *Los Angeles Times*, March 17, 1996, M6; see also Patrick J. McDonnell, "Immigrant Welfare Use Varies Widely," *Los Angeles Times*, July 30, 1997, B1; "A Minority Worth Cultivating," *The Economist*, April 25, 1998, 21; "The Keenest Recruits to the Dream," *The Economist*, April 25, 1998, 27.

50 Nancy Foner, *From Ellis Island to JFK: New York's Two Great Waves of Immigration* (New Haven, CT: Yale University Press, 2000), 64.

51 *Statistical Abstract of the United States 1999*, Table 74, p. 62.

52 Ibid., Table 84, p. 68.

53 Ibid., Table 62, p. 57.

54 Author's interview with Gregory Rodriguez, July 30, 1997.

55 Francis Fukuyama, "Immigrants and Family Values," *Commentary*, May 1993, 29.

56 Ibid.

57 Skerry, "E Pluribus Hispanic?" in Garcia, *Pursuing Power*, 18–19.

58 De Soto, *The Other Path*, 4; Lawrence E. Harrison, *The Pan-American Dream*, 38–39.

59 Christine Haughney, "Religion Revives the Bronx," *Washington Post*, September 11, 2000, A3.

60 Blaine Harden, "Hispanic Evangelicals Flock to Hear a Force in Their Faith," *New York Times*, September 5, 2000, B1.

61 *Statistical Abstract of the United States 1999*, Table 263, p. 169.

62 Ibid., Table 260, p. 167.

63 Ibid., Table 263, p. 169.

64 See Diane Ravitch, *Left Back: A Century of Failed School Reforms* (New York: Simon & Schuster, 2000).

65 "Index of Hispanic Economic Indicators 1997" (Washington, DC: National Council of La Raza, 1997), 5.

66 Glenn Garvin, "Loco, Completamente Loco," *Reason*, January 1998, 22.

67 Ron Unz, "Bilingualism Is a Damaging Myth," *Los Angeles Times*, October 19, 1997, M5.

68 Garvin, "Loco, Completamente Loco," 18–29.

69 John Miller, *The Unmaking of Americans*, 195–197.

70 "The Importance of Learning English: A National Survey of Hispanic Parents" (Washington, DC: Center for Equal Opportunity, 1996), 5, 14.

71 See, for example, Michael Bazeley, "English-Only Test Scores Up," *San Jose Mercury News*, December 26, 1999; Joanne Jacobs, "No Celebration for Success of Proposition 227," *San Jose Mercury News*, December 30, 1999; Jennifer Karr, "English Learners Show Gains As State Releases More Figures," Associated Press, August 14, 2000.

72 James Traub, "The Class of Prop. 209," *New York Times Magazine*, May 2, 1999, 44.

73 Ibid.

74 See, for example, Crystal Yednak, "Laws Meant to Boost Diversity Paying Off," *Fort Worth Star-Telegram*, January 13, 2001.

75 John J. Miller and Moore, "The Index of Leading Immigration Indicators," 18.

76 *Statistical Abstract of the United States 1999*, Table 345, p. 216.

77 David E. Hayes-Bautista and Gregory Rodriguez, "The Criminalization of Latino Identity Makes Fighting Gangs That Much Harder," *Los Angeles Times*, September 15, 1996, M1.

78 David E. Hayes-Bautista and Gregory Rodriguez, "The Chicano Movement: More Nostalgia Than a Reality," *Los Angeles Times*, September 17, 1995, M6.

79 William Branigin, "Capital of 'Chicano Power' Wants to Shed Militant Political Image," *Washington Post*, October 2, 1998, A3.

80 Hayes-Bautista and Rodriguez, "The Chicano Movement: More Nostalgia Than a Reality," M6.

81 Ibid.

82 Walker Conner, "Who Are the Mexican-Americans?" in Conner, *Mexican-Americans in Comparative Perspective*, 15.

83 Quoted in Dirk Kirschten, "American Dreamers," *National Journal*, July 5, 1997, 1367.

84   Krauze, *Mexico*, 694–731. For Krauze, one of Mexico's leading intel-
      lectuals, Tlatelolco was the central event in recent Mexican history, the
      point at which the PRI regime began to lose moral authority. "Today,"
      he wrote in 1997, "the great majority of the leaders of the Student
      Movement of 1968—now in their fifties—are seeking some way to
      change the life of Mexico in the direction of democracy, so as to give
      meaning to the sacrifice that 'broke' them. Many of them—and their
      generation—will always bear profound scars, but they have mended
      themselves, and are acting 'for Mexico.'" Ibid., 723.
85   Peter Skerry, "Do We Really Want Immigrants to Assimilate?" *Society*
      (March/April 2000), citing Tomas Almaguer et al., "The Diversity
      Project: An Interim Report to the Chancellor" (Berkeley, CA:
      Institute for the Study of Social Change, 1990).
86   Hayes-Bautista and Rodriguez, "The Chicano Movement: More Nos-
      talgia Than a Reality," M6.
87   Philip Pan, "Naturalization: An Unnatural Process," *Washington Post*,
      July 4, 2000, A1.
88   Ibid.
89   Kirschten, "American Dreamers," 1365–1366.
90   "Profile of the Foreign-Born Population in the United States" (Wash-
      ington, DC: Bureau of the Census, 1997), quoted in Pan, "Natural-
      ization: An Unnatural Process," A1.
91   Clifford J. Levy, "Hispanic Voters Emerge As Powerful and Unpre-
      dictable Force," *New York Times*, November 9, 1997, 37.
92   VNS Exit Poll.
93   Michael Barone and Grant Ujifusa, *The Almanac of American Politics,
      2000* (Washington, DC: National Journal, 1999), 265, 255.
94   Author's interview with Jose Legaspi, July 31, 1997.
95   Author's interview with Rodriguez, July 30, 1997.
96   VNS Exit Poll.
97   Ibid.
98   Ibid.
99   Skerry, "E Pluribus Hispanic?" in Garcia, *Pursuing Power*, 24–25.
100   "The Keenest Recruits to the Dream," 27.
101   Dennis Farney, "Both Candidates Woo Newsman with a Line to the
      Hispanic Vote," *Wall Street Journal*, October 3, 2000, A1; Christopher
      Stern, "Univision to Buy Diller TV Stations," *Washington Post*, Decem-
      ber 8, 2000, E4.
102   Farney, "Both Candidates Woo Newsman with a Line to the Hispanic
      Vote," A1.

103   Eduardo Porter, "Hispanic TV Takes Off in the U.S.," *Wall Street Journal*, September 7, 2000, B1.

104   Dale Russakoff, "Keeping Up with the Garcias," *Washington Post*, September 24, 2000, A1, A8–A9.

105   Farney, "Both Candidates Woo Newsman with a Line to the Hispanic Vote," A1.

106   Skerry, "E Pluribus Hispanic?" in Garcia, *Pursuing Power*, 26.

107   David E. Hayes-Bautista and Gregory Rodriguez, "Technobanda," *New Republic*, April 11, 1994, 10.

108   Rodriguez, "Rethinking Latino Identity," M6.

109   John J. Miller and Moore, "The Index of Leading Immigration Indicators," 14.

110   Dowell Myers, "The Changing Immigrants of Southern California," Research Project for California Immigration and the American Dream, October 25, 1995, Exhibit 4.1.

111   Ibid., 20.

112   "The Importance of Learning English: A National Survey of Hispanic Parents."

113   Author's interview with Sergio Sarmiento, July 1, 2000.

114   Skerry, "Do We Really Want Immigrants to Assimilate?" citing Almaguer et al., "The Diversity Project: An Interim Report to the Chancellor."

115   Greta Gilbertson et al., "Hispanic Intermarriage in New York City: New Evidence from 1991," *International Migration*, Summer 1996, 445–459, cited in John Miller, *The Unmaking of Americans*, 145.

116   John Miller, *The Unmaking of Americans*, 145.

117   Author's interview with Rodriguez, July 30, 1997; Rodriguez, "Rethinking Latino Identity," M6.

CHAPTER 5: JEWS

1   Simon Schama, *Landscape and Memory* (New York: Knopf, 1995), 26.

2   Ibid., 23.

3   Ibid., 25.

4   Anne Applebaum, *Between East and West: Across the Borderlands of Europe* (New York: Pantheon Books, 1994), xx.

5   Paul Johnson, *A History of the Jews* (New York: Harper & Row, 1987), 231.

6   Ibid., 250–251.

7   Ibid., 259.

8   Ibid., 358.

9   Ibid., 357–358.

10   Arthur Hertzberg, *The Jews in America: Four Centuries of an Uneasy Encounter* (New York: Simon & Schuster, 1989), 163. Hertzberg estimates that from 1827 to 1856, when Russian draft policy changed, nearly 100,000 Jewish boys were "forced into this slavery."

11   Johnson, *A History of the Jews*, 358–363.

12   Howe, *World of Our Fathers*, 10–11.

13   Johnson, *A History of the Jews*, 357, 365.

14   Gerald Sorin, *A Time for Building: The Third Migration, 1880–1920* (Baltimore: Johns Hopkins University Press, 1992), 23.

15   Johnson, *A History of the Jews*, 339.

16   Howe, *World of Our Fathers*, 12.

17   Sorin, *A Time for Building*, 14.

18   Sowell, *Migrations and Cultures*, 262–263.

19   Sorin, *A Time for Building*, 15.

20   Richard Pipes, *Russia Under the Old Regime* (New York: Scribner, 1974), 305; Richard Pipes, *The Russian Revolution* (New York: Knopf, 1990), 74; Martin Gilbert, *Jewish History Atlas* (New York: Collier Books, 1969), 71. Pipes and Johnson both argue that the police state created by tsarist Russia laid the groundwork for the police state created by the Soviets after 1917. Johnson, *A History of the Jews*, 569.

21   Pipes, *Russia Under the Old Regime*, 311. See also Sachar, *A History of the Jews in America*, 117–118.

22   Johnson, *A History of the Jews*, 455–457; Sachar, *A History of the Jews in America*, 313.

23   Johnson, *A History of the Jews*, 363.

24   Sorin, *A Time for Building*, 203.

25   Gilbert, *Jewish History Atlas*, 71; Sorin, *A Time for Building*, 34.

26   Johnson, *A History of the Jews*, 448–452. Needless to say, none of these was an observant Jew.

27   Ibid., 452–454.

28   William O. McCagg, *A History of Habsburg Jews, 1670–1918* (Bloomington, IN: Indiana University Press, 1989), 26.

29   Ibid., 2, 27–28.

30   See Carl E. Schorske, *Fin-de-Siècle Vienna: Politics and Culture* (New York: Knopf, 1980); Allan Janik and Stephen Toulmin, *Wittgenstein's*

Vienna (New York: Simon & Schuster, 1973); Steven Beller, *Vienna and the Jews, 1867–1938: A Cultural History* (New York: Cambridge University Press, 1989).

31 McCagg, *A History of Habsburg Jews, 1670–1918*, 164–216.

32 Ibid., 161–164.

33 Sachar, *A History of the Jews in America*, 119–121.

34 Ibid., 121–123; Howe, *World of Our Fathers*, 28–30.

35 Johnson, *A History of the Jews*, 460.

36 Gerald Sorin gives the number of Jewish immigrants from 1881 to 1914 as 2,019,215. Sorin, *A Time for Building*, 58, citing Samuel Joseph, *Jewish Immigration to the United States from 1881 to 1910* (New York: Columbia University, 1914), and Simon Kuznets, "Immigration of Russian Jews to the United States: Background and Structure," *Perspectives in American History* 9 (1975), 35–124. See also Johnson, *A History of the Jews*, 365; Howe, *World of Our Fathers*, 30. Some 85 percent of the Jewish immigrants from Austria-Hungary were from Galicia. McCagg, *A History of Habsburg Jews, 1670–1918*, 183.

37 Howe, *World of Our Fathers*, 36–46.

38 Kessner, *The Golden Door*, 31–32.

39 Joseph, *Jewish Immigration to the United States from 1881 to 1910*, 126–129, cited in Howe, *World of Our Fathers*, 58.

40 Howe, *World of Our Fathers*, 58, 30.

41 Ibid., 62–63.

42 Sorin, *A Time for Building*, 7, 12.

43 Sowell, *Migrations and Cultures*, 282, 292–293.

44 Arthur Goren, "Jews," in Thernstrom, *Harvard Encyclopedia of American Ethnic Groups*, 571–575.

45 Sachar, *A History of the Jews in America*, 81–82, Freeman, *Washington*, 585.

46 Goren, "Jews," in Thernstrom, *Harvard Encyclopedia of American Ethnic Groups*, 576, 571.

47 Ibid., 576. See also Sowell, *Migrations and Cultures*, 294–295.

48 Sorin, *A Time for Building*, 3.

49 Ibid., 4.

50 For the story of the Jews in the South, see Eli N. Evans, *The Provincials: A Personal History of Jews in the South* (New York: Free Press Paperbacks, 1997, revised edition).

51 Eli N. Evans, *Judah P. Benjamin, The Jewish Confederate* (New York: Free Press, 1988).

52 Goren, "Jews," in Thernstrom, *Harvard Encyclopedia of American Ethnic Groups*, 576–578.

53 Johnson, *A History of the Jews*, 369–370.

54 Goren, "Jews," in Thernstrom, *Harvard Encyclopedia of American Ethnic Groups*, 578–579.

55 Johnson, *A History of the Jews*, 370. On efforts by German Jews to prevent immigration of Russian Jews, see Sachar, *A History of the Jews in America*, 123–125.

56 Sowell, *Migrations and Cultures*, 296.

57 Sachar, *A History of the Jews in America*, 150–153.

58 Roger Daniels, *Coming to America: A History of Immigration and Ethnicity in American Life* (New York: HarperCollins, 1990), 226; Goren, "Jews," in Thernstrom, *Harvard Encyclopedia of American Ethnic Groups*, 581.

59 Howe, *World of Our Fathers*, 69; Sachar, *A History of the Jews in America*, 141.

60 Goren, "Jews," in Thernstrom, *Harvard Encyclopedia of American Ethnic Groups*, 581.

61 See Howe, *World of Our Fathers*, 151–152.

62 Sachar, *A History of the Jews in America*, 144.

63 Eric Homberger, *The Historical Atlas of New York City* (New York: Henry Holt and Company, 1994), 132.

64 Sachar, *A History of the Jews in America*, 196–200.

65 Binder and Reimers, *All the Nations Under Heaven*, 120–121; Sorin, *A Time for Building*, 86–87.

66 Quoted in Binder and Reimers, *All the Nations Under Heaven*, 116.

67 Johnson, *A History of the Jews*, 372.

68 See the map in Homberger, *The Historical Atlas of New York City*, 136–137.

69 Sachar, *A History of the Jews in America*, 214; Binder and Reimers, *All the Nations Under Heaven*, 117.

70 Goren, "Jews," in Thernstrom, *Harvard Encyclopedia of American Ethnic Groups*, 581.

71 Glazer and Moynihan, *Beyond the Melting Pot*, 140.

72 Sachar, *A History of the Jews in America*, 194–196.

73 Ibid., 143.

74 Joel Kotkin, *Tribes: How Race, Religion, and Identity Determine Success in the New Global Economy* (New York: Random House, 1992), 47.

75 Kessner, *The Golden Door*, 37–38.

76 Ronald H. Bayor, *Neighbors in Conflict: The Irish, Germans, Jews, and Italians of New York City, 1929–1941* (Baltimore: Johns Hopkins University Press, 1978), 14–15.

77 Sowell, *Migrations and Cultures*, 285; Sachar, *A History of the Jews in America*, 145.

78 Kotkin, *Tribes*, 48–49; Sowell, *Migrations and Cultures*, 297.

79 Kotkin, *Tribes*, 49.

80 Thomas Sowell, "Cultural Diversity: A World View," lecture presented at the American Enterprise Institute's Annual Policy Conference, December 5, 1990, quoted in Kotkin, *Tribes*, 48–49.

81 Sorin, *A Time for Building*, 75–76.

82 Sachar, *A History of the Jews in America*, 145–147.

83 Howe, *World of Our Fathers*, 154–159.

84 Burrows and Wallace, *Gotham*, 1116–1117.

85 Sachar, *A History of the Jews in America*, 182–186.

86 Ibid., 186–88.

87 Goren, "Jews," in Thernstrom, *Harvard Encyclopedia of American Ethnic Groups*, 584.

88 Perlman and Waldinger, "Immigrants Past and Present: A Reconsideration," in Hirschman, Kasinitz, and DeWind, *The Handbook of International Migration*, 225.

89 Howe, *World of Our Fathers*, 140.

90 Sorin, *A Time for Building*, 76.

91 Ibid., 76–77.

92 Howe, *World of Our Fathers*, 139, 159–162.

93 Hertzberg, *The Jews in America*, 209–210; Kotkin, *Tribes*, 43.

94 Sachar, *A History of the Jews in America*, 335–337.

95 Ibid., 344–346.

96 Ibid., 333–334; Howe, *World of Our Fathers*, 139.

97 Hertzberg, *The Jews in America*, 245–246.

98 Glazer and Moynihan, *Beyond the Melting Pot*, 148.

99 Kotkin, *Tribes*, 55.

100 Bayor, *Neighbors in Conflict*, 19.

101 Goren, "Jews," in Thernstrom, *Harvard Encyclopedia of American Ethnic Groups*, 589.

102 Glazer and Moynihan, *Beyond the Melting Pot*, 146.

103 Hertzberg, *The Jews in America*, 247–249.

104 Ibid., 248.

105 There was still a Jewish working class in New York in the early 1960s, although Jewish workers "as they retire or die … are not replaced by

either their children or new Jewish immigrants." Glazer and Moynihan, *Beyond the Melting Pot*, 144.

106 Binder and Reimers, *All the Nations Under Heaven*, 130; Howe, *World of Our Fathers*, 167.

107 Sowell, *Ethnic America*, 87–88.

108 Hertzberg, *The Jews in America*, 246; Binder and Reimers, *All the Nations Under Heaven*, 130.

109 Hertzberg, *The Jews in America*, 246.

110 Goren, "Jews," in Thernstrom, *Harvard Encyclopedia of American Ethnic Groups*, 583.

111 Sachar, *A History of the Jews in America*, 152–158.

112 Ibid., 158–162.

113 Perlman and Waldinger, "Immigrants Past and Present: A Reconsideration," in Hirschman, Kasinitz, and DeWind, *The Handbook of International Migration*, 225.

114 Binder and Reimers, *All the Nations Under Heaven*, 130.

115 Howe, *World of Our Fathers*, 167.

116 Glazer and Moynihan, *Beyond the Melting Pot*, 155. The number of Jewish graduates of medical schools in ten American cities increased from 25 from 1881 to 1885 to 1,273 from 1916 to 1920. See Howe, *World of Our Fathers*, 167.

117 Sachar, *A History of the Jews in America*, 326–331.

118 Howe, *World of Our Fathers*, 411–412.

119 Hertzberg, *The Jews in America*, 246.

120 Sachar, *A History of the Jews in America*, 332.

121 Hertzberg, *The Jews in America*, 246; Glazer and Moynihan, *Beyond the Melting Pot*, 156–157.

122 Sowell, *Migrations and Cultures*, 298.

123 Glazer and Moynihan, *Beyond the Melting Pot*, 165.

124 Ibid., 154.

125 Hertzberg, *The Jews in America*, 200–201.

126 Glazer and Moynihan, *Beyond the Melting Pot*, 150.

127 Bayor, *Neighbors in Conflict*, 19.

128 See, for example, Norman Podhoretz, Irving Kristol, and many others.

129 Sorin, *A Time for Building*, 175. The 2,000 synagogues included 70 in the West, 130 in the South, 340 in the Midwest, and about 1,500 in the Northeast.

130 Goren, "Jews," in Thernstrom, *Harvard Encyclopedia of American Ethnic Groups*, 582–583.

131 Sorin, *A Time for Building*, 175.

132 Hertzberg, *The Jews in America*, 171.

133 Goren, "Jews," in Thernstrom, *Harvard Encyclopedia of American Ethnic Groups*, 583.

134 Sachar, *A History of the Jews in America*, 386–390.

135 Ibid., 390–391.

136 Ibid., 398–403.

137 Sorin, *A Time for Building*, 175.

138 See Abrams, *Faith or Fear?*

139 Sorin, *A Time for Building*, 84; Glazer and Moynihan, *Beyond the Melting Pot*, 165; Sachar, *A History of the Jews in America*, 149. Sachar quotes a New Jersey health commissioner's conclusion that "alcoholism, together with syphilis and other genitourinary diseases—all prime killers among the non-Jewish population—rarely were encountered among immigrant Jews."

140 Hertzberg, *The Jews in America*, 206.

141 Sachar, *A History of the Jews in America*, 164–168; Hertzberg, *The Jews in America*, 204–206; Johnson, *A History of the Jews*, 466.

142 Binder and Reimers, *All the Nations Under Heaven*, 109.

143 Sorin, *A Time for Building*, 85.

144 Hertzberg, *The Jews in America*, 205.

145 Sorin, *A Time for Building*, 84–86.

146 Sachar, *A History of the Jews in America*, 349; Hertzberg, *The Jews in America*, 207. Sachar believes that Rothstein bribed the White Sox; Hertzberg believes that he did not.

147 Sachar, *A History of the Jews in America*, 348.

148 Ibid., 349–351.

149 Ibid., 353.

150 Ibid., 277–278, 304; Hertzberg, *The Jews in America*, 190–191.

151 Sachar, *A History of the Jews in America*, 278–283.

152 Quoted in John Miller, *The Unmaking of Americans*, 77.

153 See George F. Kennan, *The Decision to Intervene* (Princeton, NJ: Princeton University Press, 1958).

154 Sachar, *A History of the Jews in America*, 293–295, 298–299.

155 Quoted in Johnson, *A History of the Jews*, 459.

156 Sachar, *A History of the Jews in America*, 307.

157 Ibid., 313–319.

158 Ibid., 319–324; Johnson, *A History of the Jews*, 460. Presidents Cleveland, Taft, and Wilson vetoed immigration restriction bills. Sachar, *A History of the Jews in America*, 284–288.

159   Johnson, *A History of the Jews*, 370.

160   Sachar, *A History of the Jews in America*, 326; Glazer and Moynihan, *Beyond the Melting Pot*, 160.

161   Sachar, *A History of the Jews in America*, 326–327; Glazer and Moynihan, *Beyond the Melting Pot*, 160–161.

162   Hertzberg, *The Jews in America*, 173.

163   Sorin, *A Time for Building*, 197.

164   Ibid., 193–196.

165   Ibid., 196.

166   Sachar, *A History of the Jews in America*, 224–225.

167   Roosevelt was interested in attracting Jewish votes for Charles Evans Hughes, the Republican candidate for governor of New York, running against William Randolph Hearst, who had made strong appeals for Jewish votes. Hughes won, ending Hearst's ambitions to be president. Hertzberg, *The Jews in America*, 191; Sachar, *A History of the Jews in America*, 217.

168   Sorin, *A Time for Building*, 196–197, 199.

169   Sachar, *A History of the Jews in America*, 181.

170   Ibid., 174–175, 176–177.

171   Seymour Martin Lipset and Gary Marks, *It Didn't Happen Here: Why Socialism Failed in the United States* (New York: W. W. Norton & Co., 2000), 141–142.

172   Ibid., 138.

173   Sachar, *A History of the Jews in America*, 177–178.

174   Ibid., 462–463.

175   Ibid., 251–255, quotation at 252; Walter Laqueur, *A History of Zionism* (New York: Holt, Rinehart and Winston, 1972), 159–160.

176   Sachar, *A History of the Jews in America*, 254–258.

177   Ibid., 258–273.

178   Glazer and Moynihan, *Beyond the Melting Pot*, 167–169.

179   Barone, *Our Country*, 64.

180   Sachar, *A History of the Jews in America*, 459–460.

181   Alan Brinkley, *Voices of Protest: Huey Long, Father Coughlin, and the Great Depression* (New York: Vintage Books, 1982), 266–267; Sachar, *A History of the Jews in America*, 452–455.

182   Sachar, *A History of the Jews in America*, 455–457.

183   Ibid., 481–482.

184   A. Scott Berg, *Lindbergh* (New York: Putnam, 1998), 425–428, quotation at 427.

185 See the searing indictment in Howe, *World of Our Fathers*, 392–394.

186 Johnson, *A History of the Jews*, 470.

187 Sachar, *A History of the Jews in America*, 523.

188 Johnson, *A History of the Jews*, 470.

189 Theodore Draper, *American Communism and Soviet Russia* (New York: Viking Press, 1960), 191; Sachar, *A History of the Jews in America*, 433.

190 Sachar, *A History of the Jews in America*, 432–437.

191 Ibid., 437–446.

192 Ibid., 449–450.

193 Ibid., 445.

194 Ibid., 628–639.

195 Glazer and Moynihan, *Beyond the Melting Pot*, 137–138.

196 David G. McCullough, *Truman* (New York: Simon & Schuster, 1992), 608–618; Robert J. Donovan, *Conflict and Crisis: The Presidency of Harry S. Truman*, 1945–1948 (New York: Norton, 1977), 379–387.

197 Howe, *World of Our Fathers*, 73.

198 Sachar, *A History of the Jews in America*, 352–353.

199 Hertzberg, *The Jews in America*, 207.

200 William B. Mead, *Baseball Goes to War* (Washington: Farragut, 1985), 32.

201 Johnson, *A History of the Jews*, 463.

202 Sachar, *A History of the Jews in America*, 209–213.

203 Ibid., 354–355, 356–357.

204 Ibid., 367–370.

205 Howe, *World of Our Fathers*, 165.

206 Johnson, *A History of the Jews*, 465.

207 *Historical Statistics of the United States*, 400. Box office receipts were $732 million annually—an enormous sum.

208 Howe, *World of Our Fathers*, 165–166. Cf. Hertzberg, *The Jews in America*, 209. "These men were themselves the incarnation of the Horatio Alger myth which Hollywood often celebrated. Yet, even as they told the story of poor farm children rising from the log cabin to the presidency, or to a Fifth Avenue mansion, they were not yet ready to tell their own story, of rising from the streets of the ghetto to sit beside the swimming pools of Beverly Hills."

209 Howe, *World of Our Fathers*, 556–568.

210 Ibid., 568–573.

211 Steven D. Stark, *Glued to the Set: The 60 Television Shows and Events That Made Us Who We Are Today* (New York: The Free Press, 1997), 12–13.

212 Glazer and Moynihan, *Beyond the Melting Pot*, 160–161.

213 Ibid., 137–138.

214 Sachar, *A History of the Jews in America*, 75.

215 Ibid., 669.

216 Abrams, *Faith or Fear?*, 143.

217 Robert Dallek, *Flawed Giant: Lyndon Johnson and His Times, 1961–1973* (New York: Oxford University Press, 1998), 427–432.

218 Abrams, *Faith or Fear?*, 137, 141–142, 149.

219 Hertzberg, *The Jews in America*, 380.

220 Ibid., 377.

221 Johnson, *A History of the Jews*, 570. Johnson, a Briton sympathetic to both America and Jews, has an interesting observation on the place of Jews in American society: "[With] the transformation of the Jewish minority into a core element of American society ... Jews ceased to be a lobby in American society. They began to operate not from without the American body inwards, but from within it outwards. With their historic traditions of democracy, tolerance, and liberalism, they assumed to some extent the same role in America as the Whigs had once played in England: an elite seeking moral justification for its privileges by rendering enlightened service to those less fortunate. In short, they were no longer a minority seeking rights but part of the majority conferring them; their political activity switched imperceptibly from influencing leadership to exercising it." Johnson, *A History of the Jews*, 567.

222 Sowell, *Ethnic America*, 299.

223 Abrams, *Faith or Fear?*, 99.

224 Ibid., 106–110.

225 Ibid., 111.

226 See the diagram in Alan Dershowitz, *The Vanishing American Jew* (Boston: Little, Brown, 1997), 26.

227 Abrams, *Faith or Fear?*, 164.

228 Hertzberg, *The Jews in America*, 386.

CHAPTER 6: ASIANS

1 Figure calculated from *Statistical Abstracts* for the years covering 1971–1997 and from *Historical Statistics of the United States, 1789–1870* for the years 1965–1970. The latter provides a large total of "other

Asians," and I have assumed that two-thirds of them were from East and South Asia; this rough and ready estimate produces a total of 4,933,000 East and South Asian immigrants, or approximately 5 million.

2 Fukuyama, *Trust*, 70–71.

3 Kotkin, *Tribes*, 174–175.

4 Fukuyama, *Trust*, 128–131.

5 Min Zhou and Carl L. Bankston III, *Growing Up American: How Vietnamese Children Adapt to Life in the United States* (New York: Russell Sage Foundation, 1998), 83–84.

6 Kotkin, *Tribes*, 178.

7 Pyong Gap Min, *Changes and Conflicts: Korean Immigrant Families in New York* (Boston: Allyn and Bacon, 1998), 25–27.

8 Fukuyama, *Trust*, 85–86.

9 Kotkin, *Tribes*, 175–176.

10 Fukuyama, *Trust*, 70–80; Kotkin, *Tribes*, 166.

11 "The Chinese communities, like those of the Jews in Europe, certainly remained separate from others, choosing to maintain their own subeconomies, community associations, and community leaders, as well as the inevitable criminal gangs." Kotkin, *Tribes*, 171.

12 "Resentments against the overseas Chinese have been quite real, however little relationship these resentments have had with the reasons given for it. Nor is simple envy a sufficient explanation. Other groups, both domestic and foreign, have often been much more prosperous than the Chinese, without arousing as much hostility.... Not only did the overseas Chinese usually begin destitute in a foreign country at a given historical period; new destitute Chinese continued arriving over the years, even after the original immigrants and their descendants had achieved prosperity. Thus the indigenous populations had continuously before their eyes the spectacle of foreigners arriving poorer than they were and yet rising to surpass them." Sowell, *Migrations and Cultures*, 228.

13 Kotkin, *Tribes*, 172.

14 Ibid., 180.

15 "Conditions of chronic insecurity, much like those facing the Jews of Europe, led the overseas Chinese to treasure the instruments of self-reliance—whether in the form of a business, a hoard of cash or gold, real estate, or simply the money to pay for their children's education, so they might then develop useful skills." Ibid., 185.

16 Fukuyama, *Trust*, 94.

17 Daniels, *Coming to America*, 332.

18 Ibid., 338–339.

19   Dallek, *Flawed Giant*, 192, 227–228.

20   Glazer, *Clamor at the Gates*, 7.

21   Stephan Thernstrom, "Plenty of Room for All," *Times Literary Supplement*, May 26, 2000, 5.

22   Daniels, *Coming to America*, 338; Millman, *The Other Americans*, 61. "If Congress had known in 1965 that its reforms would open the door to more than 18 million immigrants over the next three decades— about one-third of them from Asia—they may not have passed the new law.... Ideals were what motivated reform in the first place, and in the end they were enough to trump popular fears about an Asian invasion." John Miller, *The Unmaking of Americans*, 105.

23   Daniels, *Coming to America*, 341.

24   Min, *Changes and Conflicts*, 11.

25   Since the males did not reproduce, the Chinese population of the United States declined from 107,000 in 1890 to 61,000 in 1920. Daniels, *Coming to America*, 238–241.

26   Daniels, *Coming to America*, 250–255.

27   Gunther, *Inside U.S.A.*, 46–47.

28   Roger Daniels, *Asian America: Chinese and Japanese in the United States Since 1850* (Seattle: University of Washington Press, 1988), 317–321.

29   William Petersen, "Success Story, Japanese Style," *New York Times Magazine*, January 6, 1966, 20, quoted in Daniels, *Asian America*, 319.

30   John J. Miller and Moore, "The Index of Leading Immigration Indicators," 21.

31   Joe Mathews, "The Three Chinatowns," *Baltimore Sun*, May 7, 1997, E1, E10.

32   There is a good review of this literature in Timothy Fong, *The First Suburban Chinatown: The Remaking of Monterey Park, California* (Philadelphia: Temple University Press, 1994), 6–10.

33   Daniels, *Asian America*, 324–325.

34   Kotkin, *Tribes*, 167.

35   Peter Kwong, *The New Chinatown* (New York: Hill and Wang, 1996, revised edition), 5.

36   Binder and Reimers, *All the Nations Under Heaven*, 232.

37   Kwong, *The New Chinatown*, 40.

38   Foner, *From Ellis Island to JFK*, 58–59.

39   Illsoo Kim, "The Koreans: Small Business in an Urban Frontier," in Nancy Foner, ed., *New Immigrants in New York* (New York: Columbia University Press, 1987), 223.

40   Fukuyama, *Trust*, 141–42.

41   Millman, *The Other Americans*, 275–276.

42   Seth Mydans, "25 Years Later, Vietnamese Still Flock to the U.S.,"
      New York Times, November 7, 2000, A1, A14. See the tables in Zhou
      and Bankston, *Growing Up American*, 44.

43   Zhou and Bankston, *Growing Up American*, 74–75.

44   H. L. Kitano and Roger Daniels, *Asian Americans: Emerging Minorities*
      (Englewood Cliffs, NJ: Prentice Hall, 1988), 145.

45   Michael Fletcher, "Asian Americans Using Politics as a Megaphone,"
      Washington Post, October 2, 2000, A3.

46   Min, *Changes and Conflicts*, 16–17.

47   Kotkin, *Tribes*, 189.

48   Kitano and Daniels, *Asian Americans*, 145.

49   John J. Miller and Moore, "The Index of Leading Immigration Indi-
      cators," 15.

50   Min, *Changes and Conflicts*, 22–24.

51   Richard Alba and Victor Nee, "Rethinking Assimilation Theory for a
      New Era of Immigrants," in Hirschman, Kasinitz, and DeWind, *The
      Handbook of International Migration*, 152.

52   Fukuyama, *Trust*, 300–301.

53   Kim, "The Koreans: Small Business in an Urban Frontier," in Foner,
      New Immigrants in New York, 227. Another scholar estimates that 75
      to 80 percent of Korean immigrants either own or work for Korean
      businesses: "the vast majority of the Korean work force is segregated
      in the Korean sub-economy." Min, *Changes and Conflicts*, 16–17.

54   Bernard Wong, "The Chinese: New Immigrants in New York's
      Chinatown," in Foner, *New Immigrants in New York*, 254–255.

55   Kwong, *The New Chinatown*, 26.

56   Ibid., 175–179.

57   Kotkin, *Tribes*, 168.

58   Zhou and Bankston, *Growing Up American*, 59.

59   Min, *Changes and Conflicts*, 32–33.

60   Fukuyama, *Trust*, 302. "Most of the Asian subgroups whose original
      cultures are dominated by Confucianism, Taoism, or Buddhism—such
      as the Chinese, Koreans, Japanese, and Vietnamese—often selectively
      unpack from their cultural baggage traits such as two-parent families, a
      strong work ethic, delayed gratification, and thrift that are suitable to
      the new environment. They either leave packed or keep strictly to
      themselves other traits not so well considered, such as nonconfronta-
      tion, passivity, submissiveness, and excessive obligation within the fam-
      ily." Zhou and Bankston, *Growing Up American*, 11–12.

61 Kim, "The Koreans: Small Business in an Urban Frontier," in Foner, *New Immigrants in New York*, 223.

62 Foner, *From Ellis Island to JFK*, 73.

63 Or in central city neighborhoods known for their good schools, such as School District 26 in Bayside, Little Neck, and Douglaston, Queens. Min, *Changes and Conflicts*, 66–69.

64 Zhou and Bankston, *Growing Up American*, 220.

65 Thernstrom and Thernstrom, *America in Black and White*, 399.

66 Foner, *From Ellis Island to JFK*, 205.

67 Min, *Changes and Conflicts*, 67–68.

68 Foner, *From Ellis Island to JFK*, 215.

69 Brooke Lea Foster, "Golden Children," *Washingtonian*, June 2000, 108.

70 John J. Miller and Moore, "The Index of Leading Immigration Indicators," 13.

71 Zhou and Bankston, *Growing Up American*, 138.

72 Michael Fletcher, "Asian Americans Coping with Success," *Washington Post*, March 4, 2000, A3.

73 Kotkin, *Tribes*, 168.

74 Ibid., 179.

75 Tamar Jacoby, "In Asian America," *Commentary*, July–August 2000, 21–28.

76 Ibid., 27–28.

77 Fukuyama, *Trust*, 85.

78 Ibid., 88.

79 Ibid., 91.

80 See, for example, Brooke Lea Foster, "Golden Children," 108–109.

81 "Despite all the risks, many Vietnamese families have adjusted to life in America remarkably well. The path to adjustment has involved incorporating traditional values, communal solidarities, and refugee experiences into a lifestyle adapted to American ways." Zhou and Bankston, *Growing Up American*, 86

82 John J. Miller and Moore, "The Index of Leading Immigration Indicators," 10–12.

83 Zhou and Bankston, *Growing Up American*, 55.

84 Ibid., 75.

85 Kwong, *The New Chinatown*, 175–179. "With few work alternatives, many Fujianese have turned to lives of crime, say law enforcement authorities and community leaders. Fujianese gangs are deeply involved in illegal smuggling of immigrants, though many Fujianese deny it." Mathews, "The Three Chinatowns," E10.

86   Kwong, *The New Chinatown*, 110–111, 184–185. Kwong writes that
      Fujianese immigrants in New York "have established a reign of terror
      in Chinatown. The old residents who remember quieter, more peace-
      ful days live in constant fear for their livelihood and personal safety."
      Ibid., 185. See the chart and map of gang activity in New York's
      Chinatown in Ko-lin Chin, *Chinatown Gangs: Extortion, Enterprise, and
      Ethnicity* (New York: Oxford University Press, 1996), 8–11.
87   Barone and Ujifusa, *The Almanac of American Politics, 2000*, 495–496.
88   Ibid., 283–285.
89   Fletcher, "Asian Americans Using Politics as a Megaphone," A3.
90   John J. Miller and Moore, "The Index of Leading Immigration Indi-
      cators," 14.
91   Daniels, *Coming to America*, 353.
92   Irving Kristol, "Faith à la Carter," *Times Literary Supplement*, May 26,
      2000, 14.
93   Jacoby, "In Asian America," 28.

ACKNOWLEDGMENTS

There are many people who are due thanks for helping me to write this book, starting with my parents, C. Gerald Barone and Alice Darcy Barone—many more than I can mention here. Special thanks has to go to my editors at *U.S. News & World Report*, who have encouraged me to write about today's minorities and have printed at least two articles in which I have advanced the central thesis of this book. They include Michael Ruby, Merrill McLoughlin, and Harrison Rainie, who are no longer with *U.S. News*, and current *U.S. News* editors Stephen G. Smith and Brian Kelly. Thanks should also go to William Schulz of *Reader's Digest*, who encouraged me to write articles on America's Hispanics and on bilingual education.

Thanks are also due to the American Enterprise Institute and its president, Christopher Demuth, for the invitation to deliver the Bradley Lecture in October 1999, which I entitled "We've

Been Here Before." Several who heard the lecture or read it later suggested that I expand it into a book, most notably Ambassador Max Kampelman, who took the trouble to write a letter urging me to do so. Thus a 9,000-word lecture was followed by a 900-word column in *U.S. News*, and both are now followed by this 90,000-word book. Do not wait for the 900,000-word version.

I wish to thank Vincent Cannato, a scholar who took time off from putting the finishing touches on his own fine book *The Ungovernable City: John Lindsay and His Struggle to Save New York*, scheduled for publication at the same time as this book. Without Vin's research, this book could not have been finished in time, so he deserves credit for putting out two books in 2001.

Thanks should go as well to my agent, Rafe Sagalyn, and to all the folks at Regnery, especially Alfred Regnery and Jed Donahue. Trish Bozell did a splendid job of copy-editing the manuscript.

Many individuals mentioned in the text and cited in the notes have helped me gain an understanding of America's different ethnic and racial groups. This has been the enterprise of a lifetime, starting in the supposedly white-bread 1950s when I was growing up in a neighborhood that was one-third Protestant, one-third Catholic and one-third Jewish, in a Detroit that was undergoing rapid racial change. Kind and generous guidance along the way has been provided over the years by, among others, Daniel Patrick Moynihan, Stephan and Abigail Thernstrom, Grant Ujifusa, Joel Kotkin, and Gregory Rodriguez. My conclusions and this book are, of course, my own, and not necessarily theirs. But I think we all do share a faith that today's minority groups can be interwoven into the fabric of American life, as were the immigrant groups of the past, and a gratefulness that we live in the country which, of all those that have existed in the history of the world, has done the most to enable people of every conceivable background and ancestry to reach their full potential—and which is still in the process of doing more.

INDEX